Swift for Beginners

SECOND EDITION

DEVELOP AND DESIGN

Boisy G. Pitre

PEACHPIT PRESS
WWW.PEACHPIT.COM

Swift for Beginners: Develop and Design, Second Edition
Boisy G. Pitre

Peachpit Press
www.peachpit.com

To report errors, please send a note to errata@peachpit.com.

Peachpit Press is a division of Pearson Education.

Copyright © 2016 by Boisy G. Pitre

Editor: Connie Jeung-Mills
Production editor: David Van Ness
Development editor: Robyn G. Thomas
Copyeditor and proofreader: Scout Festa
Technical editor: Steve Phillips
Compositor: Danielle Foster
Indexer: Valerie Haynes Perry
Cover design: Aren Straiger
Interior design: Mimi Heft

ISBN-13: 978-0-13-428977-9
ISBN-10: 0-13-428977-3

9 8 7 6 5 4 3 2 1

Printed and bound in the United States of America

To the girls: Toni, Hope, Heidi, Lillian, Sophie, and Belle

ACKNOWLEDGMENTS

When Peachpit's executive editor Cliff Colby approached me about writing a second edition of *Swift for Beginners*, I readily agreed for several reasons. First, Apple has continued to evolve the Swift language to the point where a book update was necessary—the first edition was already outdated with respect to Swift 2 language enhancements and Xcode improvements. Second, I was eager to work with the same great team of people who were part of the first edition.

Shortly after the project started, Cliff left Peachpit and moved on to another adventure, but not before introducing me to Connie Jeung-Mills, who took over as executive editor. She brought together the original team from the first edition: Robyn Thomas as editor and Steve Phillips as technical editor. Rounding out the team was an addition, Scout Festa, who provided additional editorial support. Each one of them was indispensable and critical to the process, and I want to thank them for their assistance.

On the technical side, I continue to draw inspiration from the works of a number of friends who are authors in the iOS and Mac OS developer community: Chris Adamson, Bill Cheescman, James Dempsey, Bill Dudney, Daniel Steinberg, and Richard Warren. Thanks go to MacTech's Ed Marczak and Neil Ticktin, as well as CocoaConf maestro Dave Klein, for the writing and speaking opportunities that they have provided me at those venues. My friends at Dave et Ray's Camp Jam/Supper Club always serve as inspiration for several of the coding examples I used in this edition. I also would like to thank Troy Deville for contributing the source code for his game Downhill Challenge.

Thanks also go to the minds at Apple for creating and enhancing Swift, currently in its second major release. The language has solidified since its introduction just over a year ago, and has already reached a popularity that is uncharacteristic for a computer language so young.

Lastly, my family and my wife, Toni, deserve special mention for the patience and encouragement they've shown while I worked on yet another book.

ABOUT THE AUTHOR

Boisy G. Pitre is Mobile Visionary and lead iOS developer at Affectiva, the leading emotion technology company and a spin-off of the MIT Media Lab. His work there has led to the creation of the first mobile SDK for delivering emotions to mobile devices. Prior to that he was a member of the Mac Products Group at Nuance Communications, where he worked with a team of developers on Dragon Dictate.

He also owns Tee-Boy, a software company focusing on Mac and iOS applications for the weather and data-acquisition markets, and he has authored the monthly "Developer to Developer" column in *MacTech* magazine.

Along with Bill Loguidice, Boisy co-authored the book *CoCo: The Colorful History of Tandy's Underdog Computer* (2013), published by Taylor & Francis.

Boisy holds a Master of Science in Computer Science from the University of Louisiana at Lafayette, is working toward his doctorate in computer science, and resides in the quiet countryside of Prairie Ronde, Louisiana. Besides Mac and iOS development, his hobbies and interests include retro-computing, ham radio, vending machine and arcade game restoration, farming, and playing the French music of South Louisiana.

CONTENTS

INTRODUCTION

Welcome to *Swift for Beginners*! Swift is Apple's new language for developing apps for iOS and Mac OS, and it is destined to become the premier computer language in the mobile and desktop space. As a new computer language, Swift has the allure of a shiny new car—everybody wants to see it up close, kick the tires, and take it for a spin down the road. That's probably why you're reading this book—you've heard about Swift and decided to see what all the fuss is about.

The notion that Swift is an easy language to use and learn certainly has merit, especially when compared to the capable but harder-to-learn programming language it's replacing: Objective-C. Apple has long used Objective-C as its language of choice for developing software on its platforms, but that is changing with the introduction of Swift.

WHO IS THIS BOOK FOR?

This book was written with the beginner in mind. In a sense, we're all beginners with Swift because it's such a new language. However, many of those who want to learn Swift as a first or second computer language haven't had any exposure to Objective-C or to the related languages C and C++.

Ideally, the reader will have some understanding and experience with a computer language; even so, the book is styled to appeal to the neophyte who is sufficiently motivated to learn. More experienced developers will probably find the first few chapters to be review material and light reading because the concepts are ubiquitous among many computer languages but nonetheless important to introduce Swift to the beginner.

HOW TO USE THIS BOOK

Like other books of its kind, *Swift for Beginners* is best read from start to finish. The material in subsequent chapters tends to build on the knowledge attained from previous ones. However, with a few exceptions, code examples are confined to a single chapter.

The book is sized to provide a good amount of material, but not so much as to overwhelm the reader. Interspersed in the text are a copious number of screenshots to guide the beginner through the ins and outs of Swift as well as the Xcode tool chain.

HOW YOU WILL LEARN

The best way to learn Swift is to use it, and using Swift is emphasized throughout the book with plenty of code and examples.

Each chapter contains code that builds on the concepts presented. Swift has two interactive environments you will use to test out concepts and gain understanding of the language: the REPL and playgrounds. Later, you'll build two simple but complete apps: a loan calculator for Mac OS and a memory game for iOS. In the final chapter, you will be introduced to the source code for a complete 2D game that uses several Apple gaming technologies.

Swift concepts will be introduced throughout the text—classes, functions, closures, and more, all the way to the very last chapter. You're encouraged to take your time and read each chapter at your leisure, even rereading if necessary, before moving on to the next one.

Source code for all the chapters is available at www.peachpit.com/swiftbeginners2. You can download the code for each chapter, which cuts down considerably on typing; nonetheless, I am a firm believer in typing in the code. By doing so, you gain insight and comprehension you might otherwise miss if you just read along and rely on the downloaded code. Make the time to type in all of the code examples.

For clarity, code and constructs such as class names are displayed in monospace font.

Highlighted code identifies the portions of the code that are intended for you to type:

```
 1> let candyJar = ["Peppermints", "Gooey Bears", "Happy Ranchers"]
candyJar: [String] = 3 values {
  [0] = "Peppermints"
  [1] = "Gooey Bears"
  [2] = "Happy Ranchers"
}
 2>
```

Bold code identifies an error returned from the REPL:

```
 8> x = y
repl.swift:8:5: error: cannot assign a value of type 'Double'
→ to a value of type 'Int'
x = y
    ^
 8>
```

You'll also find notes containing additional information about the topics.

NOTE: Dictionary keys are not necessarily placed in alphabetical order. Swift will always use the order that is the most efficient for retrieval and access.

WHAT YOU WILL LEARN

Ultimately, this book will show you how to use Swift to express your ideas in code. When you complete the final chapter, you should have a good head start, as well as a solid understanding of what the language offers. Additionally, you'll have the skills to begin writing an app. Both iOS and Mac OS apps are presented as examples in the later chapters.

What this book does not do is provide an all-inclusive, comprehensive compendium on the Swift programming language. Apple's documentation is the best resource for that. Here, the emphasis is primarily on learning the language itself, with various Cocoa and CocoaTouch frameworks introduced to facilitate examples.

WELCOME TO SWIFT

Swift is a fun, new, and easy-to-learn computer language from Apple.
With the knowledge you'll gain from this book, you can begin writing
apps for iOS and Mac OS. The main tool you'll need to start learning Swift
is the Xcode integrated development environment (IDE). Xcode includes
the Swift compiler, as well as the iOS and Mac OS software development
kits (SDKs) that contain the infrastructure required to support the
apps you develop.

THE TECHNOLOGIES

The following technologies are all part of your journey into the
Swift language.

SWIFT 2

Swift 2 is the language
you'll learn in this book.
Swift is a modern lan-
guage designed from the
ground up to be easy to
learn as well as powerful.
It is the language that
Apple has chosen to fuel
the continued growth of
the apps that make up
their iOS, watchOS, tvOS,
and Mac OS ecosystems.

XCODE 7

Xcode is Apple's premier
environment for writing
apps. It includes an editor,
a debugger, a project
manager, and the com-
piler tool chain needed to
take Swift code and turn
it into runnable code. You
can download Xcode from
Apple's Mac App Store.

LLVM

Although it works behind
the scenes within Xcode,
LLVM is the compiler
technology that powers
the elegance of the Swift
language and turns it
into the digestible bits
and bytes needed by the
processors that power
Apple devices.

```
23> for loopCounter in 0..<9{
24.     print("value at index \(loopCounter) is \(numbersArray[loopCounter])")
25. }
value at index 0 is 11
value at index 1 is 22
value at index 2 is 33
value at index 3 is 44
value at index 4 is 55
value at index 5 is 66
value at index 6 is 77
value at index 7 is 88
value at index 8 is 99
26> for loopCounter = 0; loopCounter < 9; loopCounter = loopCounter + 2 {
27.     print("value at index \(loopCounter) is \(numbersArray[loopCounter])")
28. }
value at index 0 is 11
value at index 2 is 33
value at index 4 is 55
value at index 6 is 77
value at index 8 is 99
29> for loopCounter = 8; loopCounter >= 0; loopCounter = loopCounter - 2 {
30.     print("value at index \(loopCounter) is \(numbersArray[loopCounter])")
31. }
value at index 8 is 99
value at index 6 is 77
value at index 4 is 55
value at index 2 is 33
value at index 0 is 11
32> 
```

```
1  //: Playground - noun: a place where people can play
2
3  import Cocoa
4
5  var str = "Chapter 4 Playground"                                    "Chapter 4 Playground"
6
7  func fahrenheitToCelsius(fahrenheitValue : Double) -> Double {
8      var result : Double
9
10     result = (((fahrenheitValue - 32) * 5) / 9)                      31.2222222222222
11
12     return result;                                                   31.2222222222222
13 }
14
15 var outdoorTemperatureInFahrenheit = 88.2                            88.2
16 var outdoorTemperatureInCelsius = fahrenheitToCelsius               31.2222222222222
       (outdoorTemperatureInFahrenheit)
17
18 func celsiusToFahrenheit(celsiusValue : Double) -> Double {
19     var result : Double
20
21     result = (((celsiusValue * 9) / 5) + 32)                         88.2
22
23     return result                                                    88.2
24 }
25
26 outdoorTemperatureInFahrenheit = celsiusToFahrenheit                 88.2
       (outdoorTemperatureInCelsius)
27
28 func buildASentenceUsingSubject(subject : String, verb : String, noun :
       String) -> String {
29     return subject + " " + verb + " " + noun + "!"                   (2 times)
30 }
31
32 buildASentenceUsingSubject("Swift", verb: "is", noun: "cool")        "Swift is cool!"
33 buildASentenceUsingSubject("I", verb: "love", noun: "languages")     "I love languages!"
```

THE REPL

The Read-Eval-Print-Loop (REPL) is a command-line tool you can use to try out Swift code quickly. You run it from the Terminal application on Mac OS.

PLAYGROUNDS

Their interactivity and immediate results make Xcode's playgrounds a great way to try out Swift code as you learn the language.

SECTION I
The Basics

Learning something new always starts with "the basics." The Swift language is no exception. This section covers everything you need to know about this cool new language to start making your next great app!

- Chapter 1, Introducing Swift
- Chapter 2, Working with Collections
- Chapter 3, Taking Control
- Chapter 4, Writing Functions and Closures
- Chapter 5, Organizing with Classes and Structures
- Chapter 6, Formalizing with Protocols and Extensions

CHAPTER 1

Introducing Swift

Welcome to the brave new world of Swift! In just one year, since its introduction at Apple's World Wide Developer Conference (WWDC) in 2014, Swift has emerged as a powerful new programming language. With Apple's encouragement and feedback from developers, the language has adapted and grown to become the dominant language for creating iOS, watchOS, and Mac apps. Swift is not only powerful but also easy to learn... so easy that you'll be writing simple apps before you know it.

Swift gives you powerful new ways to write code. Its readability is refreshingly simple compared to its worthy and powerful predecessor, Objective-C. With Swift, you'll find new and interesting ways to express yourself as a developer and to learn the language and its capabilities.

Even as a year-old computer language, Swift is still considered new and is subject to changes and additions by Apple. Never before has a computer language with such exposure and potential usage been subject to nearly immediate modifications and revisions. It's all part of the excitement and innovation that Swift represents.

EVOLUTIONARY YET REVOLUTIONARY

Language is the vehicle through which we share, exchange, and co-opt information. As humans, we express intent through language to our friends, family members, and co-workers. It's no different when we communicate with a computer system.

Just like human languages, computer languages aren't new—in fact, they have been with us in some form or another for many, many years. Their *raison d'etre* has always been to allow us to communicate with and instruct a computer to perform a specific operation.

What has changed and evolved are the computer languages themselves. Early computer pioneers understood that telling a computer what to do in terms of 0s and 1s was tedious and error prone. Compromises between the richness of a language's syntax and the computing power needed to process and interpret that language were made along the way, and languages such as C and C++ became the entrenched *lingua franca* of modern computer applications.

And while C and C++ were widely adopted and used on major computing platforms, Apple brought something different to the party with Objective-C. Built upon the foundation of C, Objective-C brought object-oriented design methodologies to the programmer's toolbox. For many years, Objective-C has been the underpinning of applications written for Apple's ecosystem of Macintosh computers and iOS devices.

Yet despite its power and elegance, Objective-C carried the baggage of its predecessor, C. For many of us who know C quite well, this isn't an impediment; however, the crop of new developers who have come to the Mac and iOS platforms in recent years pined for something easier to comprehend and develop with.

Apple answered the call and at the same time lowered the barrier to entry. Now, writing apps has become much easier, and our ability to express what we want our apps to do is one step closer to "easy."

PREPARING FOR SUCCESS

You may be wondering what you need in order to learn Swift successfully. Actually, you've taken your first step by starting to read this book. Learning a new computer language can be daunting, and that's why this book was written for the Swift beginner. If you are new to Swift, this book is for you. If you have never used C, C++, or Objective-C, this book is also for you. Yet even if you are a seasoned developer with knowledge of the aforementioned languages, you'll still find this book helpful in getting up to speed with Swift.

Although not an absolute necessity, possessing a basic understanding of, and familiarity with, an existing programming language is valuable while reading this book. This book isn't written to teach you how to program or to provide you the underlying fundamentals of developing software. It assumes a certain familiarity with the basic concepts of computer languages; therefore, you should have had *some* exposure to a computer language already.

Despite this requirement, the book is written to help you along as much as possible. Terminology is explained thoroughly when it is introduced, and concepts are described as clearly as possible.

TOOLS OF THE TRADE

So you're ready to learn Swift. Great! First, you need to get your "supplies" in order. Think back to when you were in grade school. Just prior to the start of the term, your parents were given a list of supplies you needed: notebooks, scissors, construction paper, glue, No. 2 pencils, and the like. Well, you won't need those for this book, but you must nevertheless prepare for learning Swift by obtaining the proper tools of the trade.

First, I highly recommend that you interactively run the code presented here, and to do that, you will need a Macintosh computer running OS X 10.10 Yosemite or 10.11 El Capitan. You'll also need Xcode 7, which has the Swift compiler and accompanying environment. Most importantly, you will want to become a member of the Apple Developer Program in order to get the most out of El Capitan and Xcode 7. If you're not already a member of the Apple Developer Program, you can read all about joining by visiting https://developer.apple.com/programs.

Once you've downloaded and installed Xcode 7 on your Mac, you're ready to learn Swift.

INTERACTING WITH SWIFT

To start out, you'll be exploring the Swift language through a fun and interactive environment known as the REPL. REPL stands for Read-Eval-Print-Loop and indicates the nature of the tool: It reads instructions, evaluates them, prints the results, and loops back around to do it all over again.

In fact, this interactivity is one of Swift's nifty features, and it evades many compiled languages, such as C and Objective-C. This isn't something new if you're coming from scripting languages such as Ruby or Python, which offer their own REPL environments, but for a compiled language, it is a novel idea. Ask C, C++, or Objective-C developers how many times they've wished for a way to "try out" code without the overhead of creating a source file with debug statements, compiling it, running it, and then observing the results. The beauty of the Swift REPL is that it makes that kind of long-winded, repetitious workflow a thing of the past.

Another huge benefit of this interactivity is that it helps make the inherently strenuous task of learning a new language much, much easier. You can put off learning the complexity of compiler tool chains and the nuances of integrated development environments, and instead focus on the language. In fact, very early on in this book, you'll be exploring, testing, and prodding the nooks and crannies of Swift. You'll quickly find that doing this interactively will help you formulate an understanding of the language much quicker.

Having the ability to run your code in real time, without the context of an encompassing run-time environment, may feel odd at first, but you'll soon fall in love with the instant gratification it provides. In fact, the REPL reminds some of us "old-timers" of the interactive nature of early interpretive languages such as BASIC, which was around in the early days of the home computer revolution. Talk about coming full circle!

READY, SET...

FIGURE 1.1 Using Spotlight to find the Terminal application

FIGURE 1.2 The Go menu in the Finder menu bar

FIGURE 1.3 Locating Terminal from the Finder

FIGURE 1.4 The Terminal window

OK, have you downloaded Xcode 7? Very good. Now, forget about Xcode for the time being. Actually, I encourage you to explore Xcode 7 and its new features, but we're going to focus our attention completely on the REPL in Terminal for the first few chapters.

If you haven't run the Terminal app before, don't worry. It's accessible from the Utilities folder, which is located in your Mac's Applications folder. The easiest way to get to it is to click the Spotlight icon and type **Terminal** (**Figure 1.1**).

Alternatively, you can click the Finder icon in the Dock and then choose Go > Utilities (**Figure 1.2**).

A new Finder window shows the contents of this folder; you may have to scroll down in the window to find the Terminal app (**Figure 1.3**). Double-click the icon to launch the app.

When you launch Terminal, you'll see a window similar to **Figure 1.4**. The text and background color of your Terminal window may vary from what you see here.

You're almost ready to start your first foray into Swift. But before you start your adventure, you'll need to type a few commands in this newly created Terminal window.

FIGURE 1.5 Enter your name and password.

Start by typing this line and pressing Return:

```
sudo xcode-select -s /Applications/Xcode.app/Contents/Developer/
```

You'll be prompted for your administrator password; type it. This command is necessary because it ensures that Xcode 7 is the default version of Xcode running on your Mac. It is required just in case you've already installed a previous version of Xcode. The good news is that you'll have to type this command only once. The setting stays in place, and you need not worry about typing it again, unless you want to switch to another version of Xcode.

Typing this next command and pressing Return takes you into the Swift REPL:

```
xcrun swift
```

Depending on your previous use of Xcode, you may be presented with a dialog asking for your password, similar to **Figure 1.5**. If so, type the password as instructed.

In short order, you're greeted with this message:

```
Welcome to Apple Swift version 2.0.  Type :help for assistance.
  1>
```

Congratulations for making it this far! Now the adventure begins.

DIVING INTO SWIFT

So here you are running the Swift REPL as it sits in the Terminal window and patiently awaits your command. Swift is in control and gently reminds you that you can type something by showing you a prompt. Every time you start the REPL, the prompt is shown with the number 1 followed by the greater-than sign. Let's do a sanity check by pressing Return:

```
Welcome to Apple Swift version 2.0.  Type :help for assistance.
  1>
  2>
```

As you type a line, the prompt increments to the next ordinal position—easy enough. The constantly increasing number acts as a reference point as you type commands.

HELP AND QUIT

Swift has built-in help for REPL commands. Typing `:help` at the prompt will show a list of these commands, which are always prepended with a colon character. This is how Swift distinguishes a REPL command from a Swift statement.

Go ahead and type `:help` (which is itself a command) to see the list of commands. There are quite a few commands in the list, and you'll notice that a number of them are related to debugging. We won't worry about most of these commands.

If you want to quit Swift at any time and return to the Terminal's default shell, you can type the `:quit` command. If you do quit the REPL, you can simply retype the `xcrun swift` command at the shell prompt to get right back into Swift.

HELLO, WORLD!

All right, this is the moment you've been waiting for. Every programmer's introduction to a new language involves the initial ritual of writing the necessary code to tell the world "Hello!" In Swift, it's surprisingly easy, as you'll soon see.

Whet your appetite a bit by typing a one-liner, which is emblematic of your first encounter with this new language. Let's tell the world hello... in French. Type the following text, and press Return at the 2> prompt:

```
print("Bonjour, monde")
```

And you see the following:

```
Welcome to Apple Swift version 2.0.  Type :help for assistance.
  1>
  2> print("Bonjour, monde")
Bonjour, monde
  3>
```

Congratulations on writing your first line of code in Swift. Granted, it's a bit minimal, but hey, it's a start. And it shows just how quickly you can get something working.

It's a rather innocuous line. `print` is a Swift method that directs the computer to display whatever is enclosed in quotation marks (the *string*) and bounded by parentheses. A *method* is a collection of instructions that can be executed by invoking a given name. The `print` method is just one of many common Swift methods you'll be using throughout the book. You'll use it often.

Now is a good time to learn a shortcut that can help you use the REPL more effectively. Let's use the `print` method again, but this time, add an exclamation mark (!) to the end of the string. You might be inclined to type the whole command again, but the REPL keeps a history of the previously typed input. Simply press the Up Arrow key and the previous line you typed appears, with the cursor positioned at the end of the line. You can then use the Left Arrow key to back up two characters, then type the exclamation mark. Press the Right Arrow key twice to reposition the cursor at the end of the line, then press the Return key.

```
  3> print("Bonjour, monde!")
Bonjour, monde!
  4>
```

As you type each line, the REPL remembers it, and you can keep pressing the Up Arrow key to go through all the previous commands you typed.

All right, you've mastered the very basics... you can tell Swift to print a string of text. This is a small but important start to your understanding of the language. Let's take things a little further by looking at some basic but important Swift constructs.

THE POWER OF DECLARATION

If you hark back to your high school algebra class, you'll remember that a variable is a placeholder that represents some quantity. When you say "x equals 12" or "y equals 42" you are in essence making a *declaration*. You declare that some variable is equal to some number.

Swift would make your algebra teacher proud, because it too can declare variables, albeit with a slightly different syntax. Type the following:

```
  4> var x = 12
x: Int = 12
  5>
```

You've just declared your first variable using Swift's var keyword. Line 4 instructed Swift to declare the variable x to be equal to 12, and Swift dutifully followed that instruction by declaring that indeed, x is now equal to 12. Not only that, but it went further: Swift declares that "x is an Int whose value is equal to 12."

What is Int? It's short for "integer," which is simply a whole number with no fractional component. By typing the number 12 as you did, Swift inferred something about the variable it was being assigned to: x is a number whose value is 12, and furthermore, x is an integer. In Swift's response, it uses the notation x: Int as a way of advertising the variable's type. You'll see this notation again in a short while.

OK, so you've declared a variable named x with seemingly little effort. Let's up the ante a bit by declaring a second variable, with a twist:

```
  5> var y = 42.0
y: Double = 42
  6>
```

Here, you've added a decimal point followed by a zero. That nomenclature is enough of a hint to Swift that y is a Double, which simply means a number with a fractional component; it's not a whole number but a representation of a real number, also known as a *floating point number*.

Here's a quick review. What Swift has done in both of these cases is assign a type to the variable. The variables x and y exist as an integer and as a double, respectively, and will hold that distinction for as long as this REPL session runs.

Variables can be assigned different values once they have been declared. For example, you assigned x the number 12 earlier. Giving a different value to the variable is as simple as using the equals sign:

```
6> x = 28
7>
```

Notice that Swift is silent on the assignment of x to the number 28. Now verify that the new value has been assigned:

```
7> print(x)
28
```

And as expected, x is shown to hold the value of its last assignment, 28.

Variables can also be assigned the contents of other variables. Test this idea by assigning the variable y to the variable x. What do you think will happen?

```
8> x = y
repl.swift:8:5: error: cannot assign a value of type 'Double'
→ to a value of type 'Int'
x = y
    ^

8>
```

Swift's errors are very detailed, providing both the line number and the column location where the error occurred (in this case, line 8 and column 5), separated by a colon. The content of the line is even reprinted after the error, with a caret reinforcing the error position. Finally, due to the error, the succeeding prompt did not increase to number 9. Instead you received a prompt with the number 8 once more (it's Swift's way of saying "hey, relax… try again!").

So what went wrong here? Very simply, you attempted to assign the variable y, whose type is Double, to the variable x, whose type is Int. Such assignments are a violation of Swift's type rules. I'll get into types in more detail in a little while, but for now, let's see if this "rule" can be bent.

Assume that you stubbornly want to assign the value of y to x, even though they are of different types. You can do it after all, but it takes a little persuasion. Recall that x is an Int and y is a Double. With this in mind, type the following statements:

```
 8> x = Int(y)
 9> print(x)
42
10>
```

With some coaxing, the assignment worked. So what's going on here?

On line 8, you are "casting" the Double value of y into an Int, which is the type of x. Swift allows such assignments if they are explicitly written. I'll talk more about casting shortly.

For good measure, you used the print command to show the value of x. And as you would expect, x is now equal to the integer value of 42.

CONSTANTS ARE CONSISTENT

Variables are useful in so many ways because their values can change over time. They come in handy for iterating loops, holding temporary numbers, strings, and other objects that I'll discuss later.

Another construct in Swift can hold values: the *constant*. Constants are just what their name implies: They hold a value constantly and unwaveringly. Unlike a variable, the value of a constant doesn't change once it's assigned. It's literally locked into place. Yet like a variable, a constant has a type, and types, once assigned, never change.

Let's see constants in action by declaring a new variable and assigning a new constant, z, to the value of the variable x:

```
10> let z = x
z: Int = 42
11>
```

On line 10, we're using the let command, which is Swift's keyword for creating a constant. The constant z has taken on both the type and the value of the variable x: It's an integer with a value of 42.

Now, if a constant is truly constant, you should not be able to assign another number or variable to it. Let's test that theory:

```
11> z = 4
repl.swift:11:3: error: cannot assign to value: 'z' is a 'let' constant
z = 4
~ ^
repl.swift:10:1: note: change 'let' to 'var' to make it mutable
let z = x
^~~
var

11>
```

The attempt to reassign the constant z to a value raised an error. Again, Swift's concise error reporting leads the way, advertising the line number (11) and the column number (3) where the offense took place. Swift even goes a bit further here; it suggests that a change from the let keyword to the var keyword on line 10 would allow the assignment. How about that for cleverness?

So why does Swift have constants *and* variables? Isn't a variable more flexible, since it can change and constants cannot? These are good questions, and the answers lie in the underlying compiler technology. The Swift compiler can make better decisions and code optimizations when it knows that a location in memory holding a value will not change. Always use constants in your code when this is the case. Use variables only when you truly anticipate that the value will change at some point. In short, constants don't require as much overhead as variables, precisely because they don't change.

As you learn to develop with Swift, you'll find yourself using constants in more and more situations in which you recognize that a value doesn't change. Indeed, Apple encourages their use in your code for that very reason.

THIS THING CALLED A TYPE

Earlier, did you notice that Swift inferred the type of your declared variables automatically? Recall that you didn't have to do any extra typing to tell Swift that a variable was an integer or a double. Swift infers the type of a variable or a constant by simply looking at what is on the right side of the equals sign.

A type is a construct that computer languages use to classify values and the containers that hold them. Types bring clarity of intent to code and eliminate ambiguity by clearly defining the characteristics of a value, variable, or constant. They tightly couple a variable or constant to its value, like an ironclad contract. Swift is very much a type-aware language, and you've seen this already in some of the previous examples.

Table 1.1 illustrates Swift's basic types. There are others, and as you'll see later, you can create our own types, but for now you'll work with these:

TABLE 1.1 Variable Types

TYPE	CHARACTERISTICS	EXAMPLES
Bool	A binary type that is either true or false	true, false
Int, Int32, Int64	A 32- or 64-bit positive or negative whole number value used to represent larger numbers; no fractional component	3, 117, −502001, 10045
Int8, Int16	An 8- or 16-bit positive or negative whole number value used to represent smaller numbers; no fractional component	−11, 83, 122
UInt, UInt32, UInt64	A 32- or 64-bit positive whole number value used to represent larger numbers; no fractional component	3, 117, 50, 10045
UInt8, UInt16	An 8- or 16-bit positive whole number value used to represent smaller numbers; no fractional component	44, 86, 255
Float, Double	A positive or negative floating point number; may have a fractional component	324.147, −2098.8388, 16.0
Character	A single letter, number, or other symbol bounded by double quotes	"A", "!", "*", "5"
String	A sequence of characters bounded by double quotes	"Jambalaya", "Crawfish Pie", "Filet Gumbo"

You have already learned about Int, but Int8, Int32, and Int64 may be new to you, as well as UInt, UInt8, UInt32, and UInt64. Integers that can be positive and negative are known as *signed integers* and come in 8-, 16-, 32-, and 64-bit representations; integers that are positive only are known as *unsigned integers*. They also come in 8-, 16-, 32-, and 64-bit flavors. If you don't specify 32- or 64-bit types, the 64-bit values are assumed in Int and UInt. In fact, in development you rarely need to concern yourself with the size of a type. For now, don't worry about this detail.

TESTING THE LIMITS

Each of the numeric types in Table 1.1 has an upper and lower limit. That is, each type can store a number that can be no smaller than its minimum and no larger than its maximum. That's because numeric types have a finite number of bits that can be used to represent them. Swift conveniently allows you to interrogate each type for its minimum and maximum stored value:

```
 11> print(Int.min)
-9223372036854775808
 12> print(Int.max)
9223372036854775807
 13> print(UInt.min)
0
 14> print(UInt.max)
18446744073709551615
 15>
```

By adding .min or .max to the end of the type name, you can determine its minimum and maximum value capacity. Lines 11 through 14 show the ranges for the Int and UInt type. Feel free to explore the ranges of the other types listed in the table.

CAN A LEOPARD CHANGE ITS STRIPES?

Since types are an inherent characteristic of a value, constant, or variable, you may be curious as to what the rules are when different types interact with each other. Remember in the earlier example where you tried assigning a variable of one type to the variable of another? The initial assignment attempt caused an error, and some nudging was required to convince Swift to assign the Double variable to an Int one. Let's look at that example again (don't retype it; just scroll up in the Terminal to see what you typed earlier):

```
  4> var x = 12
x: Int = 12
  5> var y = 42.0
y: Double = 42
```

You assigned x and y values of Int and Double, respectively, and then shortly thereafter attempted to assign the value of y to x:

```
 8> x = y
rep.swift:8:5: error: cannot assign a value of type 'Double'
→ to a value of type 'Int'
x = y
    ^
```

```
 8> x = Int(y)
 9> print(x)
42
```

The assignment of the newly declared variable x to the number 12 on line 4 established it as an Int, followed by declaring y as a Double. Then an assignment of y to x failed with the error, which forced you to cast y into an Int on line 8. We refer to this process as *casting*, whereby a value of one type is coerced into being a value of another type. In computer language–speak, this feature is known as a *type conversion*. Every language has rules for handling type conversions, and Swift is certainly no exception.

One typical rule is that type conversions can take place only between "like" types. In popular computer languages such as C, you can convert an integer to a double, or vice versa, because both are numeric types. However, coercing an integer to become a string is not a valid type conversion because the types are inherently different. Swift is a bit more flexible in this regard, however. Try the following.

```
15> var t = 123
t: Int = 123
16> var s = String(t)
s: String = "123"
17>
```

Here, the variable t is being declared and assigned what is clearly an Int number. That is followed by another declaration of the variable s to the String type casted version of the Int variable t.

Can you cast a string into an Int, or even a Double?

```
17> var u = Int(s)
u: Int? = 123
18> var v = Double(s)
v: Double? = 123
```

Yes, you can. Swift allows you the flexibility of bringing your data from one type to the next. But let's get a little naughty and try to trip up Swift with something bogus:

```
19> var w = Int("this is not a number")
w: Int? = nil
20>
```

Obviously, there isn't an intelligible way to convert a string to an integer, so Swift doesn't allow it, but instead of returning an error, it simply returns nothing: `nil`. You are probably puzzled by the Int? shown in Swift's response for lines 17 to 19, and rightly wondering "What is that question mark doing there?" It's an indicator that `myConvertedInt` is a special type of Int: an optional Int. I'll talk a lot more about optionals later, but for now, just know that they allow a variable to take on a special value known as `nil`.

BEING EXPLICIT

Having Swift infer the type of your variables or constants is pretty handy. You don't have to tell Swift what an integer is or what a number with a fractional component is—it just knows. However, sometimes you may want to explicitly declare a variable or constant to be a certain type. Swift allows you to advertise the type as part of the declaration:

```
20> var myNewNumber : Double = 3
myNewNumber: Double = 3
21>
```

Declaring a variable or constant with a specific type is as easy as adding a colon, followed by the type name, after the variable or constant name. Here, you've declared myNewNumber as a Double and assigned the number 3 to it, and Swift dutifully reports the declaration.

What would have happened if you left off the : Double on line 18? Swift would have evaluated the assignment, determined that the value was an Int, and made myNewNumber that type. In this particular case, you overrode Swift's inherent assumption and forced it to type the variable according to our wishes.

Let's consider what happens if you leave off the assignment of the variable or constant to a value:

```
21> var m : Int
repl:swift:21:1 error: variables currently must have an initial value when
→ entered at the top level of the REPL
var m : Int
^
```

```
21> let rr : Int
repl:swift:21:1: error: variables currently must have an initial value when
→ entered at the top level of the REPL
let rr : Int
^
```

On line 21, a variable named m was declared to be an Int, but was not assigned a value at declaration time. Swift returned an error indicating that an initial value must be assigned in the context of the REPL.

On the next line, the let command declares rr as an Int but does not assign a value. Notice that Swift returns the same error. In the context of the REPL, both constants and variables must have a value assigned to them at the time they are declared.

STRINGS AND THINGS

So far, you've delved a bit into the numeric types, but another type in Swift is used quite a bit: the String type. As you saw earlier, a string in Swift is one or more characters bounded by double quotes ("").

Here is a perfectly valid declaration of a string:

```
21> let myState = "Louisiana"
myState: String = "Louisiana"
22>
```

So is this:

```
22> let myParish : String = "St. Landry"
myParish: String - "St. Landry"
23>
```

Again, these examples underscore type inference versus type explicitness. In the first case, Swift looks at the value to determine the type; in the second case, you specified the type explicitly. Both are correct.

STRINGING THINGS TOGETHER

Strings can be connected, or *concatenated*, to form larger strings using the plus sign (+) operator. Here are a number of constant declarations that are used to form a larger constant string:

```
23> let noun = "Wayne"
noun: String = "Wayne"
24> let verb = "drives"
verb: String = "drives"
25> let preposition = "to Cal's gym"
preposition: String = "to Cal's gym"
26> let sentence = noun + " " + verb + " " + preposition + "."
sentence: String = "Wayne drives to Cal's gym."
27>
```

On line 26, you concatenated six individual pieces of text and assigned that result to the sentence constant.

CHARACTERS HAVE CHARACTER

So far, you've seen three types in action: Int (for whole numbers), Double (for numbers with a fractional component), and String (for a series of characters). Another type you will use in Swift is the Character type, which is actually a special case of a String. A variable or constant of type Character contains a single character bound in double quote marks.

It's worth a try:

```
27> let myFavoriteLetter = "A"
myFavoriteLetter: String = "A"
28>
```

You may be scratching your head wondering why the variable myFavoriteLetter is identified by Swift as a String. Without explicitly specifying the type Character, Swift assumes a string type when even just one letter is enclosed in double quotes. The Character type is one type that isn't inferred by Swift. Let's rectify this:

```
28> let myFavoriteLetter : Character = "A"
myFavoriteLetter: Character = "A"
29>
```

Now you get the expected result!

If a String is a composition of one or more Character types, you should be able to build a String from a Character. And indeed you can, using the same plus sign (+) operator you used earlier for strings, but with a caveat: The character must be cast to a String type.

```
29> let myFavoriteLetters = String(myFavoriteLetter) +
String(myFavoriteLetter)
myFavoriteLetters: String = "AA"
30>
```

If you are coming from languages like C or Objective-C, where string concatenation is much more obtuse, this should feel extremely simple. After all, bringing characters and strings together with a simple plus sign operator is a lot less typing than using C's strcat() function or Objective-C's Foundation class NSString method stringWithFormat: to perform string concatenation. You're witnessing the conciseness and beauty of the Swift language in action here. String concatenation is as naturally expressive as adding two numbers. Speaking of adding numbers, let's get back to them and take a look at doing some simple math in Swift.

MATH AND MORE

Swift can do math very, very well. You just saw how the String type uses the plus sign for concatenating strings. However, the plus sign is used for more than just bringing together strings. It's also the universal expression for addition, and now is as good a time as any to explore Swift's math capabilities. Let's look at a few simple arithmetic examples of mathematical expressions:

```
30> let addition = 2 + 2
addition: Int = 4
31> let subtraction = 4 - 3
subtraction: Int = 1
32> let multiplication = 10 * 5
multiplication: Int = 50
33> let division = 24 / 6
division: Int = 4
34>
```

The basic four operations are here: addition (+), subtraction (–), multiplication (*), and division (/). Swift gave you the answers you anticipated and also typed the constants as you would expect: Int. Again, this decision to type the constants as integers is based on the value on the right side of the equals sign.

You can also perform the modulo math operation (using the % operator), which returns the remainder value of a division operation:

```
34> let modulo = 23 % 4
modulo: Int = 3
35>
```

In Swift, the modulo operator even works with Double values:

```
35> let modulo = 23.5 % 4.3
modulo: Double = 2.0000000000000009
36>
```

In addition, the plus and minus signs are honored as unary operators. Prepending a + to the value infers a positive number, whereas a – implies a negative number:

```
36> var positiveNumber : Int = +33
positiveNumber: Int = 33
37> var negativeNumber : Int = -33
negativeNumber: Int = -33
38>
```

EXPRESSIONS

Mathematical expressions are fully supported, including the standard operator order of precedence (multiplication and division evaluated first from left to right, and then addition and subtraction):

```
38> let r = 3 + 5 * 9
r: Int = 48
39> let g = (3 + 5) * 9
g: Int = 72
40>
```

Line 38 yields the result of multiplying 5 times 9 first and then adding 3, and line 39 yields the same expression with parentheses around the first two values to enforce the addition first, and then the multiplication of the result by 9. Swift honors the canonical order of precedence of mathematical operations just like other modern languages.

MIXING NUMERIC TYPES

What happens if you get clever and mix a number with a fractional component with an integer?

```
40> let anotherDivision = 48 / 5.0
anotherDivision: Double = 9.5999999999999996
41>
```

Here you are dividing the integer 48 by the number 5 with a decimal point and a 0 behind it. The decimal point is just enough of a hint to Swift that its type is Double. Even the type of the resulting constant anotherDivision is assigned a type of Double. What you are witnessing here is Swift's notion of *type promotion*. The Int 48 has been promoted to a Double simply by the presence of another Double in the equation. Likewise, the type of the constant being assigned also takes on the same type. It's a good idea to be aware of this rule.

When numeric values of different types are used in a common expression, type promotion always goes from the type with the least possible representation to the type with the most possible representation. Since a Double can represent Int value, but not the other way around, Int values are promoted to Double values.

NUMERIC REPRESENTATIONS

Numeric values can be represented different ways in Swift. Up to now, we've been focused on the most common and natural way of thinking of numbers: decimal, or base 10. Let's explore other ways to express a numeric value.

BINARY, OCTAL, AND HEXADECIMAL NOTATION

If you have done any amount of programming, you've encountered base 2, base 16, and possibly even base 8 numbers. Known as binary, hexadecimal, and octal, respectively, these number systems come up often enough in software development that having a shorthand notation to refer to them in their natural state is helpful:

```
41> let binaryNumber = 0b110011
binaryNumber: Int = 51
42> let octalNumber = 0o12
octalNumber: Int = 10
43> let hexadecimalNumber = 0x32
hexadecimalNumber: Int = 50
44>
```

The prefix for binary numbers is 0b, for octal numbers it's 0o, and for hexadecimal numbers it's 0x. Of course, no prefix implies a decimal number.

SCIENTIFIC NOTATION

An alternative way of representing a number is to provide it in scientific notation. Such notation is useful for expressing numbers with a large number of decimal places in a compact form:

```
44> let scientificNotation = 4.434e-10
scientificNotation: Double = 0.00000000044339999999999999
45>
```

The e represents the exponent of a base 10 number; in this case, 4.434×10^{-10}.

LARGE NUMBER NOTATION

If you've ever sat in front of your Mac counting the number of zeros behind a number to determine its magnitude, you'll love this next feature. Swift allows you to demark large numbers in such a way that their size is immediately clear:

```
45> let fiveMillion = 5_000_000
fiveMillion: Int = 5000000
46>
```

The underscores are ignored but help immensely with the readability of the number.

TRUE OR FALSE

Another type that Swift supports is Bool, or the Boolean type; it holds a single value—true or false—and is often used in comparative expressions to answer questions like "is 12 greater than 3?" or "does 55 equal 12?" These logical comparisons are used heavily in software development, from terminating the iteration of a list of objects to determining the execution path of a set of conditional statements:

```
 46> 100 > 50
$R0: Bool = true
 47> 1.1 >= 0.3
$R1: Bool = true
 48> 66.22 < 7
$R2: Bool = false
 49> 44 <= 1
$R3: Bool = false
 50> 5.4 == 9.3
$R4: Bool = false
 51> 6 != 7
$R5: Bool = true
 52>
```

The comparisons above are: greater than, greater than or equal, less than, less than or equal, equal to, and not equal to. Based on the "trueness" of the comparison, a Bool of either true or false is returned. You're also comparing both Int and Double literals to illustrate that both numeric types are comparable, even amongst each other.

THE RESULT

Notice that you have not used the let or var keyword to assign the result of the Boolean expression to a variable or constant. Also, the results of the conditional expression evaluations are different, as in the result of line 49:

```
$R3: Bool = false
```

What is $R3? This is known in the Swift REPL as a temporary variable, and it holds the value of the result: in this case, false. You can reference a temporary variable as though it were a variable:

```
52> print($R3)
false
53>
```

You can assign values to these temporary variables as though they were declared variables as well.

WHAT ABOUT STRINGS?

Wouldn't it be great if you could use the same comparator operators to test the equality of strings? If you've come from C or Objective-C, you know how tedious testing for equality of two strings is.

In C, it's like this:

```
int result = strcmp("this string", "that string")
```

In Objective-C, it's like this:

```
NSComparisonResult result = [@"this string" compare:@ "that string"];
```

Swift makes this operation super easy to read and type:

```
53> "this string" == "that string"
$R6: Bool = false
54> "b" > "a"
$R7: Bool = true
55> "this string" == "this string"
$R8: Bool = true
56> "that string" <= "a string"
$R9: Bool = false
57>
```

The results speak for themselves: Swift's string comparison feature is much more natural and expressive.

PRINTING MADE EASY

So far you have used the print method to print strings in the REPL. Let's revisit this method and examine how you can use it to construct more complex strings.

One of the conveniences of the print method is its ability to effortlessly print the contents of variables in-line with other text. If you happen to know C or Objective-C, you'll recall that the amount of typing required to express formatted text is rather large, with printf in C and NSLog() in Objective-C being prime examples. Consider this Objective-C code excerpt:

```
NSString *myFavoriteCity = "New Orleans";
NSString *myFavoriteFood = "Seafood Gumbo";
NSString *myFavoriteRestaurant = "Mulates";
NSInteger yearsSinceVisit = 3;
NSLog(@"When I visited %@ %d years ago, I went to %@ and ordered %@.",
→ myFavoriteCity, yearsSinceVisit, myFavoriteRestaurant, myFavoriteFood);
```

If this looks familiar to you, you know that it's problematic for several reasons. First, the variables are not in the exact position they would be when the string is printed, which requires you to "line up" variables in the correct order or else you will get unexpected results. Second, you are dealing with two different types of variables with different formatting codes: NSString, which uses %@, and NSInteger, which uses %d. (If you aren't familiar with the concept of formatting codes, don't worry, you won't use them in Swift.)

With Swift you avoid the cumbersome dance of using a format string and worrying about ordering and formatting codes. Instead, you can simply place your variables right inside the string, exactly where they would naturally go, and they will be printed right alongside the other text. Here's the Swift version of the Objective-C code:

```
 57> let myFavoriteCity = "New Orleans"
myFavoriteCity: String = "New Orleans"
 58> let myFavoriteFood = "Seafood Gumbo"
myFavoriteFood: String = "Seafood Gumbo"
 59> let myFavoriteRestaurant = "Mulates"
myFavoriteRestaurant: String = "Mulates"
 60> let yearsSinceVisit = 3
yearsSinceVisit: Int = 3
 61> print("When I visited \(myFavoriteCity) \(yearsSinceVisit) years ago,
      → I went to \(myFavoriteRestaurant) and ordered \(myFavoriteFood).")
When I visited New Orleans 3 years ago, I went to Mulates and ordered
→ Seafood Gumbo.
 62>
```

The markup to do this on line 61 is amazingly simple. There, the embedded notation \() is used to reference all four constants you declared earlier on lines 57 through 60. This notation is very handy, especially when compared to how the aforementioned languages handle this feature.

Of course, assigning the result of the string to a variable or constant is just as easy as printing it:

```
62> let sentence = "When I visited \(myFavoriteCity) \(yearsSinceVisit)
  → years ago, I went to \(myFavoriteRestaurant) and ordered \
  → (myFavoriteFood)."
sentence: String = "When I visited New Orleans 3 years ago, I went to Mulates
  → and ordered Seafood Gumbo."
63>
```

USING ALIASES

I talked about types earlier and how they are central to Swift's idea of identifying and classifying variables and constants. As an *immutable* (non-changing) property, the type is an integral component of every number and string in your program. Sometimes, however, you may want to enhance the readability of your source code by using a type alias.

A *type alias* is simply a way of telling Swift to give an alternate name to a type:

```
63> typealias EightBits = UInt8
64> var reg : EightBits = 0
reg: EightBits = 0
65>
```

Here, the native Swift type UInt8 has been aliased to EightBits, which can then be used in subsequent declarations. You can even get clever and assign a type alias to another type alias:

```
65> typealias NewBits = EightBits
66> var reg2 : NewBits = 0
reg2: NewBits = 0
67>
```

Of course, NewBits and EightBits are really a UInt8 under the hood. Nothing new has been created in terms of a type, but the readability of your code changes. Although type aliases are great ways to enhance your code, use them with care and document their use, especially if you are sharing your work with other developers. Nothing is more confusing than encountering a new type and not knowing exactly what it is or what it represents.

GROUPING DATA WITH TUPLES

Sometimes bringing different data elements together to form a larger type is useful. Up to now, you've worked with single pieces of data: integers, strings, and so on. These elemental types are the foundation of Swift's data storage and manipulation capabilities, but they can also be combined in interesting ways, as you'll see throughout the book.

One such combination that we will explore here is the *tuple*. A tuple is a grouping of one or more variables, constants, or literal values into a single entity. A tuple is defined by a comma-separated list bounded with parentheses:

```
67> let myDreamCar = (2016, "Mercedes-Benz", "M-Class")
myDreamCar: (Int, String, String) = {
  0 = 2016
  1 = "Mercedes-Benz"
  2 = "M-Class"
}
68>
```

The constant myDreamCar is defined as a tuple with three elements: an Int and two String literals. Note that Swift inferred the type of each member of the tuple, because you did not provide an explicit type. Also, the members of the tuple retain the order in which they are defined.

So now that you've defined a tuple, what can you do with it? You can inspect it, of course. Using dot notation, you can explore the tuple's contents, starting with the 0 index element, as follows:

```
68> print(myDreamCar.0)
2016
69> print(myDreamCar.1)
Mercedes-Benz
70> print(myDreamCar.2)
M-Class
71> print(myDreamCar)
(2016, "Mercedes-Benz", "M-Class")
72>
```

If you attempt to reference a non-existing member of the tuple, Swift will remind you with an error:

```
72> print(myDreamCar.3)
repl:swift::72:7: error: '(Int, String, String)' does not have a member
→ named '3'
print(myDreamCar.3)
       ^         ~

72>
```

Tuples come in handy when returning multiple pieces of information as a single grouping. You will find them useful as you become more familiar with Swift.

OPTIONALS

You may recall earlier that you used the Int() method on a String variable s to convert its contents to an Int so that it could be assigned to a new variable of the same type:

```
17> var u = Int(s)
u: Int? = 123
18>
```

I glossed over the question mark following the type designator returned by Swift. That question mark signifies that u is more than just an Int. It's an *optional* Int.

So what exactly is an optional? It's actually a qualifier on a type that alerts Swift that the variable or constant could be nothing, or *nil*. The value nil has long standing in programming languages. In Objective-C, it's also known as nil, and in C/C++, it's NULL. The meaning is essentially the same: empty.

Recall line 19 earlier, where you tried to convert a string into an integer:

```
19> var w = Int("this is not a number")
w: Int? = nil
20>
```

Recall that w was set to type Int? (an optional Int), but its value was not the string; it was nil. And that is precisely because there is no numeric representation for the letters "this is not a number" to convert to an Int. Returning nil is Swift's way of admitting defeat. The optional gives a variable an alternative path to success. In this case, the Int() method is returning nil as a way of saying "I cannot convert this into a number."

Declaring a variable as an optional is as simple as adding a question mark at the end of the type at declaration time:

```
72> var v : Int?
v: Int? = nil
73>
```

Swift responds with the indication that v is indeed an optional Int. Since you didn't provide an assignment to a value at declaration time, the default assigned value is not 0, but nil.

Try setting the variable to an actual value:

```
73> v = 3
74>
```

Finally, let's show the value. Instead of using the print method, just type the name of the variable; Swift will assign it to a temporary.

```
74> v
$R10: Int? = 3
75>
```

And as you can see, Swift reports that the value is indeed 3.

Optionals work on more than just Int types. In fact, any type can be declared as an optional. Here's an example of two variables, one String and one Character, as declared optionals:

```
75> var s : String? = "Valid text"
s: String? = "Valid text"
76> var u : Character? = "a"
u: Character? = "a"
77> u = nil
78>
```

On line 77, u is set to the nil value, underscoring that any variable declared as an optional can be set to nil.

I'll explore optionals much more in a subsequent chapter. For now, knowing that they exist and recognizing the notation surrounding them is enough.

SUMMARY

Congratulations, Swift beginner, you've made it through the first chapter. And what a whirl-wind it has been. You have been thrown quite a lot of information to digest, so don't hesitate to go back and review the chapter if you need to.

Here are the topics that were introduced in this chapter:

- Variables
- Constants
- The `print` method
- Types (`Int`, `Double`, `Character`, and `String`, just to name a few)
- Mathematical operators
- Numeric notations (binary, hexadecimal, scientific, and so on)
- String concatenation
- Type inference and explicit declarations
- Type aliases
- Tuples
- Optionals

Remember: These are the basic concepts you need to master in order to become a Swift artisan. Know and understand them well, because in subsequent chapters you'll build on what you learned here and learn even more features of the language.

Working with Collections

The last chapter covered a lot of Swift's basics, with plenty of examples (including intentional mistakes) in order to reinforce the concepts of variables, constants, and types. As you'll see, the information in Chapter 1 will come in handy in this and subsequent chapters.

For this chapter, get ready to turn your attention to the notion of collections.

When you think of a collection, what comes to mind? Here are several examples of collections you might have had at one time or another:

- Assortment of toy action figures and accessories
- Postage stamps or coins from different countries
- Shopping list of items to buy at the grocery store

Collections can also be more general categorizations:

- Make and model of vehicles in a parking lot
- Names of people on a wedding invitation list

All these examples evoke the notion of a grouping or organization of individual elements or items (toys, stamps, vehicles, and so on). Collections of related (or even unrelated) items are important in the Swift language. And as you'll see shortly, collections come in different flavors.

For the bulk of this chapter, you'll focus on collections, which are essentially structures that allow you to group information and data in various ways. You'll use collections quite a bit later in this book and in your general Swift development, so take the time to understand them.

THE CANDY JAR

Let's explore the idea of collections in Swift by imagining an empty candy jar sitting on a store counter. Now, think of all the various candies you could put into that jar. Let's call the jar a *container*, which holds one or more candies, or *values*. Representing that candy jar and its contents in Swift can be modeled in a number of ways, starting with an *array*.

An array is nothing more than an ordered list of values of some length. Arrays are common constructs in computer languages, and declaring one in Swift is easy.

STARTING FROM SCRATCH

In this chapter, you'll continue to use the REPL to explore concepts. The line numbers shown in the code snippets in this chapter start with line number 1, which presumes you have restarted the REPL. Remember: To quit the REPL, type

```
:quit
```

and to restart the REPL from the Terminal, type

```
xcrun swift
```

Here is an array of three candy values that would go into the virtual candy jar:

```
1> let candyJar = ["Peppermints", "Gooey Bears", "Happy Ranchers"]
candyJar: [String] = 3 values {
  [0] = "Peppermints"
  [1] = "Gooey Bears"
  [2] = "Happy Ranchers"
}
  2>
```

Recognize the `let` keyword? That's the constant declaration keyword. In this case you're declaring a constant named `candyJar` and using a special notation: the opening and closing brackets, [and]. The items in the array are bounded by these two characters, and this is how Swift recognizes that an array is being declared.

This array has three `String` constants:

- `"Peppermints"`
- `"Gooey Bears"`
- `"Happy Ranchers"`

The comma between each value in the array denotes where one value ends and the other begins. Also, notice that once again, Swift inferred the types of each of these items by simply looking at how they are represented—as strings. That's because each value is surrounded by double quotes.

Notice how Swift reported the declaration to you after you typed it. It explicitly points to `candyJar` being an array of `String` values:

```
candyJar: [String] = 3 values {
  [0] = "Peppermints"
  [1] = "Gooey Bears"
  [2] = "Happy Ranchers"
}
```

Here, Swift is confirming that the array holds three values and that they are ordered, starting with the number 0. In fact, all arrays in Swift begin with the "0th value" and continue in ordinal fashion. This number is known as the *array index* and maps directly to the value it represents.

So far, so good? Great. Now, let's learn how to interrogate an array for a particular value. Let's say you wanted to see the second element in the array. Remember that since arrays are ordered starting at 0, the second element will have an index of 1.

```
  2> candyJar[1]
$R0: String = "Gooey Bears"
  3>
```

> **NOTE:** To print or not to print? Remember that simply typing the name of the item without using `print` is acceptable when using the REPL. When you do so, the result of the expression is assigned to a temporary variable—in this case, `$R0`.

Swift politely responds with the value "Gooey Bears" as the second element in the array and also reminds you of the type: `String`.

As expected, replacing the [1] with another array index will reference the value at that location:

```
3> candyJar[2]
$R1: String = "Happy Ranchers"
4>
```

That notation is quite handy. You can access individual elements in the array by simply using the index number bounded by brackets.

Now, what happens if you reference a nonexistent location? Use an index that is clearly out of the range of the currently available index values:

```
4> candyJar[5]
fatal error: Array index out of range
Execution interrupted. Enter Swift code to recover and continue.
Enter LLDB commands to investigate (type :help for assistance.)
5>
```

Not surprisingly, you have hit a nerve with Swift because you requested a nonexistent element. The array doesn't have a sixth element (the array has only three elements, with subscripts 0, 1, and 2). Being the ever so careful language that it is, Swift reminds us of the infraction with a fatal error.

And here's where Swift is ahead of the pack compared to some other computer languages: It emphasizes *safety*. Swift creates a safe environment where exceptional and anomalous behavior, like referencing nonexistent array subscripts, is not tolerated. If you have any experience with arrays in C, you might already know that accessing nonexistent parts of an array is possible. In fact, very similar methods have been used in the past by writers of Trojan horse virus software to compromise computer systems.

This error presents an opportunity to bring up a very good question: "What if I wanted to add more values to an array? How would I do that?" Swift has a special method that works on arrays: append(). To add a value to an array, simply append it. Let's add my favorite candy to the jar:

```
5> candyJar.append("Candy Canes")
repl.swift:5:1: error: immutable value of type '[String]' only has mutating
→ members named 'append'
candyJar.append("Candy Canes")
^        ~~~~~~


5>
```

Another error! It seems you just can't catch a break. We all learn by making mistakes, though, and this is certainly part of learning the ins and outs of Swift.

Can you spot why this error occurred? Look carefully at the text of the error message:

```
error: immutable value of type '[String]' only has mutating members
→ named 'append'
```

Swift is telling you that the array of String values is immutable (nonchangeable), and you are trying to change the contents of a constant array. Remember that you declared the array as a constant array with let. You cannot modify the value of a constant, and that includes arrays declared as constants.

You'll need to create a second array, a mutable (changeable) one. You can do that easily, and at the same time, start with the contents of the immutable array:

```
5> var refillableCandyJar = candyJar
refillableCandyJar: [String] = 3 values {
  [0] = "Peppermints"
  [1] = "Gooey Bears"
  [2] = "Happy Ranchers"
}
  6>
```

That was easy! You just declared a variable refillableCandyJar and initialized it with the contents of the candyJar constant array. All the same values that exist in the constant array are now part of this variable array.

BIRDS OF A FEATHER...

Can an array contain values of different types? Try the following:

```
6> var arrayTest - ["x", 3]
rcpl.swift:6:23: error: 'Int' is not convertible to 'IntegerLiteralConvertible'
var arrayTest = ["x", 3]
                      ^


  6>
```

Clearly, Swift prevents this from happening, underscoring that, indeed, values in an array must be of the same type.

Speaking of types, what if you want to be specific about the value type in the array declaration itself?

```
6> var h2o:[String] = ["Hydrogen", "Hydrogen", "Oxygen"]
h2o: [String] = 3 values {
  [0] = "Hydrogen"
  [1] = "Hydrogen"
  [2] = "Oxygen"
}
  7>
```

Declaring an array to hold specific type values involves adding the colon, followed by the name of the type bounded by brackets [ ].

EXTENDING THE ARRAY

Let's bring our focus back to the `refillableCandyJar` array, which is a mutable array, thanks to the previous assignment on line 5. Now, can you actually append to this new array? Let's find out:

```
7> refillableCandyJar.append("Candy Canes")
8>
```

Other than the prompt, there's no indication whether or not this was successful. But hey, at least you didn't get an error. Let's see the contents of the variable array and verify that Candy Canes was added:

```
8> refillableCandyJar
$R2: [String] = 4 values {
  [0] = "Peppermints"
  [1] = "Gooey Bears"
  [2] = "Happy Ranchers"
  [3] = "Candy Canes"
}
  9>
```

And indeed, it occupies the fourth location (array subscript 3) in the array, just as we hoped it would.

Let's add a few more candies to the jar. This time, use a different syntax:

```
 9> refillableCandyJar += ["Peanut Clusters"]
10> refillableCandyJar += ["Banana Taffy", "Bubble Gum"]
11> refillableCandyJar
$R3: [String] = 7 values {
  [0] = "Peppermints"
  [1] = "Gooey Bears"
  [2] = "Happy Ranchers"
  [3] = "Candy Canes"
  [4] = "Peanut Clusters"
  [5] = "Banana Taffy"
  [6] = "Bubble Gum"
}
 12>
```

Instead of adding a single `String` value, lines 9 and 10 instead append another array, which demonstrates the flexibility that Swift brings here. You can simply add the contents of one array to another with the += operator. Finally, on line 11, you requested the contents of the variable `refillableCandyJar`, which shows the entire contents of the virtual candy jar—all seven delicious varieties.

So far, you have created a constant array and a variable array. You've also assigned the constant array to the variable array, creating a mutable array that can be changed. And you've successfully modified the array contents using both the append() method and the += operator. Let's do some further exploration into arrays.

REPLACING AND REMOVING VALUES

Replacing an array value is as simple as specifying the array subscript and assigning it a new value. Let's replace Happy Ranchers with another type of candy:

```
12> refillableCandyJar[2] = "Lollipops"
13> refillableCandyJar
$R4: [String] = 7 values {
  [0] = "Peppermints"
  [1] = "Gooey Bears"
  [2] = "Lollipops"
  [3] = "Candy Canes"
  [4] = "Peanut Clusters"
  [5] = "Banana Taffy"
  [6] = "Bubble Gum"
}
 14>
```

Replacements work great. But what if you want to remove a value? Perhaps you don't like Gooey Bears. Can it be removed from the virtual candy jar? Of course. You've grown a variable array by appending to it, and now you'll remove some items completely:

```
14> refillableCandyJar.removeAtIndex(1)
$R5: String = "Gooey Bears"
15> refillableCandyJar
$R6: [String] = 6 values {
  [0] = "Peppermints"
  [1] = "Lollipops"
  [2] = "Candy Canes"
  [3] = "Peanut Clusters"
  [4] = "Banana Taffy"
  [5] = "Bubble Gum"
}
 16>
```

On line 14, you employed the array method removeAtIndex(), which takes a single parameter: the index of the value you wish to remove. The method's result is the value removed, and the value is assigned to $R5.

A quick review of the variable refillableCandyJar on line 15 shows that, indeed, the Gooey Bears are gone, and the contents of the entire array have "shifted" up. Instead of seven items in the candy jar, you have only six now.

Remember that anytime an item is removed from an array, the other values "fill in the gap" and move up to accommodate the empty space.

Here's another handy way to remove the last value of the array:

```
16> refillableCandyJar.removeLast()
$R7: String = "Bubble Gum"
17>
```

Again, the removed value is returned, and the array is shortened from six to five values:

```
17> refillableCandyJar
$R8: [String] = 5 values {
  [0] = "Peppermints"
  [1] = "Lollipops"
  [2] = "Candy Canes"
  [3] = "Peanut Clusters"
  [4] = "Banana Taffy"
}
18>
```

INSERTING VALUES AT A SPECIFIC LOCATION

So far, you have added values (via the append( ) method) to the end of an array, and you have directed Swift to remove a value at a specific position from the array. Now, let's see how easy inserting a value is.

Let's add "Twirlers" at the position where "Candy Canes" is currently. That's position 2, or the third position in the array:

```
18> refillableCandyJar.insert("Twirlers", atIndex: 2)
19>
```

Now let's review the contents of the array to see if it worked:

```
19> refillableCandyJar
$R9: [String] = 6 values {
  [0] = "Peppermints"
  [1] = "Lollipops "
  [2] = "Twirlers"
  [3] = "Candy Canes"
  [4] = "Peanut Clusters"
  [5] = "Banana Taffy"
20>
```

And indeed it did. "Twirlers" now occupies location 2. The values have also been shifted down one place to accommodate the new value thanks to the insert() method.

Notice that the insert() method took two parameters: the value to insert into the array, as well as the index (or position) where the insertion takes place. What's interesting to note about this method is the second parameter, which is prefixed by the name atIndex:. These named parameters increase the readability of Swift's code by providing context for the parameter being passed. You'll learn more about the composition of method names in Swift a little later.

COMBINING ARRAYS

Swift's syntax for combining arrays is natural for concatenating strings. To illustrate, create another candy jar array with a different set of confectionaries:

```
20> var anotherRefillableCandyJar = ["Sour Tarts", "Cocoa Bar",
  → "Coconut Rounds"]
anotherRefillableCandyJar: [String] = 3 values {
  [0] = "Sour Tarts"
  [1] = "Cocoa Bar"
  [2] = "Coconut Rounds"
}
 21>
```

Now create a third array with the array combination syntax using the earlier array refillableCandyJar, with six values, and the new anotherRefillableCandyJar, with three values:

```
21> var combinedRefillableCandyJar = refillableCandyJar +
  → anotherRefillableCandyJar
combinedRefillableCandyJar: [String] = 9 values {
  [0] = "Peppermints"
  [1] = "Lollipops"
  [2] = "Twirlers"
  [3] = "Candy Canes"
  [4] = "Peanut Clusters"
  [5] = "Banana Taffy"
  [6] = "Sour Tarts"
  [7] = "Cocoa Bar"
  [8] = "Coconut Rounds"
}
 22>
```

The new array has nine values (six from the first array, and three from the second). Also, the values are ordered in the same way they were in the original arrays.

We've covered a lot about arrays. They are excellent for storing lists of values, whether they are related or not. They can be immutable (by declaring them constant with the let command), or they can be mutable arrays that can change (values can be added, removed, or replaced). And finally, all values within an array must be of the same type.

The next section takes a look at another type of collection: the dictionary.

THE DICTIONARY

When you think of a dictionary, Daniel Webster probably comes to mind. The dictionary on a shelf in the library is composed of pages of definitions for words. You look up a word in alphabetical order to determine its definition. In Swift, dictionaries work in a similar fashion.

Like an array, a dictionary in Swift is composed of one or more entities. Unlike an array, the entity in a dictionary contains two distinct components: a *key* and a *value*. Although the key and the value themselves can be different types, all keys must be of the same type; likewise, all values must also share the same type.

To start out learning about dictionaries, I'll use one of my favorite food additives: peppers. Some peppers are hotter than others, and this "heat" can be quantified using a measurement known as Scoville units. You'll use a dictionary to define a subset of the Scoville scale. The key for each entry will be the name of the pepper, and the value will be the Scoville unit for that pepper:

```
 22> var scovilleScale = ["Poblano":1_000, "Serrano":700, "Red Amazon":
   → 75_000, "Red Savina Habanero" : 500_000]
scovilleScale: [String : Int] = 4 key/value pairs {
  [0] = {
   key = "Serrano"
   value = 700
  }
  [1] = {
   key = "Red Savina Habanero"
   value = 500000
  }
  [2] = {
   key = "Poblano"
   value = 1000
  }
  [3] = {
   key = "Red Amazon"
   value = 75000
```

```
      }
    }
    23>
```

You've just created a dictionary with four entries: Poblano, with a score of 1000; Serrano, with a score of 700; Red Amazon, with a score of 75,000; and Red Savina Habanero, with a score of 500,000! (That's a really hot pepper!)

> **NOTE:** Dictionary keys are not necessarily placed in alphabetical order. Swift will always use the order that is the most efficient for retrieval and access.

When you declared the dictionary, Swift once again inferred the type of both the key and the value. The key is clearly a String type; the value is an Int type. This is confirmed by the REPL report showing the result of the declaration. Also, the underscore was used to visually mark the thousands place in the number. Remember that this is purely syntactic sugar. It has no bearing on the value of the Int; the numbers show up without underscores in the result.

Do you notice something unusual? Look closely at the REPL output. The order in which you declared the dictionary and the order in which the dictionary is reported are not the same. Swift ordered the dictionary differently than you declared it. This difference illustrates an important tenet of dictionaries: Swift orders keys to determine the best method for quick retrieval and access. You cannot rely on the order in which you declared a dictionary to be the order in which it will be stored.

LOOKING UP AN ENTRY

Accessing an entry in a dictionary looks very similar to accessing a value in an array—except for the value bounded in the brackets. Recall that in an array, the ordinal position of the value is used (0, 1, 2, 3, and so on). In a dictionary, you use the actual key to look up the value of that entry:

```
23> scovilleScale["Serrano"]
$R10: Int? = 700
 24>
```

Notice the question mark again following the Int declaration. Remember that the question mark signifies an optional value—one that can be nil. The return value of a dictionary value is always an optional, but that doesn't mean you can use nil as a value, as shown in this example:

```
24> var myNilArray = ["someKey" : nil]
repl.swift:24:19: error: 'String' is not convertible to 'StringLiteralConvertible'
var myNilArray = ["someKey" : nil]
                 ^~~~~~~~~~

 24>
```

The somewhat mystical error is telling us that nil is not a valid value. Nor would it be for the key:

```
24> var myNilArray = [nil : "x"]
repl.swift:24:19: error: expression does not conform to type
→ 'NilLiteralConvertible'
var myNilArray = [nil : "x"]
                  ^~~


24>
```

So why would Swift bother to return a value as an optional type when you ask for a value in a dictionary? Let's consider the dictionary of Scoville units again:

```
24> scovilleScale
$R11: [String : Int] = 4 key/value pairs {
  [0] = {
   key = "Serrano"
   value = 700
  }
  [1] = {
   key = "Red Savina Habanero"
   value = 500000
  }
  [2] = {
   key = "Poblano"
   value = 1000
  }
  [3] = {
   key = "Red Amazon"
   value = 75000
  }
}
25>
```

You still have the same four entries in the dictionary. What if you asked for a value with a key that didn't exist? Let's find out if there is a Scoville unit for the Tabasco pepper:

```
25> scovilleScale["Tabasco"]
$R12: Int? = nil
26>
```

Lo and behold, the value returned is nil. This is precisely why Swift dictionary values return an optional type: the possibility that the dictionary will be queried with a nonexistent key.

ADDING AN ENTRY

Now that you've established what happens when you ask your Scoville unit dictionary for a nonexistent pepper, let's add that same pepper to your dictionary. Remember that because the dictionary was created as a mutable dictionary with var, extending it with the following syntax is possible:

```
26> scovilleScale["Tabasco"] = 50_000
27>
```

And for verification:

```
27> scovilleScale
$R13: [String : Int] = 5 key/value pairs {
  [0] = {
   key = "Serrano"
   value = 700
  }
  [1] = {
   key = "Red Savina Habanero"
   value = 500000
  }
  [2] = {
   key = "Tabasco"
   value = 50000
  }
  [3] = {
   key = "Poblano"
   value = 1000
  }
  [4] = {
   key = "Red Amazon"
   value = 75000
  }
}
 28>
```

Notice that the newly added pepper finds its way into the dictionary in an unpredictable order.

UPDATING AN ENTRY

If you really know your peppers, you may have realized that the Serrano's Scoville unit is actually wrong. The value is off by an order of magnitude: Its Scoville rating is 7000, not 700. Let's fix that:

```
28> scovilleScale["Serrano"] = 7_000
29>
```

The syntax for updating a dictionary entry is the same as that for assigning a new value to a new key. Swift simply replaces the old value, 700, with the new value, 7000:

```
29> scovilleScale
$R14: [String : Int] = 5 key/value pairs {
  [0] = {
   key = "Serrano"
   value = 7000
  }
  [1] = {
   key = "Red Savina Habanero"
   value = 500000
  }
  [2] = {
   key = "Tabasco"
   value = 50000
  }
  [3] = {
   key = "Poblano"
   value = 1000
  }
  [4] = {
   key = "Red Amazon"
   value = 75000
  }
}
 30>
```

REMOVING AN ENTRY

Removing a dictionary entry looks a lot like the previous two examples:

```
30> scovilleScale["Tabasco"] = nil
31>
```

Setting the key value to `nil` effectively removes that dictionary entry:

```
 31> scovilleScale
$R15: [String : Int] = 4 key/value pairs {
  [0] = {
   key = "Serrano"
   value = 7000
  }
  [1] = {
   key = "Red Savina Habanero"
   value = 500000
  }
  [2] = {
   key = "Poblano"
   value = 1000
  }
  [3] = {
   key = "Red Amazon"
   value = 75000
  }
}
 32>
```

Another way to remove a dictionary item is to use the removeValueForKey() method:

```
 32> scovilleScale.removeValueForKey("Poblano")
$R16: Int? = 1000
 33>
```

In this case, the entry's value is returned (1000). Sometimes this is the preferred method of removing an entry, as you'll see in later chapters.

ARRAYS OF ARRAYS?

The parts of this chapter on arrays and dictionaries used a very specific set of data: strings and integers. But what if you wanted to declare an array of dictionaries? Or a dictionary of arrays? In Swift, arrays and dictionaries are types, just like strings and integers, so they can contain references to each other.

Let's take the candy jar analogy a bit further. Mr. Arceneaux has a candy route with three stores: Fontenot's Grocery, Dupre's Quick Mart, and Smith's Pick-n-Sack. Each store has its own candy jar, and every week, Mr. Arceneaux's route takes him to each store to fill the candy jars.

Mr. Fontenot's customers like Choppers and Jaw Bombs, while Mr. Dupre's customers are inclined to purchase chocolate candies like Butterbar, Mrs. Goodbuys, and Giggles. Mr. Smith's customers prefer Jelly Munchers and Gooey Bears.

How could you model this assortment of candies and stores using either arrays or dictionaries? To make things easy, start from the bottom up: with the candy jars.

```
33> var fontenotsCandyJar = ["Choppers", "Jaw Bombs"]
fontenotsCandyJar: [String] = 2 values {
  [0] = "Choppers"
  [1] = "Jaw Bombs"
}
34> var dupresCandyJar = ["Butterbar", "Mrs. Goodbuys", "Giggles"]
dupresCandyJar: [String] = 3 values {
  [0] = "Butterbar"
  [1] = "Mrs. Goodbuys"
  [2] = "Giggles"
}
35> var smithsCandyJar = ["Jelly Munchers", "Gooey Bears"]
smithsCandyJar: [String] = 2 values {
  [0] = "Jelly Munchers"
  [1] = "Gooey Bears"
}
36>
```

Three arrays represent three candy jars. The variable names indicate the jars' owners. Now it's simply a matter of creating an array:

```
36> let arceneauxsCandyRoute = [fontenotsCandyJar, dupresCandyJar,
     → smithsCandyJar]
arceneauxsCandyRoute: [[String]] = 3 values {
  [0] = 2 values {
  [0] = "Choppers"
  [1] = "Jaw Bombs"
  }
  [1] = 3 values {
  [0] = "Butterbar"
  [1] = "Mrs. Goodbuys"
  [2] = "Giggles"
  }
  [2] = 2 values {
  [0] = "Jelly Munchers"
  [1] = "Gooey Bears"
```

```
    }
}
  37>
```

Swift denotes the type of arceneauxCandyRoute as "an array of an array of strings" with the [[String]] nomenclature.

Interrogating the array for the first element yields the first value in the array, which itself is an array:

```
  37> arceneauxsCandyRoute[0]
$R17: [String] = 2 values {
  [0] = "Choppers"
  [1] = "Jaw Bombs"
}
  38>
```

Notice that although the candy jars are now part of the route array, there isn't really an indication of which store goes with the array. That's because the variable name is not encapsulated within the array itself, just the values.

Let's bring some clarity to this example. Instead of using an array to hold the candy jar arrays, let's use a dictionary:

```
  38> let arceneauxsOtherCandyRoute = ["Fontenot's Grocery": fontenotsCandyJar,
       → "Dupre's Quick Mart": dupresCandyJar, "Smith's Pick-n-Sack":
       → smithsCandyJar]
arceneauxsOtherCandyRoute: [String: [String]] = 3 key/value pairs {
  [0] = {
   key = "Dupre's Quick Mart"
   value = 3 values {
      [0] = "Butterbar"
      [1] = "Mrs. Goodbuys"
      [2] = "Giggles"
   }
  }
  [1] = {
   key = "Smith's Pick-n-Sack"
   value = 2 values {
      [0] = "Jelly Munchers"
      [1] = "Gooey Bears"
   }
  }
  [2] = {
```

```
     key = "Fontenot's Grocery"
     value = 2 values {
        [0] = "Choppers"
        [1] = "Jaw Bombs"
     }
   }
}
 39>
```

Swift denotes the type of arceneauxsOtherCandyRoute with [String: [String]]. In English, this is "a dictionary whose key is a string and whose value is an array of strings."

The difference between this dictionary of arrays and the array of arrays earlier is that the key (of type String) is the descriptive term that defines the value, the candy jar. Instead of using a somewhat anonymous index value to obtain the value you want, you can now specify the value by its key:

```
 39> arceneauxsOtherCandyRoute["Smith's Pick-n-Sack"]
$R18: [String]? = 2 values {
  [0] = "Jelly Munchers"
  [1] = "Gooey Bears"
}
```

Depending on what you are trying to model, you may find that a mixture of arrays, dictionaries, or both may be appropriate. Practice certainly makes perfect.

STARTING FROM SCRATCH

Up to now, the arrays and dictionaries you have created have been initialized at declaration time. At times in Swift development, however, creating an array or dictionary without initializing it will be necessary. Perhaps the values are not known at that time in the application, or an empty array or dictionary will need to be populated by a method in a library or framework.

THE EMPTY ARRAY

Two nomenclatures are used to declare an empty array:

```
 40> var myEmptyArray:Array<Int> = []
myEmptyArray: [Int] = 0 values
 41>
```

This is the "longhand" form of declaring an array, and involves the keyword Array along with the type of the array bounded by angle brackets < >. Swift also gives you a second, "short form" style you can employ:

```
41> var myEmptyArray = [Int]()
myEmptyArray: [Int] = 0 values
42>
```

In these examples, you have declared an empty mutable array that will hold Int values. Because it's a mutable array, you can change it or populate it as you would any other array. Let's add three integers to the array:

```
42> myEmptyArray += [33, 44, 55]
43> myEmptyArray
$R19: [Int] = 3 values {
  [0] = 33
  [1] = 44
  [2] = 55
}
44>
```

You can also remove all elements of an array by assigning the variable to the "empty array":

```
44> myEmptyArray = []
45> myEmptyArray
$R20: [Int] = 0 values
46>
```

The array is now void of its original values, and you can reuse it for storing other data.

THE EMPTY DICTIONARY

Creating a new, empty dictionary is similar to creating an empty array. The syntax involves the actual word Dictionary along with a set of angle bracket characters:

```
46> var myEmptyDictionary = Dictionary<String, Double>()
myEmptyDictionary: [String : Double] = 0 key/value pairs
47>
```

THE LONG AND SHORT OF IT

Swift's syntax is very rich and flexible, usually allowing more than one way to express the same operation. In the case of array and dictionary declaration, using the short form saves some typing, but using the long form declaration is clearer. Whatever method you use, it's always helpful to be consistent.

In this example, you specified the specific key type and the value that will be allowed in the dictionary: The key type is String, and the value type is Double. These types are bounded by the angle bracket characters < > and separated by a comma. You can then add entries into the dictionary as follows:

```
47> myEmptyDictionary = ["MyKey":1.125]
48> myEmptyDictionary
$R21: [String : Double] = 1 key/value pair {
  [0] = {
   key = "MyKey"
   value = 1.125
  }
}
49>
```

ITERATING COLLECTIONS

Now that you've covered the basic collection types (arrays and dictionaries), it's time to explore *iterating* them. Iterating a collection is the act of examining each value in an array or dictionary and potentially performing some work on it.

Iterating is something that we all do in our daily work. When you're following a written list of steps to complete a task, you are iterating over that list. Working with data is no different. Iteration is a very common coding task, and as you'll see shortly, Swift provides several constructs to make iterating over collections a breeze.

ARRAY ITERATION

If you're coming from programming language like C, you are intimately familiar with the notion of the for loop. Swift has several flavors of this same construct that are more naturally expressive than C's version. Even if you have little prior programming experience, you'll pick up the concept right away.

The for-in loop is constructed in the following manner:

```
for itemName in list {
 ... do something with itemName
}
```

The itemName is any name you wish to use. It becomes a variable assigned to each value in the list as the iteration occurs. The list is the object being iterated, and everything that appears between the curly braces is code that is executed.

Let's revisit the combinedRefillableCandyJar array from earlier in the chapter:

```
49> combinedRefillableCandyJar
$R22: [String] = 9 values {
  [0] = "Peppermints"
  [1] = "Lollipops"
  [2] = "Twirlers"
  [3] = "Candy Canes"
  [4] = "Peanut Clusters"
  [5] = "Banana Taffy"
  [6] = "Sour Tarts"
  [7] = "Cocoa Bar"
  [8] = "Coconut Rounds"
}
50>
```

The following is a segment of code that uses Swift's for-in construct to print individual array values. This is a multiline code segment; as you type it in the REPL, the prompt changes from a number followed by a greater-than sign to a number followed by a period. This is triggered by the addition of the opening curly brace {, which tells the REPL that a new code block is beginning.

Because of this behavior, the results don't appear until the last line, which contains the closing curly brace }, is entered:

```
50> for candy in combinedRefillableCandyJar {
51.     print("I enjoy eating \(candy)!")
52. }
I enjoy eating Peppermints!
I enjoy eating Lollipops!
I enjoy eating Twirlers!
I enjoy eating Candy Canes!
I enjoy eating Peanut Clusters!
I enjoy eating Banana Taffy!
I enjoy eating Sour Tarts!
I enjoy eating Cocoa Bar!
I enjoy eating Coconut Rounds!
53>
```

Here's the breakdown of this code block: Each item in the combinedRefillableCandyJar array is assigned to the candy variable. Since there are nine values in the array, the for-in loop iterates nine times; each time, the code bounded in the curly braces is executed. In this case, the value is combined with a formatted String value and printed to the screen.

Another variation of the for-in loop provides both the value and the index of that value in the array:

```
53> for (index, candy) in combinedRefillableCandyJar.enumerate() {
54.     print("Candy \(candy) is in position \(index) of the array")
55. }
Candy Peppermints is in position 0 of the array
Candy Lollipops is in position 1 of the array
Candy Twirlers is in position 2 of the array
Candy Candy Canes is in position 3 of the array
Candy Peanut Clusters is in position 4 of the array
Candy Banana Taffy is in position 5 of the array
Candy Sour Tarts is in position 6 of the array
Candy Cocoa Bar is in position 7 of the array
Candy Coconut Rounds is in position 8 of the array
56>
```

Here, the enumerate() method is called on the defined array named combinedRefillableCandyJar. This method conveniently returns a tuple containing both the index of the value and the value itself in the array. The variables index and candy are then referenced to create a combined string. (You will recall that tuples were introduced in Chapter 1.)

DICTIONARY ITERATION

Iterating through a dictionary using the for-in construct is identical to that of the array example we just covered. To illustrate, let's reuse the dictionary you created earlier for Mr. Arceneaux's other candy route.

```
56> for (key, value) in arceneauxsOtherCandyRoute {
57.     print("\(key) has a candy jar with the following contents: \(value)")
58. }
Dupre's Quick Mart has a candy jar with the following contents:
→ [Butterbar, Mrs. Goodbuys, Giggles]
Smith's Pick-n-Sack has a candy jar with the following contents:
→ [Jelly Munchers, Gooey Bears]
Fontenot's Grocery has a candy jar with the following contents:
→ [Choppers, Jaw Bombs]
59>
```

Since dictionaries are composed of keys and values, they automatically return a tuple. That tuple is captured, and its contents are assigned to the variables key and value. Notice that value is itself an array, and the print method displays that array quite handily. Also, remember that the order of keys in a dictionary isn't necessarily alphabetical.

To further illustrate iterations, let's go for the gold and expand the first for-in loop to contain another for-in loop, as follows:

```
59> for (key, value) in arceneauxsOtherCandyRoute {
60.       for (index, candy) in value.enumerate() {
61.           print("\(key)'s candy jar contains \(candy) at position
             → \(index)")
62.       }
63. }
Dupre's Quick Mart's candy jar contains Butterbar at position 0
Dupre's Quick Mart's candy jar contains Mrs. Goodbuys at position 1
Dupre's Quick Mart's candy jar contains Giggles at position 2
Smith's Pick-n-Sack's candy jar contains Jelly Munchers at position 0
Smith's Pick-n-Sack's candy jar contains Gooey Bears at position 1
Fontenot's Grocery's candy jar contains Choppers at position 0
Fontenot's Grocery's candy jar contains Jaw Bombs at position 1
64>:quit
```

This is an example of a *nested* for-in loop. For each iteration through arceneauxsOtherCandyRoute (a dictionary), Swift is capturing the value in the variable value (an array) and using the enumerate() method on that variable to perform further iteration.

NOTE: Just a reminder: Although array contents are stored in a consistent order, dictionary contents aren't. Don't expect the order in which you built your dictionary to be reflected when iterating through it!

SUMMARY

The whirlwind tour of collections has come to an end. As you have seen, arrays and dictionaries are great structures for organizing and grouping different types of data, from text to numbers. These collection types can even contain other collections, allowing you to concoct very elaborate data referencing schemes. Finally, you've witnessed Swift's flexible syntax for declaring new arrays and dictionaries. You can literally take your pick of how you want your code to read when creating new collections.

In the next chapter, you will begin flexing your programming muscles with control structures, which is where things will begin to get interesting.

CHAPTER 3
Taking Control

In the last chapter, you spent some time getting to know Swift's collections: arrays and dictionaries. Then you started looking at ways to iterate through those collections. In this chapter, you'll continue looking at iteration and then move on to Swift's ability to take directions on what to do at specific intervals.

If you haven't already done so, start up the REPL in the Terminal application (remember, you can type xcrun `swift` to get it going). The line numbers in the figures in this chapter assume that you are starting with a fresh REPL session.

FOR WHAT IT'S WORTH

As you saw in the previous chapter, Swift's ability to iterate through a collection, be it an array or a dictionary, uses the for-in loop. Other variations of the for-in loop are also useful for iteration, and not just through collections.

COUNTING ON IT

One common use for the for-in loop is as an enumeration mechanism. Using a special syntax Swift provides, you can construct a for-in loop that counts a specific range of numbers. The construction of this for-in loop is as follows:

```
for loopVariable in startNumber...endNumber
```

Just as in the previous chapter, the for-in loop requires a loop variable, which will hold the value for each iteration. What follows the in keyword for this variation of the loop is a start number, followed by three periods (...), followed by the end number.

The three periods are your way of telling Swift that the start and end number are part of a range. The for loop will then start by assigning the start number to the loop variable, executing the loop, adding 1 to the loop variable, and comparing it to the end number. As long as the loop variable is less than or equal to the end number, the loop will continue to execute.

Try the following code snippet:

```
  1> var loopCounter : Int = 0
loopCounter: Int = 0
  2> for loopCounter in 1...10 {
  3.     print("\(loopCounter) times \(loopCounter) equals \(loopCounter *
         → loopCounter)")
  4. }
1 times 1 equals 1
2 times 2 equals 4
3 times 3 equals 9
4 times 4 equals 16
5 times 5 equals 25
6 times 6 equals 36
7 times 7 equals 49
8 times 8 equals 64
9 times 9 equals 81
10 times 10 equals 100
  5>
```

On line 1, you declared an Int variable loopCounter that will be used as the loop variable.
Line 2 has the for-in loop with the ... variation, setting 1 as the start number and 10 as the
end number.

On line 3 is a print command that will show the result of the multiplication of the
loopCounter variable times itself. Finally, on line 4 the closing bracket cues the REPL that
the for-in loop should be executed. Swift then emits 10 lines showing the squaring of
numbers from 1 to 10.

INCLUSIVE OR EXCLUSIVE?

Another variation on the ... syntax for specifying a range is the ..< syntax, which tells
Swift to iterate the loop *one value less* than the end number. Using the previous example
again, replace ... with ..< and notice the difference:

```
5> for loopCounter in 1..<10 {
6.     print("\(loopCounter) times \(loopCounter) equals \(loopCounter *
     → loopCounter)")
7. }
1 times 1 equals 1
2 times 2 equals 4
3 times 3 equals 9
4 times 4 equals 16
5 times 5 equals 25
6 times 6 equals 36
7 times 7 equals 49
8 times 8 equals 64
9 times 9 equals 81
8>
```

The loop ended with the number 9, one less than the ending number specified, 10.

You may be wondering why this is useful. After all, couldn't you just replace the 10 with 9, use the . . . range specifier, and obtain the same effect?

Actually, the syntax is useful when iterating through a collection like the array, which has an index that always starts at 0. Enter the following lines of code:

```
8> let numbersArray = [ 11, 22, 33, 44, 55, 66, 77, 88, 99 ]
numbersArray: [Int] = 9 values {
  [0] = 11
  [1] = 22
  [2] = 33
  [3] = 44
  [4] = 55
  [5] = 66
  [6] = 77
  [7] = 88
  [8] = 99
}
  9> for loopCounter in 0..<9 {
 10.     print("value at index \(loopCounter) is \(numbersArray[loopCounter])")
 11. }
value at index 0 is 11
value at index 1 is 22
value at index 2 is 33
value at index 3 is 44
value at index 4 is 55
value at index 5 is 66
value at index 6 is 77
value at index 7 is 88
value at index 8 is 99
 12>
```

Using the array size as the loop limit value might look more natural. No matter your preference, remember that arrays always start their index at 0, which means the last element's index is one less than the total number of elements in the array. Don't forget to compensate for that fact when iterating through an array.

FOR OLD TIME'S SAKE

Swift has yet another variation of the `for` loop, one that you might recognize if you're familiar with the C language. It doesn't use the `in` keyword, but instead has three distinct parts:

for *initialization*; *evaluation*; *modification*

- *initialization*: Here, the loop variable is initialized.
- *evaluation*: A test is made at this location; as long as the result is true, the loop executes.
- *modification*: This is typically where the loop variable is modified.

One advantage to this form of `for` loop is that it allows the modification step to be more than just a simple increment of 1. It can also be an increment of another number, or even a decrement.

```
12> for loopCounter = 0; loopCounter < 9; loopCounter = loopCounter + 2 {
13.     print("value at index \(loopCounter) is \(numbersArray[loopCounter])")
14. }
value at index 0 is 11
value at index 2 is 33
value at index 4 is 55
value at index 6 is 77
value at index 8 is 99
15>
```

The choice of 2 as an increment value in the `for` loop modification component causes the iteration to skip every other element in the array. You can even construct the loop to go backward, paying close attention not to go below 0, the index of the first element of the array:

```
15> for loopCounter = 8; loopCounter >= 0; loopCounter = loopCounter - 2 {
16.     print("value at index \(loopCounter) is \(numbersArray[loopCounter])")
17. }
value at index 8 is 99
value at index 6 is 77
value at index 4 is 55
value at index 2 is 33
value at index 0 is 11
18>
```

The flexibility of this `for` loop's form makes it ideal for traversing collections in non-ordinal fashion, or for any number of computational variations.

WRITING SHORTHAND

In the previous two examples, the modification step of the for loop looks like this:

```
loopCounter = loopCounter + 2
loopCounter = loopCounter - 2
```

The first line adds 2 to `loopCounter`; the second line subtracts 2.

It's a little long, isn't it? Don't worry. Swift has a more succinct syntax for adding or subtracting a number from a variable:

```
18> var anotherLoopCounter = 3
anotherLoopCounter: Int = 3
19> anotherLoopCounter += 2
20> anotherLoopCounter
$R0: Int = 5
21>
```

Line 18 assigns 3 to the `anotherLoopCounter` variable. On line 19, the `+=` syntax takes the place of typing the variable again. It's a shorthand method of saying "add the value on the right to the variable on the left." On line 20, typing the variable name by itself causes the REPL to show the value and assign it to a temporary variable.

The same logic works for subtraction too:

```
21> anotherLoopCounter -= 3
22> anotherLoopCounter
$R1: Int = 2
23>
```

It gets better! If you simply want to increment the number by 1, you can use an even shorter syntax, `++`:

```
23> anotherLoopCounter++
$R2: Int = 2
24>
```

Did you catch that? `anotherLoopCounter` was 2 before the increment. Why did it return 2 after the increment? Shouldn't it be 3 if you are incrementing by 1?

What you are seeing here is a side effect of the increment operation. The position of the `++` after the variable name causes the value *prior* to the increment to be returned. So the value, 2, is assigned to the temporary variable `$R2`. If you request the REPL to show the variable again, it will contain the incremented value:

```
24> anotherLoopCounter
$R3: Int = 3
25>
```

This is called a *post increment*. The increment is happening *after* the evaluation of the variable. This also works for subtraction as a *post decrement*:

```
25> anotherLoopCounter--
$R4: Int = 3
26> anotherLoopCounter
$R5: Int = 2
27>
```

Just as there is a post increment, there's also a *pre increment*:

```
27> ++anotherLoopCounter
$R6: Int = 3
28>
```

Notice that anotherLoopCounter, which was 2 on line 26, is now 3. Showing anotherLoopCounter again should reveal the same number:

```
28> anotherLoopCounter
$R7: Int = 3
29>
```

And so it is.

Finally, here's the *pre decrement*:

```
29> --anotherLoopCounter
$R8: Int = 2
30> anotherLoopCounter
$R9: Int = 2
31>
```

You'll see more of these shorthand increment/decrement operators later. Just remember that they save you some typing, so be sure to recognize them in code and use them to add or subtract a number from a variable.

IT'S TIME TO PLAY

Up to this point in your journey, you've used the Swift REPL to type code and see results. The REPL works well for short, quick lines of code that provide immediate feedback. However, as you move forward, you'll be writing more and more code. Being able to save and load that code and easily edit it requires interacting with Xcode 7, Apple's development environment for writing Swift apps for iOS and OS X.

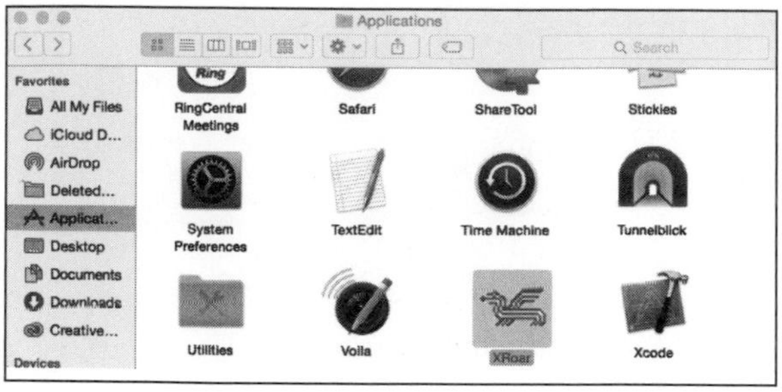

FIGURE 3.1 Finder showing Xcode 7

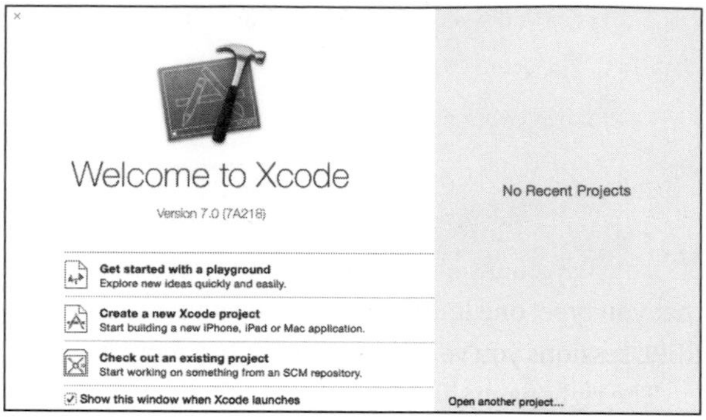

FIGURE 3.2 The Xcode startup window

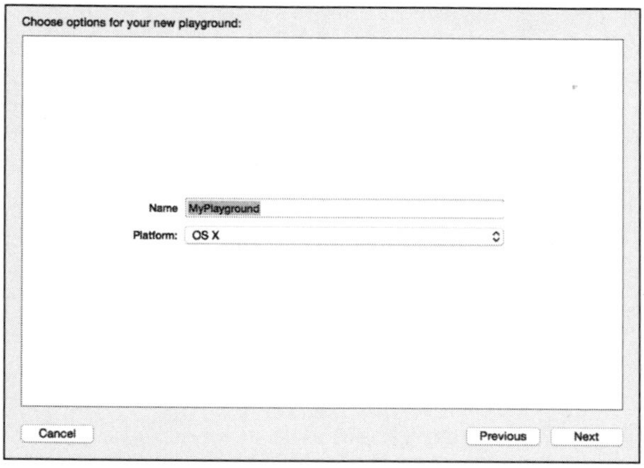

FIGURE 3.3 Saving the playground

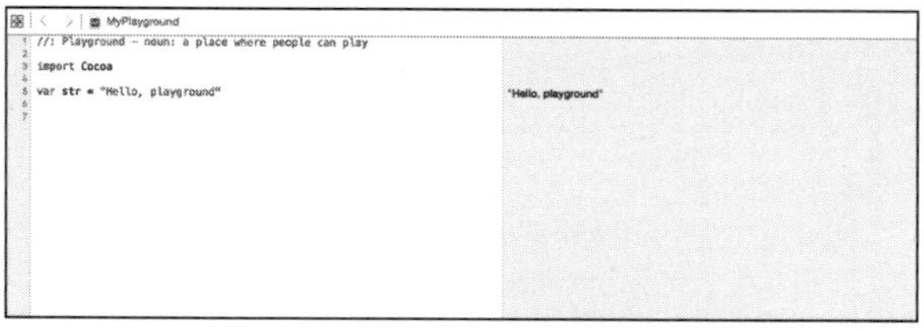

FIGURE 3.4 The newly created playground window

One of the new and fun features in Xcode is the *playground*. A playground is an interactive slate where you can type Swift instructions and see instant results—much like the REPL, but way easier to edit and change your source code.

Since you downloaded Xcode 7 in Chapter 1 in order to work with the REPL, you have everything you need to get started. To begin, use the Finder (**Figure 3.1**) to launch Xcode 7 from your Applications folder.

When starting Xcode 7, you'll be greeted with the dialog in **Figure 3.2**.

The first option is "Get started with a playground." Click it, and a new window appears, asking you to give a name to your playground and select the target platform (either iOS or OS X) (**Figure 3.3**).

For now, keep the suggested name **MyPlayground**, and leave the Platform set to OS X. Click Next. Select a location on your system, and click Create.

After the playground is saved, a new window appears (**Figure 3.4**). This is your new playground! It's like a fresh canvas with no paint—ready for you to type Swift code to your heart's content.

```
1  //: Playground - noun: a place where people can play
2
3  import Cocoa
4
5  var str = "Hello, playground"
6
```

FIGURE 3.5 The default code in the initial playground window

`"Hello, playground"`

FIGURE 3.6 The Results sidebar

The playground window is composed of two panes. The left pane shows the Swift code that you type, one line at a time, along with the line number. This pane is very similar to the REPL sessions you've used up to now, but more interactive.

The right pane shows the results of the code, corresponding to the line. This is the real power and convenience of playgrounds—seeing your code run live, along with the results. As you'll see, playgrounds are excellent for learning Swift because you can try new concepts without the overhead of waiting for the compiler to do its work.

Let's go over the five lines of code that already appear in the window (**Figure 3.5**).

Line 1 is a comment; Xcode shows comment text in green. A comment in Swift begins with two forward slashes. The Swift compiler ignores whatever follows the two forward slashes, up to the end of the current line. Developers use comments to add source code commentary, usually for the benefit of other developers who might read the code some day. Adding code comments is akin to being a good citizen; comments help others understand your app's intent. Comments also help document your own work so that months (or years) later you can quickly remember what you did.

Line 3 is an import statement. This statement tells Swift that your program needs resources (code and data) from Cocoa, which is Apple's framework for writing iOS and OS X apps

Line 5 should look familiar; it's a variable declaration, implicitly declaring a string type and assigning "Hello, playground" to the variable.

Turn your attention to the Results sidebar on the right (**Figure 3.6**). The text "Hello, playground" appears there. This is the result of Swift executing the code in the left pane.

Playgrounds make writing, editing, and understanding code so much easier. Throughout your use of playgrounds in this book, you'll appreciate that your work is preserved, and you can scroll back and modify or alter previously written code.

PLAYGROUND RULES

Wherever you use playgrounds throughout the remainder of this book, you'll see a listing of the code to type, accompanied by the code appearing in the playground along with the results. This is intended to guide you line by line through the code and show you exactly how your results will look onscreen.

MAKING DECISIONS

Can computers "think"? It's an oft-debated topic. Part of thinking is making decisions, and in that regard, computers certainly do well. An integral part of any app is decision-making, and knowing what to do and where to go is critical in the flow of a program.

Program flow is simply one long series of decisions: "If this is true, then go here, else go there." Or, "While this is not true, continue doing this operation until it is." Your life is filled with such decision-making instances—you don't even give it a second thought. Tasks like deciding which pair of shoes to wear, what time to leave for work, or when it's appropriate to cross the street are all part of the decision matrix you encounter each day.

It's no different for your Mac, iPhone, or iPad. When you're writing your app in Swift, it gives you a rich set of ways to specify what your program should do, and when. I'll spend a good part of the rest of this chapter looking at Swift's control flow constructs.

THE DECISIVENESS OF "IF"

"If" is everywhere around you. It's in your speech and is a constant presence in your mind as you go through your day making decisions. It usually indicates the start of a sentence that contains the word "then," as in:

If the light is red, **then** *apply the brake.*
If the coffee is hot, **then** *drink it.*

Swift's version isn't as wordy as the English variants, but is nonetheless easy to read. Here's the general form of the Swift if statement:

```
if predicate {
    // do something
}
```

The *predicate* is evaluated by Swift, and if found to be true will cause statements in the first set of curly braces to execute; otherwise, the evaluation is false, and the code in the curly braces is ignored.

It can also include the word "else." Carrying the previous sentence further:

If the light is red, **then** *apply the brake,* **else** *stomp on the accelerator!*
If the coffee is hot, **then** *drink it,* **else** *throw it away.*

These sentences carry a predicate and two possible outcomes, depending on the "truthfulness" of the predicate in question. Is the light red? Is the coffee hot? If so, do something; otherwise, do something else. In programming, this construct is known as the if/then/else clause.

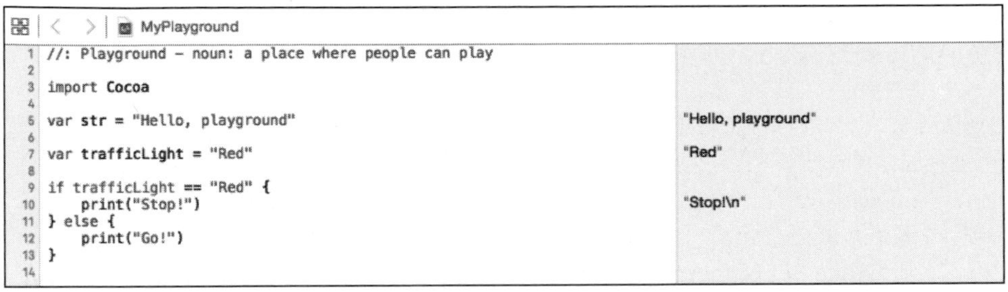

FIGURE 3.7 Using `if` in the playground

Here's the general form of the `if/then/else` as expressed in Swift:

```
if predicate {
    // do something
}
else {
    // do something else
}
```

When Swift encounters an `if` clause, it evaluates the predicate. If the predicate's result is true, the code in the first set of curly braces executes. The `else` clause provides a fallback; if the predicate evaluates to false, the code in the second set of curly braces executes.

As an illustration, let's set up the traffic light analogy in Swift's parlance. Start by typing the following code as lines 7 through 13 in the MyPlayground window (**Figure 3.7**).

```
var trafficLight = "Red"

if trafficLight == "Red" {
    print("Stop!")
} else {
    print("Go!")
}
```

On line 7, you are declaring a variable named `trafficLight` and assigning it the string "Red".

Line 9 contains the `if` statement. The predicate here is the comparison of the variable `trafficLight` to the string "Red", which is true because `trafficLight` was assigned the value "Red" on line 7.

In the Results sidebar, you can see that `"Stop!"` is shown because the comparison of `trafficLight` to the string "Red" is true.

How would you get the Results sidebar to show `"Go!"` instead of `"Stop!"`?

FIGURE 3.8 Executing the else clause

FIGURE 3.8 Executing the else clause

```
☷  <  >   🔲 MyPlayground
1  //: Playground - noun: a place where people can play
2
3  import Cocoa
4
5  var str = "Hello, playground"                              "Hello, playground"
6
7  var trafficLight = "Green"                                 "Green"
8
9  if trafficLight == "Red" {
10     print("Stop!")
11 } else {
12     print("Go!")                                           "Go!\n"
13 }
14
```

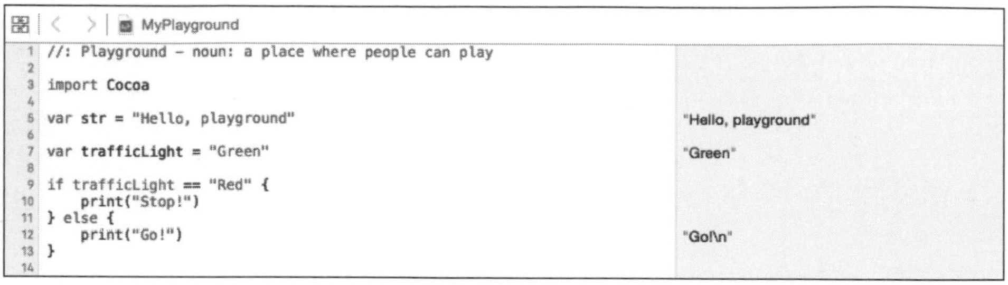

FIGURE 3.9 An alternate execution of the else clause

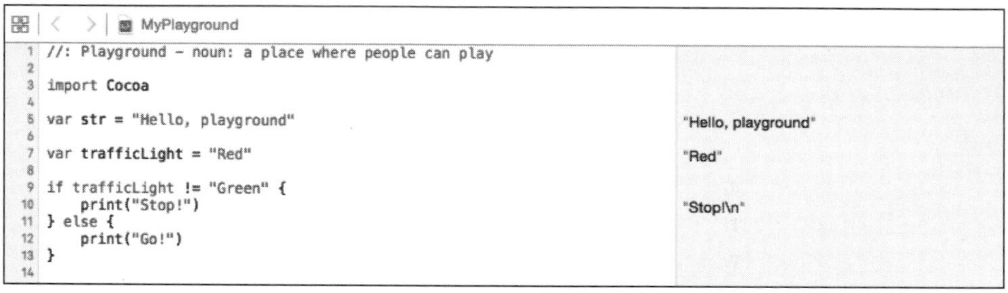

```
☷  <  >   🔲 MyPlayground
1  //: Playground - noun: a place where people can play
2
3  import Cocoa
4
5  var str = "Hello, playground"                              "Hello, playground"
6
7  var trafficLight = "Red"                                   "Red"
8
9  if trafficLight != "Green" {
10     print("Stop!")                                         "Stop!\n"
11 } else {
12     print("Go!")
13 }
14
```

You could set the trafficLight variable to something other than "Red" on line 7 (**Figure 3.8**).

Now the Results sidebar shows "Go!" as you would expect, since the comparison of trafficLight to "Red" on line 9 is false.

Another approach to checking the traffic light would be to leave the variable on line 7 set to the string "Red" and modify the comparison operator on line 9 (**Figure 3.9**).

The comparison operator != means does not equal, which is the opposite of ==. The logic of the sentence on line 9 is inverted, and literally reads: "if the trafficLight variable does not equal Green, print Stop! Otherwise, print Go!"

TESTING FOR EQUALITY IN SWIFT

Up to this point, you've seen a single equals sign when assigning a value to a variable or constant. When doing a comparison between two values, variables, or constants, the double equal (==) is used. Line 9 in Figure 3.7 uses this comparison operator, and I'll go over additional comparison operators shortly.

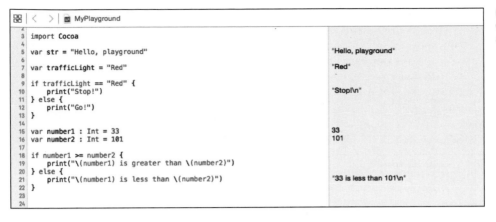

FIGURE 3.10
Comparing numbers in
an if statement

So far, you've been comparing strings. Let's try comparing numbers and look at a few new comparison operators. Just for grins, keep the existing code on lines 7 through 13, and just add the following new code beginning on line 15 (**Figure 3.10**):

```
var number1 : Int = 33
var number2 : Int = 101

if number1 >= number2 {
    print("\(number1) is greater than \(number2)")
} else {
    print("\(number1) is less than \(number2)")
}
```

Line 18 shows the greater-than-or-equal (>=) symbol as a comparison operator. In the example, number1 (value of 33) is less than or equal to number2 (value of 101), so the expression is false and the code in the second clause executes. If you replace the greater-than character on line 18 with the less-than (<) character, the condition becomes true and the code in the first clause executes. Go ahead and try it… that's what playgrounds are for!

There are more operators you can use. Swift supports the equality tests in **Table 3.1**.

TABLE 3.1 Swift's Equality Operations

OPERATOR	TEST
==	Equal
!=	Not equal
>	Greater than
<	Less than
>=	Greater than or equal
<=	Less than or equal

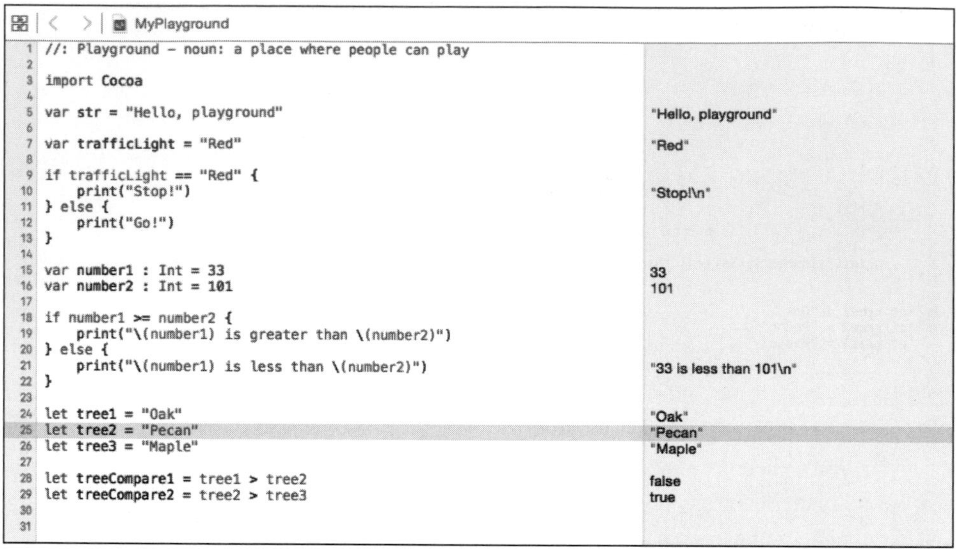

FIGURE 3.11 String comparisons

```
         < > | 🖳 MyPlayground
1  //: Playground - noun: a place where people can play
2
3  import Cocoa
4
5  var str = "Hello, playground"                                    "Hello, playground"
6
7  var trafficLight = "Red"                                         "Red"
8
9  if trafficLight == "Red" {
10     print("Stop!")
11 } else {                                                         "Stop!\n"
12     print("Go!")
13 }
14
15 var number1 : Int = 33                                           33
16 var number2 : Int = 101                                          101
17
18 if number1 >= number2 {
19     print("\(number1) is greater than \(number2)")
20 } else {
21     print("\(number1) is less than \(number2)")                 "33 is less than 101\n"
22 }
23
24 let tree1 = "Oak"                                                "Oak"
25 let tree2 = "Pecan"                                              "Pecan"
26 let tree3 = "Maple"                                              "Maple"
27
28 let treeCompare1 = tree1 > tree2                                 false
29 let treeCompare2 = tree2 > tree3                                 true
30
31
```

These operators also work on more than just numbers. You can use them to compare strings too. Strings can be compared to each other based on alphabetical order. Consider lines 24 through 29 in **Figure 3.11**.

```
let tree1 = "Oak"
let tree2 = "Pecan"
let tree3 = "Maple"

let treeCompare1 = tree1 > tree2
let treeCompare2 = tree2 > tree3
```

On lines 24 through 26, three constant strings are declared: Oak, Pecan, and Maple. Line 28 shows the comparison of tree1 (Oak) to tree2 (Pecan) and the resulting value (false). It's obvious that tree1 is not greater than tree2, because alphabetically, Oak comes before Pecan. Line 29 indicates a result of true, because tree2 (Pecan) indeed is greater than (or comes after) tree3 (Maple).

WHEN ONE CHOICE IS NOT ENOUGH

Sometimes a comparison yields more than just an either/or scenario. Take, for example, the three tree constants you just created. Each type of tree is associated with a type of product. What if you wanted to return a product for each tree type? Type the following code on lines 31 through 43 (**Figure 3.12**) and let's talk about the results.

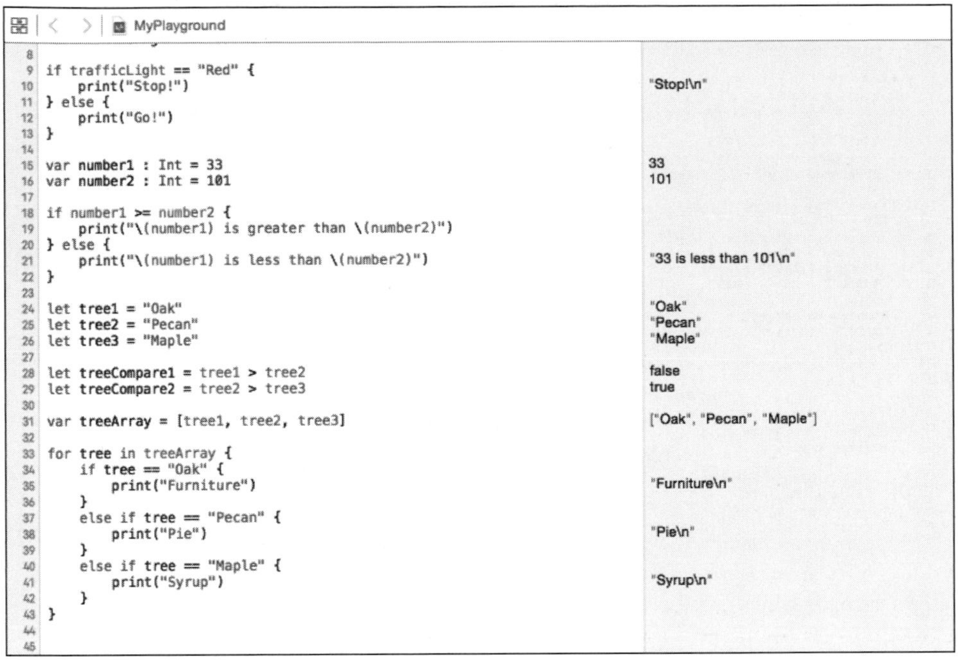

FIGURE 3.12 Multiple
if statements wrapped
in a for loop

```
8
9   if trafficLight == "Red" {
10      print("Stop!")                                              "Stop!\n"
11  } else {
12      print("Go!")
13  }
14
15  var number1 : Int = 33                                          33
16  var number2 : Int = 101                                         101
17
18  if number1 >= number2 {
19      print("\(number1) is greater than \(number2)")
20  } else {
21      print("\(number1) is less than \(number2)")                 "33 is less than 101\n"
22  }
23
24  let tree1 = "Oak"                                               "Oak"
25  let tree2 = "Pecan"                                             "Pecan"
26  let tree3 = "Maple"                                             "Maple"
27
28  let treeCompare1 = tree1 > tree2                                false
29  let treeCompare2 = tree2 > tree3                                true
30
31  var treeArray = [tree1, tree2, tree3]                           ["Oak", "Pecan", "Maple"]
32
33  for tree in treeArray {
34      if tree == "Oak" {
35          print("Furniture")                                     "Furniture\n"
36      }
37      else if tree == "Pecan" {
38          print("Pie")                                           "Pie\n"
39      }
40      else if tree == "Maple" {
41          print("Syrup")                                         "Syrup\n"
42      }
43  }
44
45
```

```
var treeArray = [tree1, tree2, tree3]

for tree in treeArray {
   if tree == "Oak" {
      print("Furniture")
   }
   else if tree == "Pecan" {
      print("Pie")
   }
   else if tree == "Maple" {
      print("Syrup")
   }
}
```

This code snippet combines several concepts. On line 31, you declare an array composed of the three tree constants declared earlier.

On line 33, the for statement is used to iterate through the newly created array, with the variable tree holding each array element throughout the iteration process. Lines 34, 37, and 40 each compare the variable tree to the known strings that were assigned earlier, and if a match is made, the product for that tree is printed.

FIGURE 3.13

The switch-case state-ment wrapped in a for loop

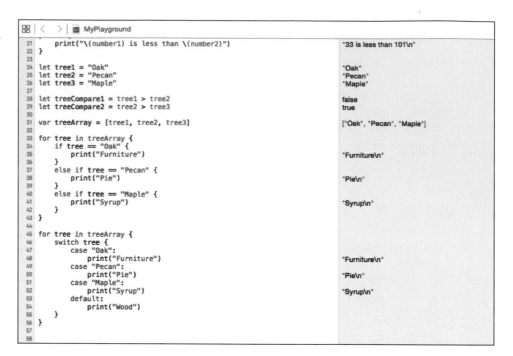

```
21      print("\(number1) is less than \(number2)")        "33 is less than 101\n"
22  }
23
24  let tree1 = "Oak"                                       "Oak"
25  let tree2 = "Pecan"                                     "Pecan"
26  let tree3 = "Maple"                                     "Maple"
27
28  let treeCompare1 = tree1 > tree2                        false
29  let treeCompare2 = tree2 > tree3                        true
30
31  var treeArray = [tree1, tree2, tree3]                  ["Oak", "Pecan", "Maple"]
32
33  for tree in treeArray {
34      if tree == "Oak" {
35          print("Furniture")                             "Furniture\n"
36      }
37      else if tree == "Pecan" {
38          print("Pie")                                   "Pie\n"
39      }
40      else if tree == "Maple" {
41          print("Syrup")                                 "Syrup\n"
42      }
43  }
44
45  for tree in treeArray {
46      switch tree {
47          case "Oak":
48              print("Furniture")                         "Furniture\n"
49          case "Pecan":
50              print("Pie")                               "Pie\n"
51          case "Maple":
52              print("Syrup")                             "Syrup\n"
53          default:
54              print("Wood")
55      }
56  }
57
58
```

SWITCHING THINGS AROUND

In the previous example, the three if statements handled the available cases, but what hap-pens if there are more possibilities to compare? Long lists of repeating if statements can be tedious to type and difficult to read. Swift gives you an alternative when handling more than just a handful of predicates: the switch statement.

You'll find that this new construct comes in handy in a number of coding scenarios. Type in the following code, and study the results in **Figure 3.13** to see exactly what is happening.

```
for tree in treeArray {
  switch tree {
    case "Oak":
        print("Furniture")
    case "Pecan":
        print("Pie")
    case "Maple":
        print("Syrup")
    default:
        print("Wood")
  }
}
```

FIGURE 3.14 The effect on the switch-case statement when adding to the array

```
24  let tree1 = "Oak"                              "Oak"
25  let tree2 = "Pecan"                            "Pecan"
26  let tree3 = "Maple"                            "Maple"
27
28  let treeCompare1 = tree1 > tree2               false
29  let treeCompare2 = tree2 > tree3               true
30
31  var treeArray = [tree1, tree2, tree3]          ["Oak", "Pecan", "Maple"]
32
33  for tree in treeArray {
34      if tree == "Oak" {
35          print("Furniture")                     "Furniture\n"
36      }
37      else if tree == "Pecan" {
38          print("Pie")                           "Pie\n"
39      }
40      else if tree == "Maple" {
41          print("Syrup")                         "Syrup\n"
42      }
43  }
44
45  treeArray += ["Cherry"]                         ["Oak", "Pecan", "Maple", "Cherry"]
46
47  for tree in treeArray {
48      switch tree {
49          case "Oak":
50              print("Furniture")                 "Furniture\n"
51          case "Pecan":
52              print("Pie")                       "Pie\n"
53          case "Maple":
54              print("Syrup")                     "Syrup\n"
55          default:
56              print("Wood")                      "Wood\n"
57      }
58  }
59
```

Line 46 in Figure 3.13 shows the switch keyword, followed by the tree variable, which is assigned each member in the treeArray throughout the for loop iteration on line 45. A closing curly brace on line 55 encompasses the various case statements that fall below it. Swift stops at each case statement and evaluates the tree variable for a match. When one is found, the code bounded between the triggered case statement and the next case statement is executed.

You may be wondering what the default keyword does. It is a "catch-all" case whose code is executed when all other cases fail. Here, it is never executed, because all three tree types are covered in case statements, but what if you were to add a fourth tree in the array? Line 45 in **Figure 3.14** does just that.

Now the default case is activated because the new value in the array does not have a matching case statement, and "Wood" is printed when "Cherry" is encountered in the for loop.

WHERE'S THE BREAK?

If you're familiar with Objective-C, you may have used switch-case statements in that language and be wondering where the break statement is in each case. Simply put, Swift does not require it. It's implicitly understood that execution will bypass the remaining case statements on a match, and the intervening code won't be executed.

FIGURE 3.15
Multiple constants on
a single case

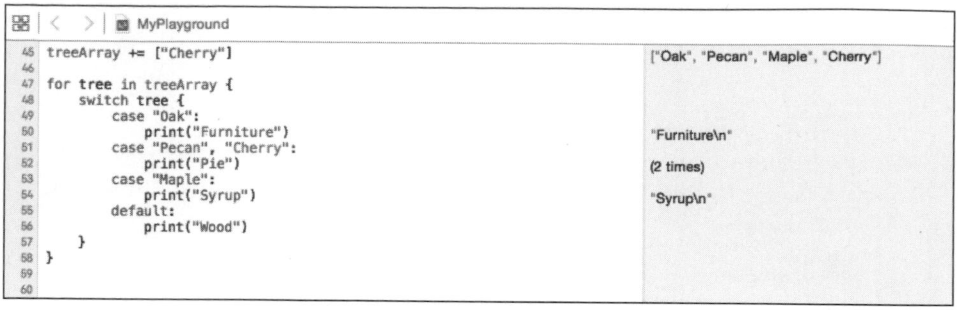

```
45  treeArray += ["Cherry"]                                    ["Oak", "Pecan", "Maple", "Cherry"]
46
47  for tree in treeArray {
48      switch tree {
49          case "Oak":
50              print("Furniture")                             "Furniture\n"
51          case "Pecan", "Cherry":
52              print("Pie")                                   (2 times)
53          case "Maple":
54              print("Syrup")                                 "Syrup\n"
55          default:
56              print("Wood")
57      }
58  }
59
60
```

How could you alter the statement to accommodate printing the word "Pie" for both Pecan and Cherry? Obviously, you could add another case statement to catch the case of the variable tree being equal to "Cherry" and that would certainly work, but there is a much more neat and tidy alternative. Swift allows you to combine two or more values in a single case for evaluation. Modify line 51 to case "Pecan", **"Cherry":** as in **Figure 3.15**.

Swift duly notes that in the case of "Pecan" and "Cherry", the code to print "Pie" was executed two times. You don't have to stop there. As an exercise, you can add other names, like "Lemon" and "Apple", to line 51. This flexibility makes switch-case a powerful alternative to other normally used conditional constructs.

You've been using switch-case to evaluate strings. That is more than can be done in languages like Objective-C and C, which can evaluate only numbers. Numbers in Swift are easy to compare. The following code snippet illustrates this by using a switch-case statement to append the appropriate ordinal abbreviation to a number between 1 and 9 (**Figure 3.16**).

```
var position = 8

switch position {
  case 1:
    print("\(position)st")

  case 2:
    print("\(position)nd")

  case 3:
    print("\(position)rd")

  case 4...9:
    print("\(position)th")

  default:
    print("Not covered")
}
```

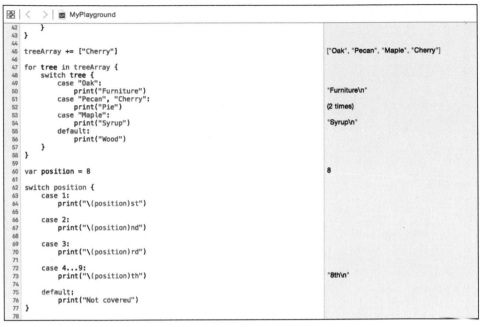

FIGURE 3.16 Using switch-case on numeric values

On line 60, `position` is declared as a variable with the number 8 and execution falls through to the `switch-case` where the variable is evaluated against the possible cases. Since numbers 4 through 9 always end in "th," line 72 takes advantage of Swift's range (...) operator to specify every whole number between 4 and 9, with the remaining cases being covered on the previous lines.

Feel free to experiment with this code by changing the value of `position` on line 60. The Results sidebar will update to indicate the code being executed when you make your change.

WHILE YOU WERE AWAY...

Up to this point, you've seen some of Swift's powerful control and iterative capabilities with `if`, `for`, and `switch-case`, but additional constructs can provide other natural ways of expressing intent.

Sometimes in the course of developing software you want to express the logic of a loop in terms of an unknown iteration count. For example, you want to iterate on something *until* a specific set of criteria is met. For example, let's say you want to compute a table of values but don't want to stop until the computed value is greater than some number.

The `while` loop is a Swift loop construct that allows you to continue executing the same code, over and over, until a condition of your choosing is met. Its basic form is:

```
while someCondition {
  // execute code
}
```

FIGURE 3.17 Iterating a value in a while loop

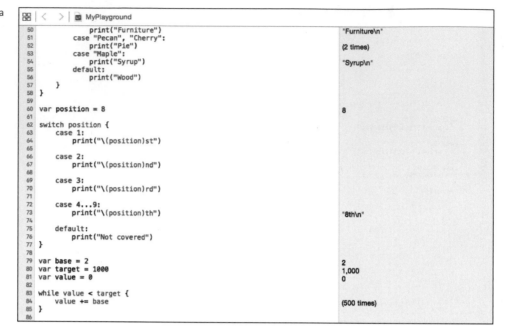

The condition someCondition is a Boolean expression that can be either true or false. If true, the code in the curly braces is executed and control goes back to the while loop. If the condition result is false, execution moves past the encapsulated code.

To see the while loop in action, type the following code on lines 79 through 85 (**Figure 3.17**), and watch the results in the Results sidebar.

```
var base = 2
var target = 1000
var value = 0

while value < target {
  value += base
}
```

A variation of the while loop is the repeat-while. This type of loop executes the code *and then* evaluates the expression before deciding whether to continue the execution or move on. Here's the form of this style of loop:

```
repeat {
  // execute code
} while someCondition;
```

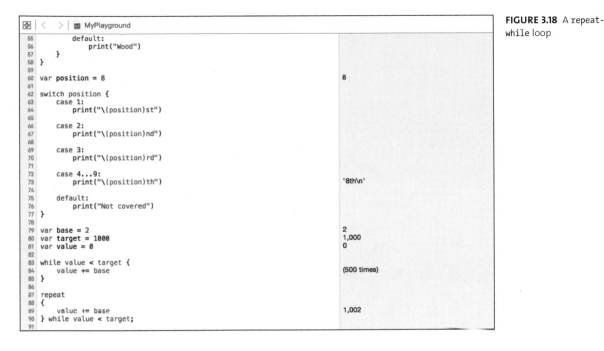

FIGURE 3.18 A repeat-while loop

```
55          default:
56              print("Wood")
57      }
58  }
59
60  var position = 8                              8
61
62  switch position {
63      case 1:
64          print("\(position)st")
65
66      case 2:
67          print("\(position)nd")
68
69      case 3:
70          print("\(position)rd")
71
72      case 4...9:
73          print("\(position)th")             "8th\n"
74
75      default:
76          print("Not covered")
77  }
78
79  var base = 2                                  2
80  var target = 1000                             1,000
81  var value = 0                                 0
82
83  while value < target {
84      value += base                          (500 times)
85  }
86
87  repeat
88  {
89      value += base                          1,002
90  } while value < target;
91
```

The condition someCondition is the same Boolean expression expected in the while loop, but is evaluated after the code in the curly braces is executed initially. In **Figure 3.18**, lines 87 through 90 show a repeat-while loop executing the same code as the earlier while loop in lines 83 through 85. Notice the difference in the value for the repeat-while loop: It is 1002 instead of the while loop's value of 1000. Why?

```
repeat
{
    value += base
} while value < target
```

When you entered the repeat-while loop, in lines 87 through 90, value was already 1000, due to being previously set by the while loop in lines 83 through 85. The repeat-while loop enforced the execution of the code, which added base (2) to value (1000) and *then* evaluated the expression. At that point, value (1002) was *not* less than target (1000); the condition was false, and the repeat-while loop exited.

INSPECTING YOUR CODE

One feature of playgrounds I've glossed over so far is the ability to inspect and see the output of the code. In the Results sidebar, Swift is constantly analyzing the code you type, even reporting how many times a code segment runs. This is helpful for analyzing how many times a loop runs, and can even be used in certain scenarios to optimize and make your code run faster and better.

FIGURE 3.19 The speed limit code snippet

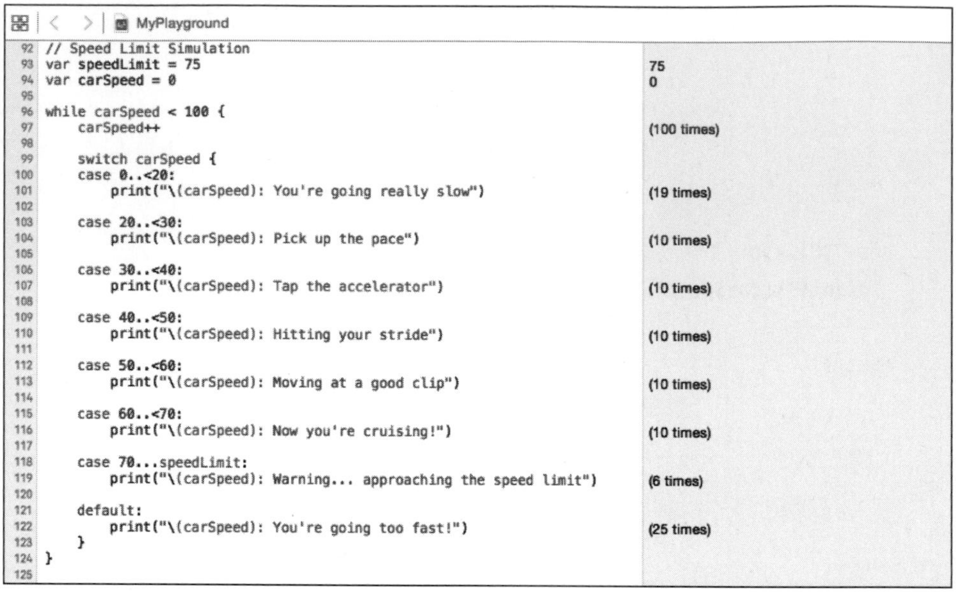

```
92  // Speed Limit Simulation
93  var speedLimit = 75                                              75
94  var carSpeed = 0                                                 0
95
96  while carSpeed < 100 {
97      carSpeed++                                                   (100 times)
98
99      switch carSpeed {
100     case 0..<20:
101         print("\(carSpeed): You're going really slow")           (19 times)
102
103     case 20..<30:
104         print("\(carSpeed): Pick up the pace")                   (10 times)
105
106     case 30..<40:
107         print("\(carSpeed): Tap the accelerator")                (10 times)
108
109     case 40..<50:
110         print("\(carSpeed): Hitting your stride")                (10 times)
111
112     case 50..<60:
113         print("\(carSpeed): Moving at a good clip")              (10 times)
114
115     case 60..<70:
116         print("\(carSpeed): Now you're cruising!")               (10 times)
117
118     case 70...speedLimit:
119         print("\(carSpeed): Warning... approaching the speed limit")  (6 times)
120
121     default:
122         print("\(carSpeed): You're going too fast!")             (25 times)
123     }
124 }
125
```

The playground environment actually offers more ways to inspect your code in the Results sidebar. Type the following code snippet, and study the results of the code on lines 92 through 128 in **Figure 3.19**. This code uses a combination of while and switch-case to monitor the increasing speed of a car.

```
// Speed Limit Simulation
var speedLimit = 75
var carSpeed = 0

while (carSpeed < 100) {
  carSpeed++

  switch carSpeed {
    case 0..<20:
      print("\(carSpeed): You're going really slow")

    case 20..<30:
      print("\(carSpeed): Pick up the pace")

    case 30..<40:
      print("\(carSpeed): Tap the accelerator")
```

FIGURE 3.20 The icons in the Results sidebar

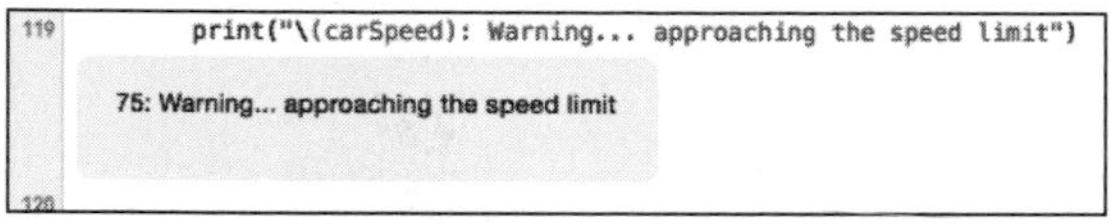

FIGURE 3.21 The icons in the Results view

```
119        print("\(carSpeed): Warning... approaching the speed limit")

      75: Warning... approaching the speed limit

120
```

```
case 40..<50:
  print("\(carSpeed): Hitting your stride")

case 50..<60:
  print("\(carSpeed): Moving at a good clip")

case 60..<70:
  print("\(carSpeed): Now you're cruising!")

case 70...speedLimit:
  print("\(carSpeed): Warning... approaching the speed limit")

default:
  print("\(carSpeed): You're going too fast!")


  }
}
```

This example monitors the ever-increasing speed of a car. On line 93, the speed limit is set to 75 (miles per hour), and on the following line, the car's speed variable is set to 0. The while loop on line 96 contains the condition that the speed is less than 100. As the loop progresses, the car's speed is incremented by 1 on line 97, then evaluated in a switch-case statement.

Each case handles a range of speeds, providing feedback on each value. After you type in the code, notice that the number of times each case is executed appears in the Results sidebar. If you hover your mouse over any of those lines in the Results sidebar, you'll see an "eye" icon (the Quick Look button) and a circle (the Results button).

For now, focus on line 119 (where you are warned about approaching the speed limit). Hovering your mouse over the line displaying the value (6 times) in the Results sidebar causes the Quick Look and Results buttons to appear to the right (**Figure 3.20**). Click the Results button (the circle) and you'll see a box appear under the line. This is a summary view (**Figure 3.21**). To see the line-by-line results, click the icon highlighted in **Figure 3.22** to expand the console view at the bottom of the window. In this area, the output of the print method shows the lines indicating the speed and the message "Warning... approaching the speed limit" 6 times, with the value of carSpeed increasing from 70 to 75.

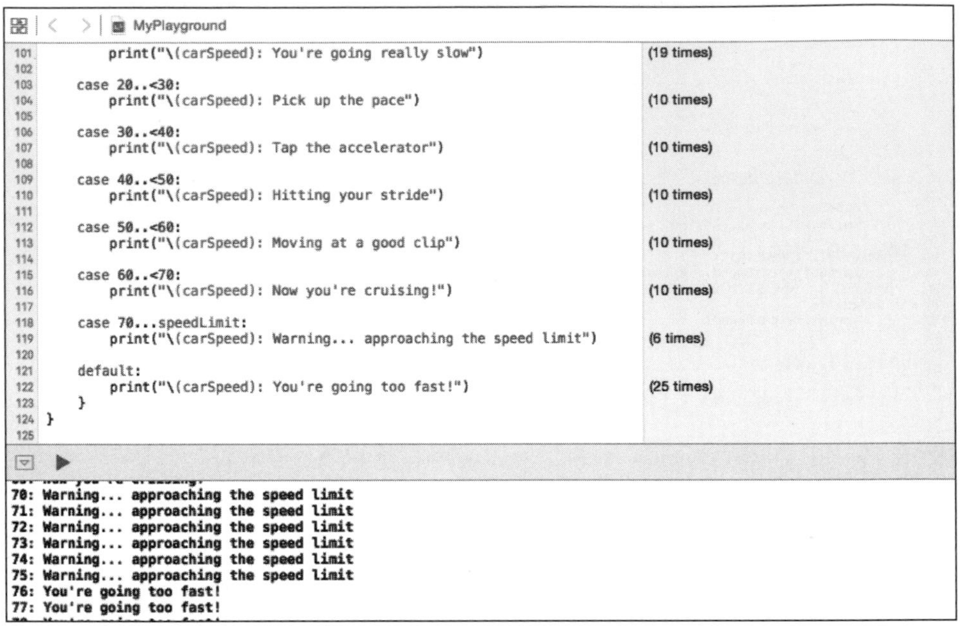

FIGURE 3.22
The expanded
Results view

```
     MyPlayground
101        print("\(carSpeed): You're going really slow")          (19 times)
102
103    case 20..<30:
104        print("\(carSpeed): Pick up the pace")                   (10 times)
105
106    case 30..<40:
107        print("\(carSpeed): Tap the accelerator")                (10 times)
108
109    case 40..<50:
110        print("\(carSpeed): Hitting your stride")                (10 times)
111
112    case 50..<60:
113        print("\(carSpeed): Moving at a good clip")              (10 times)
114
115    case 60..<70:
116        print("\(carSpeed): Now you're cruising!")               (10 times)
117
118    case 70...speedLimit:
119        print("\(carSpeed): Warning... approaching the speed limit")   (6 times)
120
121    default:
122        print("\(carSpeed): You're going too fast!")             (25 times)
123    }
124 }
125
```

```
70: Warning... approaching the speed limit
71: Warning... approaching the speed limit
72: Warning... approaching the speed limit
73: Warning... approaching the speed limit
74: Warning... approaching the speed limit
75: Warning... approaching the speed limit
76: You're going too fast!
77: You're going too fast!
```

In the console, you can review the exact behavior of your code, even down to the messages that were output, how many times they were output, and their order. This is a very insightful part of playgrounds, so feel free to scroll around and get a taste of what else is in this box. When you're finished exploring, click the down arrow icon just above the area and the console will collapse.

GIVE ME A BREAK!

Sometimes in the process of using a loop you may find yourself wanting to exit early. The previous code snippet provides such an opportunity. Once the car is speeding past the speed limit, the message "You're going too fast!" continues to print all the way to the car going to 100 miles per hour. What if you wanted to stop the while loop once the car exceeded the speed limit? This is achievable using the break keyword. Using break allows you to exit early from a loop or switch-case statement, allowing control to go immediately to the nearest encompassing block of code. Type the following code into lines 125 through 127 (**Figure 3.23**) to see how this is done.

```
if carSpeed > speedLimit {
    break
}
```

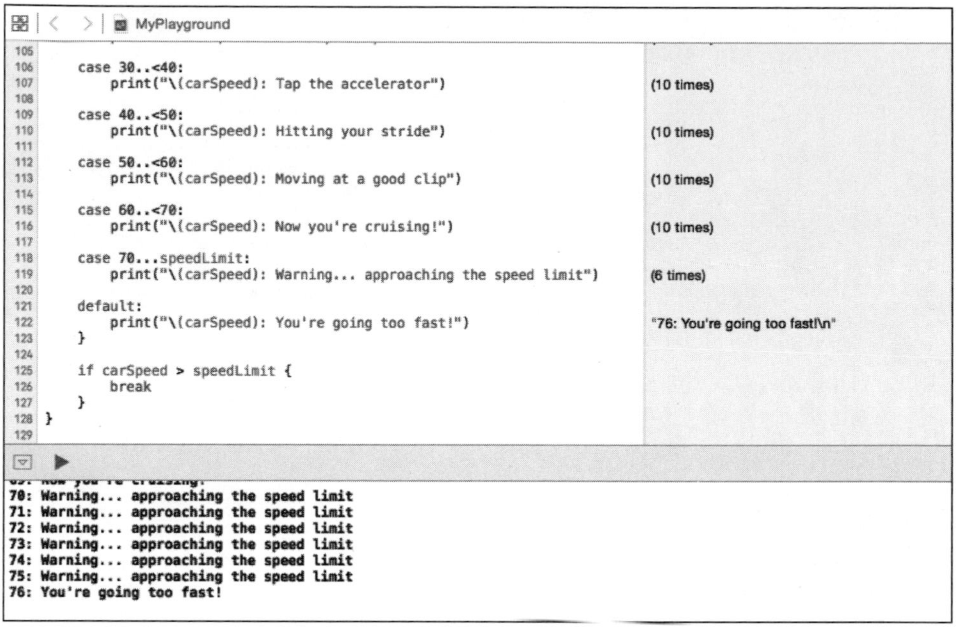

FIGURE 3.23 Using break to exit the while loop early

The `if` statement on line 125 checks to see if the car's speed has exceeded the speed limit, and if so, issues a break. Note that this breaks the encompassing `while` loop, effectively ending the iteration. What happens if you were to remove lines 125 through 127? Try it, and use the Results view to see how many additional lines would be printed.

SUMMARY

In this chapter, you've seen Swift's control constructs in action, and you have tamed the wild west of `while` and `repeat-while` loops. You've also been exposed to one of Swift and Xcode 7's neatest features: playgrounds. These interactive documents let you play with your code like putty in your hands, allowing you to see changes nearly in real time, as well as analyze the results. They're a great way to experiment and learn the Swift language.

Give your mind a rest and get ready for the next chapter, where there's more Swift goodness coming!

Writing Functions and Closures

I've covered a lot up to this point in the book: variables, constants, dictionaries, arrays, looping constructs, control structures, and the like. You've used both the REPL command-line interface and now Xcode's playgrounds feature to type in code samples and explore the language.

Up to this point, however, you have been limited to mostly experimentation: typing a line or three here and there and observing the results. Now it's time to get more organized with your code. In this chapter, you'll learn how to tidy up your Swift code into nice clean reusable components known as functions.

Let's start this chapter with a fresh new playground file. If you haven't already done so, launch Xcode and create a new playground by choosing File > New > Playground, and name it **Chapter 4.playground**. You'll explore this chapter's concepts with contrived examples in similar fashion to earlier chapters.

THE FUNCTION

Think back to your school years again. This time, remember high school algebra. You were paying attention, weren't you? In that class your teacher introduced the concept of the *function*. In essence, a function in arithmetic parlance is a mathematical formula that takes one or more inputs, performs a calculation, and provides a result, or output.

Mathematical functions have a specific notation. For example, to convert a Fahrenheit temperature value to the equivalent Celsius value, you would express that function in this way:

$$f(x) = \frac{(x-32)*5}{9}$$

The important parts of the function are:

- Name: In this case the function's name is *f*.
- Input, or independent variable: Contains the value that will be used in the function. Here it's *x*.
- Expression: Everything to the right of the equals sign.
- Result: Considered to be the value of *f(x)* on the left side of the equals sign.

Functions are written in mathematical notation but can be described in natural language. In English, the sample function could be described as:

A function whose independent variable is x and whose result is the difference of the independent variable and 32, with the result being multiplied by 5, with the result being divided by 9.

The expression is succinct and tidy. The beauty of functions is that they can be used over and over again to perform work, and all they need to do is be called with a parameter. So how does this relate to Swift? Obviously I wouldn't be talking about functions if they didn't exist in the Swift language. And as you'll see, they can perform not just mathematical calculations but a whole lot more.

CODING THE FUNCTION IN SWIFT

Swift's notation for establishing the existence of a function is a little different than the mathematical one you just saw. In general, the syntax for declaring a Swift function is:

```
func funcName(paramName : type, ...) -> returnType
```

Take a look at an example to help clarify the syntax. **Figure 4.1** shows the code in the Chapter 4.playground file, along with the function defined on lines 7 through 13. This is the function discussed earlier, but now in a notation that the Swift compiler can understand.

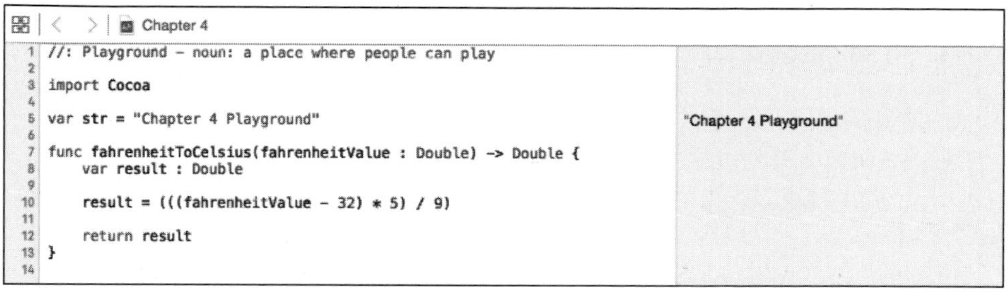

FIGURE 4.1 Temperature conversion as a Swift function

```
⊞  <  >  ▣ Chapter 4
1  //: Playground - noun: a place where people can play
2
3  import Cocoa
4
5  var str = "Chapter 4 Playground"                          "Chapter 4 Playground"
6
7  func fahrenheitToCelsius(fahrenheitValue : Double) -> Double {
8      var result : Double
9
10     result = (((fahrenheitValue - 32) * 5) / 9)
11
12     return result
13 }
14
```

Start by typing in the following code.

```
func fahrenheitToCelsius(fahrenheitValue : Double) -> Double {
  var result : Double

  result = (((fahrenheitValue - 32) * 5) / 9)

  return result
}
```

As you can see on line 7, there is some new syntax to learn. The func keyword is Swift's way to declare a function. That is followed by the function name (fahrenheitToCelsius), and the independent variable's name, or parameter name, in parentheses. Notice that the fahrenheitValue parameter's type is explicitly declared as Double.

Following the parameter are the two characters ->, which denote that this function is returning a value of a type (in this case, a Double type), followed by the open curly brace, which indicates the start of the function.

On line 8, you declare a variable of type Double named result. This will hold the value that will be given back to anyone who calls the function. Notice that it is the same type as the function's return type declared after the -> on line 7.

The actual mathematical function appears on line 10, with the result of the expression assigned to result, the local variable declared in line 8. Finally on line 12, the result is returned to the caller using the return keyword. Anytime you wish to exit a function and return to the calling party, you use return along with the value being returned.

The Results sidebar doesn't show anything in the area where the function was typed. That's because a function by itself doesn't *do* anything. It has the potential to perform some useful work, but it must be called by a caller. That's what you'll do next.

FIGURE 4.2 The result of calling the newly created function

```
     ⊞ | < > | 🖥 Chapter 4
 1   //: Playground – noun: a place where people can play
 2
 3   import Cocoa
 4
 5   var str = "Chapter 4 Playground"                            "Chapter 4 Playground"
 6
 7   func fahrenheitToCelsius(fahrenheitValue : Double) -> Double {
 8       var result : Double
 9
10       result = (((fahrenheitValue – 32) * 5) / 9)             31.22222222222222
11
12       return result                                          31.22222222222222
13   }
14
15   var outdoorTemperatureInFahrenheit = 88.2                   88.2
16   var outdoorTemperatureInCelsius = fahrenheitToCelsius        31.22222222222222
         (outdoorTemperatureInFahrenheit)
17
18
```

EXERCISING THE FUNCTION

Now it's time to call on the function you just created. Type in the following two lines of code, and pay attention to the Results sidebar in **Figure 4.2**.

```
var outdoorTemperatureInFahrenheit = 88.2
var outdoorTemperatureInCelsius = fahrenheitToCelsius(outdoorTemperature
→ InFahrenheit)
```

On line 15, you've declared a new variable, outdoorTemperatureInFahrenheit, and set its value to 88.2 (remember, Swift infers the type in this case as a Double). That value is then passed to the function on line 16, where a new variable, outdoorTemperatureInCelsius, is declared, and its value is captured as the result of the function.

The Results sidebar shows that 31.222222 (repeating decimal) is the result of the function, and indeed, 31.2 degrees Celsius is equivalent to 88.2 degrees Fahrenheit. Neat, isn't it? You now have a temperature conversion tool right at your fingertips.

Now, here's a little exercise for you to do on your own: Write the inverse method, celsiusToFahrenheit, using the following formula for that conversion:

$$f(x) = \frac{x * 9}{5} + 32$$

Go ahead and code it up yourself, but resist the urge to peek ahead. Don't look until you've written the function, and then check your work against the following code and in **Figure 4.3**.

FIGURE 4.3 Declaring the inverse function, celsiusToFahrenheit

```
      //: Playground - noun: a place where people can play

      import Cocoa

      var str = "Hello, playground"                               "Hello, playground"

      func fahrenheitToCelsius(fahrenheitValue : Double) -> Double {
          var result : Double

          result = (((fahrenheitValue - 32) * 5) / 9)            31.22222222222222

          return result;                                         31.22222222222222
      }

      var outdoorTemperatureInFahrenheit = 88.2                  88.2
      var outdoorTemperatureInCelsius = fahrenheitToCelsius      31.22222222222222
          (outdoorTemperatureInFahrenheit)

      func celsiusToFahrenheit(celsiusValue : Double) -> Double {
          var result : Double

          result = (((celsiusValue * 9) / 5) + 32)               88.2

          return result                                          88.2
      }

      outdoorTemperatureInFahrenheit = celsiusToFahrenheit       88.2
          (outdoorTemperatureInCelsius)
```

```
func celsiusToFahrenheit(celsiusValue : Double) -> Double {
  var result : Double

  result = (((celsiusValue * 9) / 5) + 32)

  return result
}
```

```
outdoorTemperatureInFahrenheit = celsiusToFahrenheit(outdoorTemperature
→ InCelsius)
```

The inverse function on lines 18 through 24 simply implements the Celsius to Fahrenheit formula and returns the result. Passing in the Celsius value of 31.22222 on line 26, you can see that the result is the original Fahrenheit value, 88.2.

You've just created two functions that do something useful: temperature conversions. Feel free to experiment with other values to see how they change between the two related functions.

MORE THAN JUST NUMBERS

The notion of a function in Swift is more than just the mathematical concept I have discussed. In a broad sense, Swift functions are more flexible and robust in that they can accept more than just one parameter, and even accept types other than numeric ones.

Consider creating a function that takes more than one parameter and returns something other than a Double (**Figure 4.4**).

FIGURE 4.4 A multi-parameter function

```
                                                    Chapter 4
 1  //: Playground – noun: a place where people can play
 2
 3  import Cocoa
 4
 5  var str = "Hello, playground"                              "Hello, playground"
 6
 7  func fahrenheitToCelsius(fahrenheitValue : Double) -> Double {
 8      var result : Double
 9
10      result = (((fahrenheitValue - 32) * 5) / 9)            31.22222222222222
11
12      return result;                                         31.22222222222222
13  }
14
15  var outdoorTemperatureInFahrenheit = 88.2                  88.2
16  var outdoorTemperatureInCelsius = fahrenheitToCelsius      31.22222222222222
        (outdoorTemperatureInFahrenheit)
17
18  func celsiusToFahrenheit(celsiusValue : Double) -> Double {
19      var result : Double
20
21      result = (((celsiusValue * 9) / 5) + 32)               88.2
22
23      return result                                          88.2
24  }
25
26  outdoorTemperatureInFahrenheit = celsiusToFahrenheit       88.2
        (outdoorTemperatureInCelsius)
27
28  func buildASentenceUsingSubject(subject : String, verb : String, noun :
        String) -> String {
29      return subject + " " + verb + " " + noun + "!"         (2 times)
30  }
31
32  buildASentenceUsingSubject("Swift", verb: "is", noun: "cool")      "Swift is cool!"
33  buildASentenceUsingSubject("I", verb: "love", noun: "languages")   "I love languages!"
34
```

```
func buildASentenceUsingSubject(subject : String, verb : String, noun : String)
→ -> String {
  return subject + " " + verb + " " + noun + "!"
}
```

```
buildASentenceUsingSubject("Swift", verb: "is", noun: "cool")
buildASentenceUsingSubject("I", verb: "love", noun: "languages")
```

After typing in lines 28 through 33, examine your work. On line 28, you declared a new function, buildASentence, with not one but three parameters: subject, verb, and noun, all of which are String types. The function also returns a String type as well. On line 29, the concatenation of those three parameters, interspersed with spaces to make the sentence readable, is what is returned.

To demonstrate the utility of the function, it is called twice on lines 32 and 33, resulting in the sentences in the Results sidebar.

If you are familiar with the C language and how parameters are passed to functions, the notation on lines 32 and 33 may appear confusing at first. Swift enforces the notion of named parameters on all but the first parameter of a function. The names that were declared in the function on line 28 (verb and noun) are specified on this line right alongside the actual string values.

```
11
12      return result;                                          31.22222222222222
13 }
14
15 var outdoorTemperatureInFahrenheit = 88.2                    88.2
16 var outdoorTemperatureInCelsius = fahrenheitToCelsius        31.22222222222222
      (outdoorTemperatureInFahrenheit)
17
18 func celsiusToFahrenheit(celsiusValue : Double) -> Double {
19      var result : Double
20
21      result = (((celsiusValue * 9) / 5) + 32)                88.2
22
23      return result                                           88.2
24 }
25
26 outdoorTemperatureInFahrenheit = celsiusToFahrenheit         88.2
      (outdoorTemperatureInCelsius)
27
28 func buildASentenceUsingSubject(subject : String, verb : String, noun :
      String) -> String {
29      return subject + " " + verb + " " + noun + "!"          (2 times)
30 }
31
32 buildASentenceUsingSubject("Swift", verb: "is", noun: "cool")     "Swift is cool!"
33 buildASentenceUsingSubject("I", verb: "love", noun: "languages")  "I love languages!"
34
35 // Parameters Ad Nauseam
36 func addMyAccountBalances(balances : Double...) -> Double {
37      var result : Double = 0                                 (3 times)
38
39      for balance in balances {
40          result += balance                                  (9 times)
41      }
42
43      return result                                           (3 times)
44 }
45
46 addMyAccountBalances(77.87)                                  77.87
47 addMyAccountBalances(10.52, 11.30, 100.60)                  122.42
48 addMyAccountBalances(345.12, 1000.80, 233.10, 104.80, 99.90) 1783.72
49
```

FIGURE 4.5 Variable parameter passing in a function

Swift enforces the notion of named parameters, which is a legacy of Objective-C. Named parameters bring clarity to your source code by documenting exactly what is being passed. From the code, you can clearly see that the verb and noun are the second and third parameters, respectively.

Feel free to replace the parameters with values of your own liking and view the results interactively.

PARAMETERS AD NAUSEAM

Imagine you're writing the next big banking app for the Mac, and you want to create a way to add some arbitrary number of account balances. Something so mundane can be done a number of ways, but you want to write a Swift function to do the addition. The problem is you don't know how many accounts will need to be summed at any given time.

Enter Swift's variable parameter passing notation. It provides you with a way to tell Swift, "I don't know how many parameters I'll need to pass to this function, so accept as many as I will give." Type in the following code, which is shown in action on lines 35 through 48 in **Figure 4.5**.

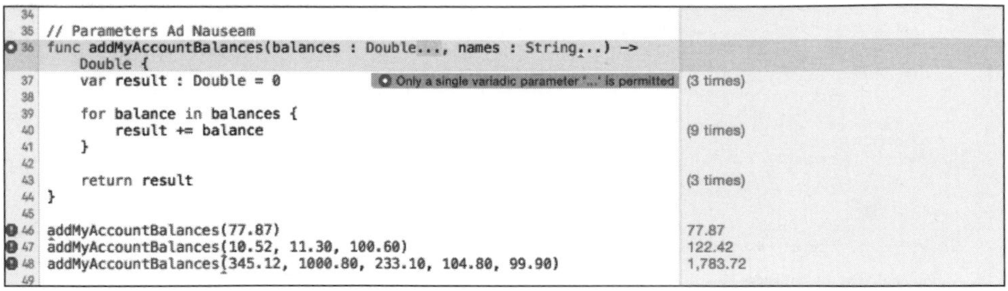

FIGURE 4.6 Adding
additional variable
parameters

```
34
35    // Parameters Ad Nauseam
36    func addMyAccountBalances(balances : Double..., names : String...) ->
        Double {
37        var result : Double = 0          ⊙ Only a single variadic parameter "..." is permitted  (3 times)
38
39        for balance in balances {                                                 (9 times)
40            result += balance
41        }
42
43        return result                                                            (3 times)
44    }
45
46    addMyAccountBalances(77.87)                                                  77.87
47    addMyAccountBalances(10.52, 11.30, 100.60)                                   122.42
48    addMyAccountBalances(345.12, 1000.80, 233.10, 104.80, 99.90)                 1,783.72
49
```

```swift
// Parameters Ad Nauseam
func addMyAccountBalances(balances : Double...) -> Double {
  var result : Double = 0

  for balance in balances {
      result += balance
  }

  return result
}

addMyAccountBalances(77.87)
addMyAccountBalances(10.52, 11.30, 100.60)
addMyAccountBalances(345.12, 1000.80, 233.10, 104.80, 99.90)
```

This function's parameter, known as a *variadic parameter*, can represent an unknown number of parameters.

On line 36, your balances parameter is declared as a Double followed by the ellipsis (...) and returns a Double. The presence of the ellipsis is the clue: It tells Swift to expect *one or more* parameters of type Double when this function is called.

The function is called three times on lines 46 through 48, each with a different number of bank balances. The totals for each appear in the Results sidebar.

You might be tempted to add additional variadic parameters in a function. **Figure 4.6** shows an attempt to extend addMyAccountBalances with a second variadic parameter, but it results in a Swift error.

This is a no-no, and Swift will quickly shut you down with an error. Only *one* parameter of a function may contain the ellipsis to indicate a variadic parameter. All other parameters must refer to a single quantity.

Since we're on the theme of bank accounts, add two more functions: one that will find the largest balance in a given list of balances, and another that will find the smallest balance. Type the following code, which is shown on lines 50 through 75 in **Figure 4.7**.

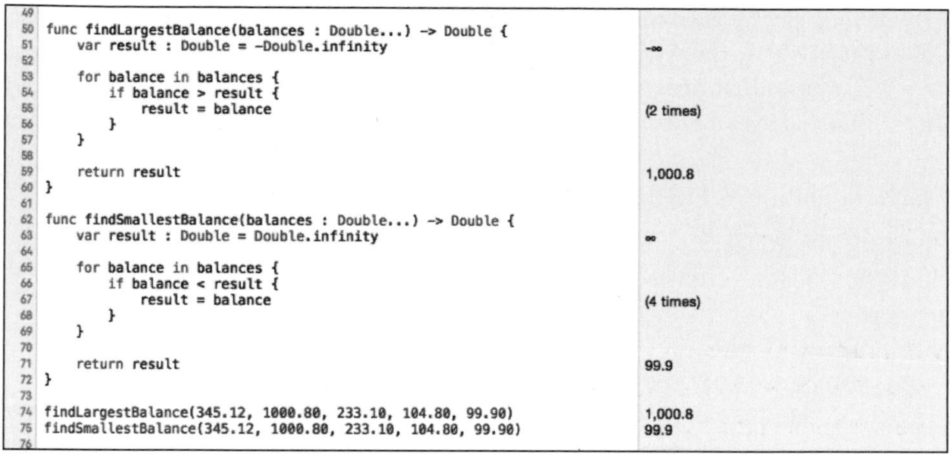

FIGURE 4.7 Functions to find the largest and smallest balance

```
func findLargestBalance(balances : Double...) -> Double {
  var result : Double = -Double.infinity

  for balance in balances {
    if balance > result {
      result = balance
    }
  }

  return result
}

func findSmallestBalance(balances : Double...) -> Double {
  var result : Double = Double.infinity

  for balance in balances {
    if balance < result {
      result = balance
    }
  }

  return result
}

findLargestBalance(345.12, 1000.80, 233.10, 104.80, 99.90)
findSmallestBalance(345.12, 1000.80, 233.10, 104.80, 99.90)
```

Both functions iterate through the parameter list to find the largest and smallest balance. Unless you have an account with plus or minus infinity of your favorite currency, these functions will work well. On lines 74 and 75, both functions are tested with the same balances used earlier, and the Results sidebar confirms their correctness.

FUNCTIONS FLY FIRST CLASS

One of the powerful features of Swift functions is that they are *first-class objects*. Sounds pretty fancy, doesn't it? What that really means is that you can handle a function just like any other value. You can assign a function to a constant, pass a function as a parameter to another function, and even return a function from a function!

To illustrate this idea, consider the act of depositing a check into your bank account, as well as withdrawing an amount. Every Monday, an amount is deposited, and every Friday, another amount is withdrawn. Instead of tying the day directly to the function name of the deposit or withdrawal, use a constant to point to the function for the appropriate day. The code on lines 77 through 94 in **Figure 4.8** provides an example.

```
var account1 = ("State Bank Personal", 1011.10)
var account2 = ("State Bank Business", 24309.63)

func deposit(amount : Double, account : (name : String, balance : Double)) ->
→ (String, Double) {
  let newBalance : Double = account.balance + amount
  return (account.name, newBalance)
}
func withdraw(amount : Double, account : (name : String, balance : Double)) ->
→ (String, Double) {
  var newBalance : Double = account.balance - amount
  return (account.name, newBalance)
}

let mondayTransaction = deposit
let fridayTransaction = withdraw

let mondayBalance = mondayTransaction(300.0, account: account1)
let fridayBalance = fridayTransaction(1200, account: account2)
```

```
56        }
57      }
58
59      return result                                              1000.8
60 }
61
62 func findSmallestBalance(balances : Double...) -> Double {
63     var result : Double = Double.infinity                       inf
64
65     for balance in balances {
66         if balance < result {
67             result = balance                                    (4 times)
68         }
69     }
70
71     return result                                               99.9000000000001
72 }
73
74 findLargestBalance(345.12, 1000.80, 233.10, 104.80, 99.90)      1000.8
75 findSmallestBalance(345.12, 1000.80, 233.10, 104.80, 99.90)     99.9000000000001
76
77 var account1 = ("State Bank Personal", 1011.10)                 (.0 "State Bank Personal", .1 1011.1)
78 var account2 = ("State Bank Business", 24309.63)                (.0 "State Bank Business", .1 24309.63)
79
80 func deposit(amount : Double, account : (name : String, balance :
       Double)) -> (String, Double) {
81     let newBalance : Double = account.balance + amount          1311.1
82     return (account.name, newBalance)                           (.0 "State Bank Personal", .1 1311.1)
83 }
84
85 func withdraw(amount : Double, account : (name : String, balance :
       Double)) -> (String, Double) {
86     let newBalance : Double = account.balance - amount          23109.63
87     return (account.name, newBalance)                           (.0 "State Bank Business", .1 23109.63)
88 }
89
90 let mondayTransaction = deposit                                 (Double, (String, Double)) -> (String, Double)
91 let fridayTransaction = withdraw                                (Double, (String, Double)) -> (String, Double)
92
93 let mondayBalance = mondayTransaction(300.0, account: account1) (.0 "State Bank Personal", .1 1311.1)
94 let fridayBalance = fridayTransaction(1200, account: account2)  (.0 "State Bank Business", .1 23109.63)
95
```

FIGURE 4.8 Demonstrating functions as first-class types

For starters, you create two accounts on lines 77 and 78. Each account is a tuple consisting of an account name and balance.

On line 80, a function named deposit is declared, and it takes two parameters: the amount (a Double) and a tuple named account. The tuple has two members: name, which is of type String, and balance, which is a Double that represents the funds in that account. The same tuple type is also declared as the return type.

At line 81, a variable named newBalance is declared, and its value is assigned the sum of the balance member of the account tuple and the amount variable that is passed. The tuple result is constructed on line 82 and returned.

The function on line 85 is named differently (withdraw) but is effectively the same, save for the subtraction that takes place on line 86.

On lines 90 and 91, two new constants are declared and assigned to the functions respectively by name: deposit and withdraw. Since deposits happen on a Monday, the mondayTransaction is assigned the deposit function. Likewise, withdrawals are on Friday, and the fridayTransaction constant is assigned the withdraw function.

Lines 93 and 94 show the results of passing the account1 and account2 tuples to the mondayTransaction and fridayTransaction constants, which are in essence the functions deposit and withdraw. The Results sidebar bears out the result, and you've just called the two functions by referring to the constants.

FIGURE 4.9 Returning a function from a function

```
     ┌─┐ ⟨  ⟩ │ ▣ Chapter 4
65       for balance in balances {
66           if balance < result {
67               result = balance                        (4 times)
68           }
69       }
70
71       return result                                   99.90000000000001
72   }
73
74   findLargestBalance(345.12, 1000.80, 233.10, 104.80, 99.90)    1000.8
75   findSmallestBalance(345.12, 1000.80, 233.10, 104.80, 99.90)   99.90000000000001
76
77   var account1 = ("State Bank Personal", 1011.10)    (.0 "State Bank Personal", .1 1011.1)
78   var account2 = ("State Bank Business", 24309.63)   (.0 "State Bank Business", .1 24309.63)
79
80   func deposit(amount : Double, account : (name : String, balance :
         Double)) -> (String, Double) {
81       let newBalance : Double = account.balance + amount    1311.1
82       return (account.name, newBalance)                (.0 "State Bank Personal", .1 1311.1)
83   }
84
85   func withdraw(amount : Double, account : (name : String, balance :
         Double)) -> (String, Double) {
86       let newBalance : Double = account.balance - amount    23109.63
87       return (account.name, newBalance)                (.0 "State Bank Business", .1 23109.63)
88   }
89
90   let mondayTransaction = deposit      (Double, (String, Double)) -> (String, Double)
91   let fridayTransaction = withdraw     (Double, (String, Double)) -> (String, Double)
92
93   let mondayBalance = mondayTransaction(300.0, account: account1)   (.0 "State Bank Personal", .1 1311.1)
94   let fridayBalance = fridayTransaction(1200, account: account2)    (.0 "State Bank Business", .1 23109.63)
95
96   func chooseTransaction(transaction : String) -> (Double, (String,
         Double)) -> (String, Double) {
97       if (transaction == "Deposit") {
98           return deposit
99       }
100
101      return withdraw
102  }
103
```

THROW ME A FUNCTION, MISTER

Just as a function can return an Int, Double, or String, a function can also return another function. Your head starts hurting just thinking about the possibilities, doesn't it? Actually, it's not as hard as it sounds. Check out lines 96 through 102 in **Figure 4.9**.

```
func chooseTransaction(transaction: String) -> (Double, (String, Double)) ->
→ (String, Double) {
  if transaction == "Deposit" {
    return deposit
  }

  return withdraw
}
```

On line 96, the function chooseTransaction takes a String as a parameter, which it uses to deduce the type of banking transaction. That same function returns a function, which itself takes a Double, and a tuple of String and Double, and returns a tuple of String and Double. Phew!

FIGURE 4.10 Calling the returned function in two different ways

```
72  }
73
74  findLargestBalance(345.12, 1000.80, 233.10, 104.80, 99.90)      1,000.8
75  findSmallestBalance(345.12, 1000.80, 233.10, 104.80, 99.90)     99.9
76
77  var account1 = ("State Bank Personal", 1011.10)                 (.0 "State Bank Personal", .1 1,011.1)
78  var account2 = ("State Bank Business", 24309.63)                (.0 "State Bank Business", .1 24,309.63)
79
80  func deposit(amount : Double, account : (name : String, balance :
        Double)) -> (String, Double) {
81      let newBalance : Double = account.balance + amount          (2 times)
82      return (account.name, newBalance)                           (2 times)
83  }
84
85  func withdraw(amount : Double, account : (name : String, balance :
        Double)) -> (String, Double) {
86      let newBalance : Double = account.balance - amount          (2 times)
87      return (account.name, newBalance)                           (2 times)
88  }
89
90  let mondayTransaction = deposit                                 (Double, (String, Double)) -> (String, Double)
91  let fridayTransaction = withdraw                                (Double, (String, Double)) -> (String, Double)
92
93  let mondayBalance = mondayTransaction(300.0, account: account1) (.0 "State Bank Personal", .1 1,311.1)
94  let fridayBalance = fridayTransaction(1200, account: account2)  (.0 "State Bank Business", .1 23,109.63)
95
96  func chooseTransaction(transaction : String) -> (Double, (String,
        Double)) -> (String, Double) {
97      if (transaction == "Deposit") {
98          return deposit                                          (Double, (String, Double)) -> (String, Double)
99      }
100
101     return withdraw                                             (Double, (String, Double)) -> (String, Double)
102 }
103
104 // option 1: capture the function in a constant and call it
105 let myTransaction = chooseTransaction("Deposit")                (Double, (String, Double)) -> (String, Double)
106 myTransaction(225.33, account2)                                 (.0 "State Bank Business", .1 24,534.96)
107
108 // option 2: call the function reuslt directly
109 chooseTransaction("Withdraw")(63.17, account1)                  (.0 "State Bank Personal", .1 947.93)
110
```

That's a mouthful. Let's take a moment to look at that line more closely and break it down a bit. The line begins with the definition of the function and its sole parameter, transaction, followed by the -> characters indicating the return type:

```
func chooseTransaction(transaction: String) ->
```

After that is the return type, which is a function that takes two parameters—the Double, and a tuple of Double and String—as well as the function return characters ->:

```
(Double, (String, Double)) ->
```

And finally, the return type of the returned function, a tuple of String and Double.

What functions did you write that meet these criteria? The deposit and withdraw functions, of course! Look at lines 80 and 85. Those two functions are bank transactions that were used earlier. Since they are defined as functions that take two parameters (a Double and a tuple of String and Double) and return a tuple of Double and String, they are appropriate candidates for return values in the chooseTransaction function on line 96.

Back to the chooseTransaction function: On line 97, the transaction parameter, which is a String, is compared against the constant string "Deposit" and if a match is made, the deposit function is returned on line 98; otherwise, the withdraw function is returned on line 101.

OK, so you have a function which itself returns one of two possible functions. How do you use it? Do you capture the function in another variable and call it?

Actually, there are two ways this can be done (**Figure 4.10**).

```
// option 1: capture the function in a constant and call it
let myTransaction = chooseTransaction("Deposit")
myTransaction(225.33, account2)

// option 2: call the function result directly
chooseTransaction("Withdraw")(63.17, account1)
```

On line 105 you can see that the returned function for making deposits is captured in the constant myTransaction, which is then called on line 106 with account2 increasing its amount by $225.33.

The alternate style is on line 109. There, the chooseTransaction function is being called to gain access to the withdraw function. Instead of assigning the result to a constant, however, the returned function is immediately pressed into service with the parameters 63.17 and the first account, account1. The results are the same in the Results sidebar: The withdraw function is called and the balance is adjusted.

A FUNCTION IN A FUNCTION IN A...

If functions returned by functions and assigned to constants isn't enough of an enigma for you, how about declaring a function inside another function? Yes, such a thing exists. They're known as *nested functions*.

Nested functions are useful when you want to isolate, or hide, specific functionality that doesn't need to be exposed to outer layers. Take, for instance, the code in **Figure 4.11**.

```
// nested function example
func bankVault(passcode : String) -> String {
  func openBankVault(_: Void) -> String {
    return "Vault opened"
  }
  func closeBankVault() -> String {
    return "Vault closed"
  }
  if passcode == "secret" {
    return openBankVault()
  }
  else {
    return closeBankVault()
  }
}

print(bankVault("wrongsecret"))
print(bankVault("secret"))
```

FIGURE 4.11 Nested functions in action

```
89
90   let mondayTransaction = deposit                                    (Double, (String, Double)) -> (String, Double)
91   let fridayTransaction = withdraw                                   (Double, (String, Double)) -> (String, Double)
92
93   let mondayBalance = mondayTransaction(300.0, account: account1)    (.0 "State Bank Personal", .1 1,311.1)
94   let fridayBalance = fridayTransaction(1200, account: account2)     (.0 "State Bank Business", .1 23,109.63)
95
96   func chooseTransaction(transaction : String) -> (Double, (String,
         Double)) -> (String, Double) {
97       if (transaction == "Deposit") {
98           return deposit                                            (Double, (String, Double)) -> (String, Double)
99       }
100
101      return withdraw                                               (Double, (String, Double)) -> (String, Double)
102  }
103
104  // option 1: capture the function in a constant and call it
105  let myTransaction = chooseTransaction("Deposit")                  (Double, (String, Double)) -> (String, Double)
106  myTransaction(225.33, account2)                                   (.0 "State Bank Business", .1 24,534.96)
107
108  // option 2: call the function reuslt directly
109  chooseTransaction("Withdraw")(63.17, account1)                    (.0 "State Bank Personal", .1 947.93)
110
111  // nested function example
112  func bankVault(passcode : String) -> String {
113      func openBankVault(_: Void) -> String {
114          return "Vault opened"                                     "Vault opened"
115      }
116      func closeBankVault() -> String {
117          return "Vault closed"                                     "Vault closed"
118      }
119      if (passcode == "secret") {
120          return openBankVault()                                    "Vault opened"
121      }
122      else {
123          return closeBankVault();                                  "Vault closed"
124      }
125  }
126
127  print(bankVault("wrongsecret"))                                   "Vault closed"
128  print(bankVault("secret"))                                        "Vault opened"
129
```

On line 112, a new function, bankVault, is defined. It takes a single parameter, passcode, which is a String, and returns a String.

Lines 113 and 116 define two functions inside the bankVault function: openBankVault and closeBankVault. Both of these functions take no parameter and return a String.

On line 119, the passcode parameter is compared with the string "secret" and if a match is made, the bank vault is opened by calling the openBankVault function. Otherwise, the bank vault remains closed.

INTO THE VOID

On line 113 you'll notice a new Swift keyword: Void. It means exactly what you might think: emptiness. The Void keyword is used mostly as a placeholder when declaring empty parameter lists, and is optional in this case. The underscore that precedes it is known as an "unnamed parameter," which is essentially an anonymous variable name. On line 116, you declare the closeBankVault function without any parameter, which assumes Void. In any case, functions that have no parameters can simply be declared without any parameters, and they're used here only for illustrative purposes. In fact, both function definitions on line 113 and 116 are equivalent for all practical purposes.

FIGURE 4.12 The result of attempting to call a nested function from a different scope

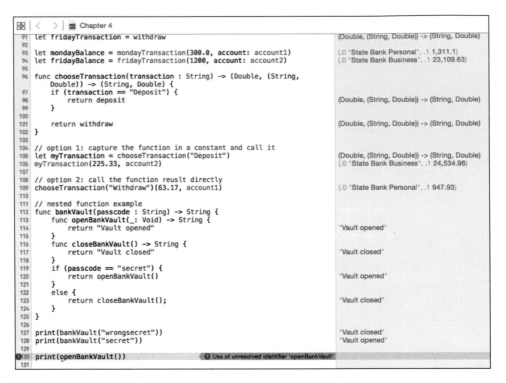

Lines 127 and 128 show the result of calling the bankVault method with an incorrect and correct passcode. What's important to realize is that the openBankVault and closeBankVault functions are "enclosed" by the bankVault function, and are not known outside of that function.

If you were to attempt to call either openBankVault or closeBankVault outside of the bankVault function, you would get an error. That's because those functions are not in *scope*. They are, in effect, hidden by the bankVault function and are unable to be called from the outside. **Figure 4.12** illustrates an attempt to call one of these nested functions.

In general, the obvious benefit of nesting functions within functions is that it prevents the unnecessary exposing of functionality. In Figure 4.12, the bankVault function is the sole gateway to opening and closing the vault, and the functions that perform the work are isolated within that function. Always consider this when designing functions that are intended to work together.

DEFAULT PARAMETERS

As you've just seen, Swift functions provide a rich area for utility and experimentation. A lot can be done with functions and their parameters to model real-world problems. Functions provide an interesting feature known as *default parameter values*, which allow you to declare functions that have parameters containing a "prefilled" value.

```
97      if (transaction == "Deposit") {
98          return deposit                              (Double, (String, Double)) -> (String, Double)
99      }
100
101     return withdraw                                 (Double, (String, Double)) -> (String, Double)
102  }
103
104  // option 1: capture the function in a constant and call it
105  let myTransaction = chooseTransaction("Deposit")    (Double, (String, Double)) -> (String, Double)
106  myTransaction(225.33, account2)                     (.0 "State Bank Business", .1 24,534.96)
107
108  // option 2: call the function reuslt directly
109  chooseTransaction("Withdraw")(63.17, account1)      (.0 "State Bank Personal", .1 947.93)
110
111  // nested function example
112  func bankVault(passcode : String) -> String {
113      func openBankVault(_: Void) -> String {
114          return "Vault opened"                       "Vault opened"
115      }
116      func closeBankVault() -> String {
117          return "Vault closed"                       "Vault closed"
118      }
119      if (passcode == "secret") {
120          return openBankVault()                      "Vault opened"
121      }
122      else {
123          return closeBankVault();                    "Vault closed"
124      }
125  }
126
127  print(bankVault("wrongsecret"))                     "Vault closed"
128  print(bankVault("secret"))                          "Vault opened"
129
130  func writeCheckTo(payee : String = "Unknown", amount : String = "10.00")
131      -> String {
         return "Check payable to " + payee + " for $" + amount   (3 times)
132  }
133
134  writeCheckTo()                          "Check payable to Unknown for $10.00"
135  writeCheckTo("Donna Soileau")           "Check payable to Donna Soileau for $10.00"
136  writeCheckTo("John Miller", amount : "45.00")   "Check payable to John Miller for $45.00"
137
```

FIGURE 4.13 Using default parameters in a function

Let's say you want to create a function that writes checks. Your function would take two parameters: a payee (the person or business to whom the check is written) and the amount. Of course, in the real world, you always want to know these two pieces of information, but for now, think of a function that would assume a default payee and amount in the event the information wasn't passed.

Figure 4.13 shows such a function on lines 130 through 132. The writeCheckTo function takes two String parameters, the payee and amount, and returns a String that is simply a sentence describing how the check is written.

```
func writeCheckTo(payee : String = "Unknown", amount : String = "10.00") ->
→ String {
  return "Check payable to " + payee + " for $" + amount
}


writeCheckTo()
writeCheckTo("Donna Soileau")
writeCheckTo("John Miller", amount : "45.00")
```

Take note of the declaration of the function on line 130:

```
func writeCheckTo(payee : String = "Unknown", amount : String = "10.00") ->
→ String
```

What you haven't seen before now is the assignment of the parameters to actual values (in this case, payee is being set to "Unknown" by default and amount is being set to "10.00"). This is how you can write a function to take default parameters—simply assign the parameter name to a value!

So how do you call this function? Lines 134 through 136 show three different ways:

- Line 134 passes no parameters when calling the function.
- Line 135 passes a single parameter.
- Line 136 passes both parameters, with the second parameter following its parameter name amount.

In the case where no parameters are passed, the default values are used to construct the returned String. In the other two cases, the passed parameter values are used in place of the default values, and you can view the results of the calls in the Results sidebar.

Recall that Swift enforces the requirement that the parameter name must be passed for all but the first parameter. On line 135, only one parameter is used, so the name is not passed:

```
writeCheckTo("Donna Soileau")
```

On line 136, two parameter names are used, and the parameter name is specified prior to the amount string:

```
writeCheckTo("John Miller", amount : "45.00")
```

Default parameters give you the flexibility of using a known value instead of taking the extra effort to pass it explicitly. They're not necessarily applicable for every function out there, but they do come in handy at times.

WHAT'S IN A NAME?

As Swift functions go, declaring them is easy, as you've seen. In some cases, however, what really composes the function name is more than just the text following the keyword func.

As I touched on earlier, each parameter in a Swift function has the parameter name preceding the parameter. This gives additional clarity and description to a function name. Up to this point, you've been told that it must be passed when calling the function. Although it is good practice, it is not entirely necessary. When declaring a function, an *implicit external parameter name* can be notated with an underscore preceding the parameter name. Consider another check writing function in **Figure 4.14**, lines 138 through 140.

```
func writeCheckFrom(payer : String, _ payee : String, _ amount : Double) ->
→ String {
    return "Check payable from \(payer) to \(payee) for $\(amount)"
}

writeCheckFrom("Dave Johnson", "Coz Fontenot", 1_000.0)
```

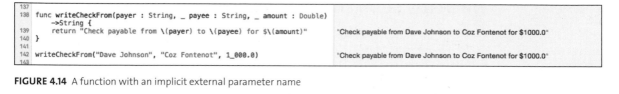

```
137
138   func writeCheckFrom(payer : String, _ payee : String, _ amount : Double)
         ->String {
139       return "Check payable from \(payer) to \(payee) for $\(amount)"      "Check payable from Dave Johnson to Coz Fontenot for $1000.0"
140   }
141
142   writeCheckFrom("Dave Johnson", "Coz Fontenot", 1_000.0)               "Check payable from Dave Johnson to Coz Fontenot for $1000.0"
143
```

FIGURE 4.14 A function with an implicit external parameter name

```
143
144   func writeBetterCheckFrom(payer : String, payee : String, amount :
         Double) -> String {
145       return "Check payable from \(payer) to \(payee) for $\(amount)"      "Check payable from Fred Charlie to Ryan Hanks for $1350.0"
146   }
147
148   writeBetterCheckFrom("Fred Charlie", payee: "Ryan Hanks", amount:    "Check payable from Fred Charlie to Ryan Hanks for $1350.0"
         1350.0)
149
```

FIGURE 4.15 A function called with parameter names

This function is different from the earlier check writing function on lines 130 through 132 in two ways:

- An underscore and a space precede the parameters named payee and amount
- There are no default parameters

On line 142, the new writeCheckFrom function is called with three parameters: two String values and a Double value. From the name of the function, its purpose is clearly to write a check. When writing a check, you need to know several things: who the check is being written for, who is writing the check, and the amount the check is for. A good guess is that the Double parameter is the amount, which is a number. But without actually looking at the function declaration itself, how would you know what the two String parameters actually mean? Even if you were to deduce that they are the payer and payee, how do you know which is which, and in which order to pass the parameters?

Swift's default behavior of insisting on the use of parameter names solves this problem and makes the intent of your code easier to understand; it makes very clear to anyone reading the calling function what the intention is and the purpose of each parameter. **Figure 4.15** illustrates this.

```
func writeBetterCheckFrom(payer : String, payee : String, amount : Double) ->
→ String {
  return "Check payable from \(payer) to \(payee) for $\(amount)"
}
```

```
writeBetterCheckFrom("Fred Charlie", payee : "Ryan Hanks", amount : 1350.0)
```

On line 144, you declare a function, writeBetterCheckFrom, which takes the same number of parameters as the function on line 138. However, each of the parameters in the new function omits the underscore.

The extra bit of typing pays off when the writeBetterCheckFrom function is called. Looking at that line of code alone, the order of the parameters and what they indicate is clear: Write a check *from* Fred Charlie *to* Ryan Hanks for a *total* of $1350.

WHEN IT'S GOOD ENOUGH

Parameter names bring clarity to functions, as you've just seen. In addition, Swift allows *external parameter names* to decorate a function declaration. This can be useful if you want to bring additional clarity to your function.

Line 150 of **Figure 4.16** shows this in action. The new method, writeBestCheck has dropped the From in the name. Instead, it has moved to the first parameter as an external parameter name. Other external parameter names in this function declaration are to and total.

On line 154, the parameter names are used as external parameter names to call the function, and the use of those names clearly shows what the function's purpose and parameter order is: a check written *from* Bart Stewart *to* Alan Lafleur for a *total* of $101. Note that when using external parameter names, the first parameter also requires the parameter name to be passed. This is different from what you saw earlier when your earlier functions weren't using external parameter names.

```
func writeBestCheck(from payer : String, to payee : String,
→ total amount : Double) -> String {
  return "Check payable from \(payer) to \(payee) for $\(amount)"
}


writeBestCheck(from: "Bart Stewart", to: "Alan Lafleur", total: 101.0)
```

TO USE OR NOT TO USE?

Parameter names bring clarity to functions, but they also require more typing on the part of the coder who uses your functions. Since they are optional parts of a function's declaration, when should you use them?

In general, if the function in question can benefit from the additional clarity of having parameter names provided for each parameter, by all means use them. The check writing example is such a case. Avoid parameter ambiguity in the cases where it might exist. On the other hand, if you're creating a function that just adds two numbers (see lines 156 through 160 in **Figure 4.17**), parameter names add little to nothing of value for the caller. You can just use the underscore (recall implicit external parameter names) and avoid passing the parameter name altogether.

```
func addTwoNumbers(number1 : Double, _ number2 : Double) -> Double {
  return number1 + number2
}


addTwoNumbers(33.1, 12.2)
```

```
149
150   func writeBestCheck(from payer : String, to payee : String, total
          amount : Double) -> String {
151       return "Check payable from \(payer) to \(payee) for $\(amount)"      "Check payable from Bart Stewart to Alan Lafleur for $101.0"
152   }
153
154   writeBestCheck(from: "Bart Stewart", to: "Alan Lafleur", total: 101.0)   "Check payable from Bart Stewart to Alan Lafleur for $101.0"
155
```

FIGURE 4.16 Using the external parameter name syntax

```
156   func addTwoNumbers(number1 : Double, _ number2 : Double) -> Double {
157       return number1 + number2                                    45.3
158   }
159
160   addTwoNumbers(33.1, 12.2)                                        45.3
161
```

FIGURE 4.17 When parameter names are not necessary

```
161
162   func cashCheck(from : String, to : String, total : Double) -> String {
163       if to == "Cash" {
164           to = from                    ⊘ Cannot assign to value: 'to' is a 'let' constant
165       }
166       return "Check payable from \(from) to \(to) for $\(total) has been
              cashed"
167   }
168
169   cashCheck("Jason Guillory", to: "Cash", total: 103.0)
170
```

FIGURE 4.18 Assigning a value to a parameter results in an error.

DON'T CHANGE MY PARAMETERS!

Functions are prohibited from changing the values of parameters passed to them, because parameters are passed as constants and not variables. Consider the function cashCheck on lines 162 through 169 in **Figure 4.18**.

```
func cashCheck(from : String, to : String, total : Double) -> String {
  if to == "Cash" {
    to = from
  }
  return "Check payable from \(from) to \(to) for $\(total) has been cashed"
}


cashCheck("Jason Guillory", to: "Cash", total: 103.00)
```

The function takes the same parameters as your earlier check writing function: who the check is from, who the check is to, and the total. On line 163, the to variable is checked for the value "Cash" and if it is equal, it is reassigned the contents of the variable from. The rationale here is that if you are writing a check to "Cash," you're essentially writing it to yourself.

Notice the error: Cannot assign to value: 'to' is a 'let' constant. Swift is saying that the parameter to is a constant, and since constants cannot change their values once assigned, this is prohibited and results in an error.

```
161
162  func cashCheck(from : String, to : String, total : Double) -> String {
163      var otherTo = to                                                    "Cash"
164      if to == "Cash" {
165          otherTo = from                                                  "Jason Guillory"
166      }
167      return "Check payable from \(from) to \(otherTo) for $\(total) has   "Check payable from Jason Guillory to Jason Guillory for $103.0 has been cas..."
         been cashed"
168  }
169
170  cashCheck("Jason Guillory", to: "Cash", total: 103.0)                   "Check payable from Jason Guillory to Jason Guillory for $103.0 has been cas..."
171
```

FIGURE 4.19 A potential workaround to the parameter change problem

```
171
172  func cashBetterCheck(from : String, var to : String, total : Double) ->
         String {
173      if to == "Cash" {
174          to = from                                                       "Ray Daigle"
175      }
176      return "Check payable from \(from) to \(to) for $\(total) has been   "Check payable from Ray Daigle to Ray Daigle for $103.0 has been cashed"
         cashed"
177  }
178
179  cashBetterCheck("Ray Daigle", to: "Cash", total: 103.0)                 "Check payable from Ray Daigle to Ray Daigle for $103.0 has been cashed"
180
```

FIGURE 4.20 Using variable parameters to allow modifications

To get around this error, you could create a temporary variable, as done in **Figure 4.19**. Here, a new variable named otherTo is declared on line 163 and assigned to the to variable, and then possibly to the from variable on line 165, assuming the condition on line 164 is met. This is clearly acceptable and works fine for your purposes, but Swift gives you a better way.

With a var declaration on a parameter, you can tell Swift that the parameter is intended to be variable and can change within the function. All you need to do is add the keyword before the parameter name (or external parameter name in case you have one of those). **Figure 4.20** shows a second function, cashBetterCheck, which declares the to parameter as a variable parameter. Now the code inside the function can modify the to variable without receiving an error from Swift, and the output is identical to the workaround function above it.

```
func cashBetterCheck(from : String, var to : String, total : Double) ->
→ String {
  if to == "Cash" {
    to = from
  }
    return "Check payable from \(from) to \(to) for $\(total) has been cashed"
}

cashBetterCheck("Ray Daigle", to: "Cash", total: 103.00)
```

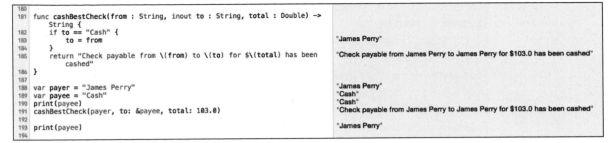

FIGURE 4.21 Using the inout keyword to establish a modifiable parameter

THE INS AND OUTS

As you've just seen, a function can be declared to modify the contents of one or more of its passed variables. The modification happens inside the function itself, and the change is not reflected back to the caller.

Sometimes having a function change the value of a passed parameter so that its new value is reflected back to the caller is desirable. For example, in the cashBetterCheck function on lines 172 through 177, having the caller know that the to variable has changed to a new value would be advantageous. Right now, that function's modification of the variable is not reflected back to the caller. Let's see how to do this in **Figure 4.21** using Swift's inout keyword.

```swift
func cashBestCheck(from : String, inout to : String, total : Double) ->
→ String {
  if to == "Cash" {
    to = from
  }
  return "Check payable from \(from) to \(to) for $\(total) has been cashed"
}


var payer = "James Perry"
var payee = "Cash"
print(payee)
cashBestCheck(payer, to: &payee, total: 103.00)

print(payee)
```

Lines 181 through 186 define the cashBestCheck function, which is virtually identical to the cashBetterCheck function on line 172, except the second parameter to is no longer a variable parameter—the var keyword has been replaced with the inout keyword. This new keyword tells Swift that the parameter's value can be expected to change in the function and that the change should be reflected back to the caller. With that exception, everything else is the same between the cashBetterCheck and cashBestCheck functions.

On lines 188 and 189, two variables are declared: payer and payee, with both being assigned String values. This is done because inout parameters must be passed a variable. A constant value will not work, because constants cannot be modified.

On line 190, the payee variable is printed, and the Results sidebar for that line clearly shows the variable's contents as "Cash". This is to make clear that the variable is set to its original value on line 189.

On line 191, you call the cashBestCheck function. Unlike the call to cashBetterCheck on line 179, you are passing variables instead of constants for the to and from parameters. More so, for the second parameter (payee), we are prepending the ampersand character (&) to the variable name. This is a direct result of declaring the parameter in cashBestCheck as an inout parameter. You are in essence telling Swift that this variable is an inout variable and that you expect it to be modified once control is returned from the called function.

On line 193, the payee variable is again printed. This time, the contents of that variable do not match what was printed on line 190 earlier. Instead, payee is now set to the value "James Perry", which is a direct result of the assignment in the cashBestCheck function on line 183.

BRINGING CLOSURE

Functions are great, and in the earlier code you've written, you can see just how versatile they can be for encapsulating functionality and ideas. Although the many contrived examples you went through may not give you a full appreciation of how useful they can be in every scenario, this will change as you proceed through the book. Functions are going to appear over and over again both here and in your code, so understand them well. You may want to re-read this chapter to retain all the ins and outs of functions.

I've got a little more to talk about before I close this chapter, however. Your tour of functions would not be complete without talking about another significant and related feature of functions in Swift: *closures*.

In layman's terms, a closure is essentially a block of code, like a function, that "closes in" or "encapsulates" all the "state" around it. All variables and constants declared and defined before a closure are "captured" in that closure. In essence, a closure preserves the state of the program at the point that it is created.

Computer science folk have another word for closures: *lambdas*. In fact, the very notion of the function you have been working with throughout this chapter is actually a special case of a closure—a function is a closure with a name.

So if functions are actually special types of closures, then why use closures? It's a fair question, and the answer can be summed up this way: Closures allow you to write simple and quick code blocks that can be passed around just like functions, but without the overhead of naming them.

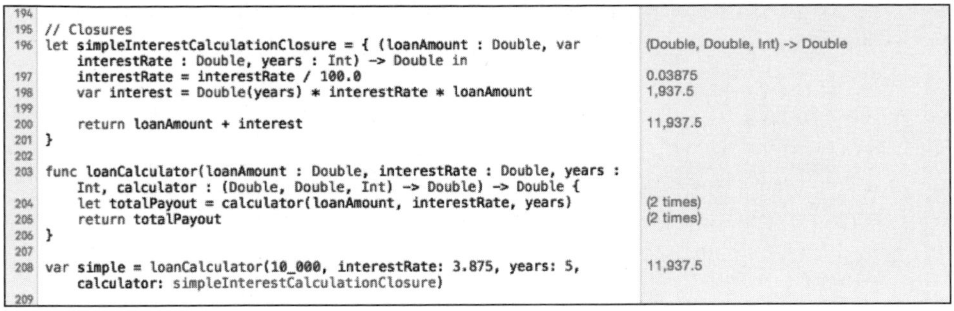

FIGURE 4.22 Using a closure to compute simple interest

In essence, closures are anonymous blocks of executable code.

Swift closures have the following structure:

```
{ (parameters) -> return_type in
  statements
}
```

This almost looks like a function, except that the keyword func and the name is missing, the curly braces encompass the entire closure, and the keyword in follows the return type.

Let's see closures in action. **Figure 4.22** shows a closure being defined on lines 196 through 201. The closure is being assigned to a constant named simpleInterestCalculationClosure. The closure takes three parameters: loanAmount, interestRate (both Double types), and years (an Int type). The code computes the future value of a loan over the term and returns it as a Double.

```
// Closures
let simpleInterestCalculationClosure = { (loanAmount : Double,
→ var interestRate : Double, years : Int) -> Double in
  interestRate = interestRate / 100.0
  var interest = Double(years) * interestRate * loanAmount

  return loanAmount + interest
}


func loanCalculator(loanAmount : Double, interestRate : Double, years :
→ Int, calculator : (Double, Double, Int) -> Double) -> Double {
  let totalPayout = calculator(loanAmount, interestRate, years)
  return totalPayout
}


var simple = loanCalculator(10_000, interestRate: 3.875, years: 5, calculator:
→ simpleInterestCalculationClosure)
```

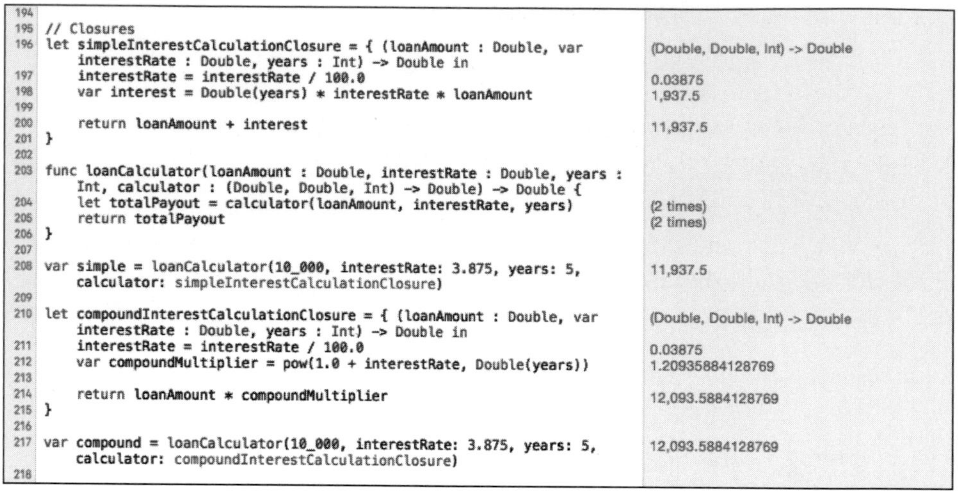

FIGURE 4.23 Adding
a second closure that
computes compound
interest

```
194
195   // Closures
196   let simpleInterestCalculationClosure = { (loanAmount : Double, var        (Double, Double, Int) -> Double
         interestRate : Double, years : Int) -> Double in
197      interestRate = interestRate / 100.0                                    0.03875
198      var interest = Double(years) * interestRate * loanAmount               1,937.5
199
200      return loanAmount + interest                                           11,937.5
201   }
202
203   func loanCalculator(loanAmount : Double, interestRate : Double, years :
         Int, calculator : (Double, Double, Int) -> Double) -> Double {
204      let totalPayout = calculator(loanAmount, interestRate, years)          (2 times)
205      return totalPayout                                                     (2 times)
206   }
207
208   var simple = loanCalculator(10_000, interestRate: 3.875, years: 5,        11,937.5
         calculator: simpleInterestCalculationClosure)
209
210   let compoundInterestCalculationClosure = { (loanAmount : Double, var      (Double, Double, Int) -> Double
         interestRate : Double, years : Int) -> Double in
211      interestRate = interestRate / 100.0                                    0.03875
212      var compoundMultiplier = pow(1.0 + interestRate, Double(years))        1.20935884128769
213
214      return loanAmount * compoundMultiplier                                 12,093.5884128769
215   }
216
217   var compound = loanCalculator(10_000, interestRate: 3.875, years: 5,      12,093.5884128769
         calculator: compoundInterestCalculationClosure)
218
```

The formula for simple interest calculation is:

futureValue = *presentValue* * *interestRate* * *years*

Lines 203 through 206 contain the function `loanCalculator`, which takes four parameters:
the same three that the closure takes, and an additional parameter, `calculator`, which is a closure that takes two `Double` types and an `Int` type and returns a `Double` type. Not coincidentally,
this is the same parameter and return type signature as your previously defined closure.

On line 208, the function is called with four parameters. The fourth parameter is the
constant `simpleInterestCalculationClosure`, which will be used by the function to compute the total loan amount.

This example becomes more interesting when you create a second closure to pass to the
`loanCalculator` function. Since you've already computed simple interest, you can now write
a closure that computes the future value of money using the compound interest formula:

futureValue = *presentValue* (1 + *interestRate*)*years*

Figure 4.23 shows the compound interest calculation closure defined on lines 210
through 215, which takes the exact same parameters as the simple calculation closure on line
196. On line 217, the `loanCalculator` function is again called with the same parameters as
before, except the `compoundInterestCalculationClosure` is passed as the fourth parameter.
As you can see in the Results sidebar, compound interest yields a higher future value of the
loan than simple interest does.

```
let compoundInterestCalculationClosure = { (loanAmount : Double,
→ var interestRate : Double, years : Int) -> Double in
  interestRate = interestRate / 100.0
  var compoundMultiplier = pow(1.0 + interestRate, Double(years))
```

```
    return loanAmount * compoundMultiplier
}

var compound = loanCalculator(10_000, interestsRate: 3.875, years: 5,
→ calculator: compoundInterestCalculationClosure)
```

On line 212 you may notice something new: a reference to a function named pow. This
is the power function, and it is part of Swift's math package. The function takes two Double
parameters: the value to be raised and the power to raise it to. It returns the result as a
Double value.

SUMMING IT UP

I've spent the entire chapter discussing functions and their use. Toward the end, you learned
about closures and how they are essentially nameless functions that can be passed around to
do useful work. As I indicated earlier, functions and closures are the foundations on which
Swift apps are written. They appear everywhere and are an integral part of the development
process. Knowing how they work and when to use them is a skill you will acquire over time.

In fact, there are even more things about functions and closures that I didn't touch on in
this chapter. There's no need to overload you on every possible feature they have; I'll cover
those extras later in the book. For now, you have enough of the basics to start doing useful
programming.

Also, feel free to work with the code in the playground for this chapter. Change it, modify
it, add to it, and make a mess of it if you want. That's what playgrounds are for, after all!

STAY CLASSY

With functions and closures covered, I'll turn your attention to the concept of the *class*. If
you are familiar with object-oriented programming (OOP), Swift's notion of a class is similar
to that of Objective-C and C++. If you're new to the idea of objects and OOP, don't worry—
I'll explain all that terminology in the next chapter.

Meanwhile, feel free to take a break and review the notes and code in this chapter, as well
as experiment with your playground file. When you're ready, proceed to Chapter 5, and I'll
get down and dirty with classes.

Organizing with Classes and Structures

Swift is an object-oriented language, and as such, it is apropos to devote considerable real estate to the subject. If you are familiar with other object-oriented languages, such as Objective-C and C++, the concepts presented here will be very familiar to you. If you are new to the idea of object-oriented programming (OOP), don't be alarmed. I'll take you through a tour of the concepts to prepare you for Swift's flavor of OOP.

No matter what your current familiarity is with OOP concepts, preparing yourself with a new playground file in Xcode 7 is a good idea. Choose File > New > Playground, and save your new playground file as **Chapter 5.playground**. You'll use this playground for all the examples in this chapter, and you can easily go back and refer to it as you need.

Ready? Let's dive in.

OBJECTS ARE EVERYWHERE

OOP is a methodology in software development that involves thinking about problems in terms of *objects*.

Look around you—objects are everywhere. Anything you can pick up and hold, or even touch and feel, could be considered an object.

If you think about an object—any object—you can immediately identify certain *properties* (also called *attributes*) of that object, as well as certain *behaviors*. In OOP parlance, objects have properties and behaviors. This is true in the real world, and it's true in Swift.

Take a moment to glance around the room. Pick out an object on the wall—a door, a window, a mirror, a picture, or a piece of furniture. Let's start with the door, which any room should have (or else you'll be stuck inside). Look at the door and ask yourself: What properties does this door have?

- Dimensions (width, height, and depth)
- Weight
- Color
- State (is it open or closed?)

These very generic properties could be applied to another item in the room—namely, the window. The door and the window share these same properties, which makes them similar but not the same—a door is not a window. This notion of similar properties will come in handy later as we study classes.

Now that you've identified the properties of the door, can you ascertain what its behaviors are? In other words, what is it that the door can do?

- A door can open and close.
- A door can lock or unlock (assuming it has a lock).

Technically, it takes someone (or something) to open or close a door, or even to lock or unlock it, so these behaviors describe a number of actions that can be performed on the object.

Let's continue this process a bit further by identifying another object. If you have a window you can look out of, perhaps you can see other objects: cars, people, trees, and so on. Set your sights on a tree if possible, and note its properties:

- Height
- Type (oak, maple, cypress, and so on)
- Foliage state (Does it have leaves or have they all fallen due to the time of year?)

Of course, a tree has many other properties, but I'll keep it simple with these three. What about behaviors of a tree? What can a tree "do?"

- A tree can sway in the breeze.
- A tree can produce seeds.
- A tree can perform photosynthesis.

This process you just went through is an important one when thinking about objects. What you have done is a common task in OOP: *modeling*. Modeling an object entails examining its properties and behaviors and then coming up with the code to describe that model in whatever programming language you want to use.

In this case, you've modeled two very different objects: a tree and a door. Other than dimensions, one has very little similarity to the other. That's where objects can get interesting.

Now that you have an idea how to model an object, it's time to look at how to express that model in Swift.

SWIFT OBJECTS ARE CLASSY

In Swift, objects are expressed using a special construct called the *class*. Just as in our modeling exercise, a Swift class contains the elements to express the model in code. The word class is an actual keyword and comprises several items:

- A namc
- One or more properties
- One or more methods

Every class has a name that uniquely identifies it, as well as properties, just like the objects you modeled earlier. A class also has methods. A *method* is a formal name for a function that exists inside a class. You explored functions in the previous chapter; now they come back to us in the form of methods, as you'll see shortly.

So to summarize, a Swift class defines the properties that make up the object, as well as the methods that perform the behaviors and act on those properties.

FIGURE 5.1 The Door object in Swift

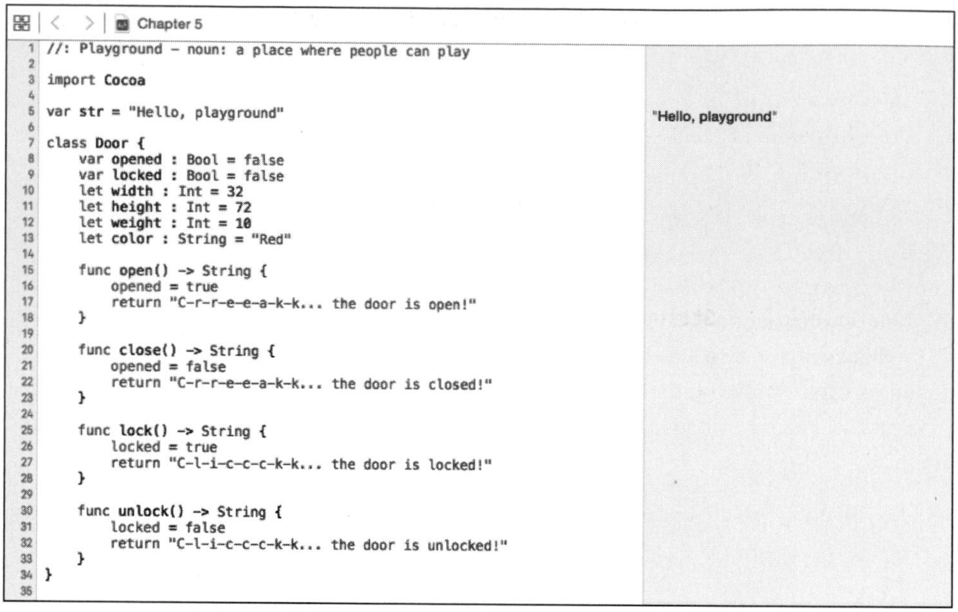

```
⊞  <  >  | 🖥 Chapter 5
1  //: Playground — noun: a place where people can play
2
3  import Cocoa
4
5  var str = "Hello, playground"                                    "Hello, playground"
6
7  class Door {
8      var opened : Bool = false
9      var locked : Bool = false
10     let width : Int = 32
11     let height : Int = 72
12     let weight : Int = 10
13     let color : String = "Red"
14
15     func open() -> String {
16         opened = true
17         return "C-r-r-e-e-a-k-k... the door is open!"
18     }
19
20     func close() -> String {
21         opened = false
22         return "C-r-r-e-e-a-k-k... the door is closed!"
23     }
24
25     func lock() -> String {
26         locked = true
27         return "C-l-i-c-c-c-k-k... the door is locked!"
28     }
29
30     func unlock() -> String {
31         locked = false
32         return "C-l-i-c-c-c-k-k... the door is unlocked!"
33     }
34 }
35
```

KNOCK, KNOCK

As we explore this idea of object modeling in Swift, let's look more closely at the door as an object, which is as good an example as any. **Figure 5.1** shows a definition for a new object you'll call Door.

Get started on the example by typing the following on lines 7 through 34:

```
class Door {
    var opened : Bool = false
    var locked : Bool = false
    let width : Int = 32
    let height : Int = 72
    let weight : Int = 10
    let color : String = "Red"

    func open() -> String {
        opened = true
        return "C-r-r-e-e-a-k-k-k... the door is open!"
    }

    func close() -> String {
        opened = false
```

```
        return "C-r-r-e-e-a-k-k-k... the door is closed!"
    }

    func lock() -> String {
        locked = true
        return "C-l-i-c-c-c-k-k... the door is locked!"
    }

    func unlock() -> String {
        locked = false
        return "C-l-i-c-c-c-k-k... the door is unlocked!"
    }
}
```

In Swift, an object is defined using the class keyword, followed by the name of the class. In this case, Door on line 7. Following that is an opening curly brace and the rest of the definition of the class.

Lines 8 through 13 define the properties of the class. Every property, be it a variable or a constant, has an assigned value. Swift requires that all properties be assigned to some value to avoid ambiguity. Notice that two of the properties are variables: opened and locked. These Booleans reflect the door's state, which can change throughout the lifetime of the object; thus they are declared as variables.

The remaining properties, however, are constants. The door's width, height, weight, and color are not expected to change once it has been created.

Lines 15 through 33 define the methods for the class. This class has four methods: open, close, lock, and unlock. In the case of the open and close methods, they set the opened variable accordingly and return a string indicating the state of the door. The lock and unlock methods perform a similar function.

LET THERE BE OBJECTS!

So now that you have defined a class, how do you use it?

In OOP parlance, the process of turning a class into an object is known as *instantiation*. This is effectively the process of creating a real, live object that can be interacted with. Without the act of instantiating an object, a class is merely just a template or blueprint to build an object. Just as blueprints don't turn a house into a home until the carpenters arrive and the hammers start swinging, a class alone cannot deliver a ready-to-run object. It requires the instantiation process.

```
30      func unlock() -> String {
31          locked = false
32          return "C-l-i-c-c-k-k... the door is unlocked!"
33      }
34  }
35
36  let frontDoor = Door()                                              Door

            opened false
            locked false
            width 32
            height 72
            weight 10
            color "Red"

37
```

```
30      func unlock() -> String {
31          locked = false
32          return "C-l-i-c-c-k-k... the door is unlocked!"     Door
33      }                                                       "C-l-i-c-c-k-k... the door is unlocked!"
34  }
35
36  let frontDoor = Door()                                      Door
37
38  frontDoor.open()                                            "C-r-r-e-e-a-k-k... the door is open!"
39  frontDoor.close()                                           "C-r-r-e-e-a-k-k... the door is closed!"
40
```

Let's see how instantiation works in **Figure 5.2**.

On line 36, an instance of the Door class is created by simply referencing the class's name, followed by open and close parentheses. This is the basic method for creating and initializing an object. The result of the assignment is a newly created object, which is assigned in this case to frontDoor. It's that simple!

If you are coming from Objective-C, you may ask, "Where is the init method defined?" That's a good question, and we'll explore that more in just a bit. For now, this Swift class does not have one.

Along with the creation of the frontDoor object, notice that the Results sidebar shows the name of the class just instantiated: Door.

OPENING AND CLOSING THE DOOR

Quiz time! How would you tell the frontDoor object to open and close?

The methods, of course. You just saw in Figure 5.2 how to call a method; lines 38 and 39 in **Figure 5.3** reveal the answer.

```
let frontDoor = Door()

frontDoor.open()
frontDoor.close()
```

Now that the object frontDoor is created, you reference the named constant and the dot notation when calling the open and close methods. The open and close parentheses indicate that the names following the dot are method names.

```
36  let frontDoor = Door()                                      Door
37
38  frontDoor.open()                                            "C-r-r-e-e-a-k-k... the door is open!"
39  frontDoor.close()                                           "C-r-r-e-e-a-k-k... the door is closed!"
40
41  frontDoor.lock()                                            "C-l-i-c-c-c-k-k... the door is locked!"
42  frontDoor.unlock()                                          "C-l-i-c-c-c-k-k... the door is unlocked!"
43
```

FIGURE 5.4 Locking and unlocking the door

DOT NOTATION—IT ISN'T JUST FOR PROPERTIES

Note how the open and close methods are called. They follow the class name you've instantiated (Door) and a dot (.) character. The dot is part of Swift's *dot notation*, and it applies to both accessing properties and calling methods in a class. The dot acts as a syntactical element that delineates an object from its properties or methods. In the case of calling methods, the method name is always followed by open and close parentheses ().

Dot notation is a very common element of Swift; you'll see it used over and over again.

LOCKING AND UNLOCKING THE DOOR

In the same way you opened and closed the door with the available methods, you can lock and unlock the door. Type in the following code on lines 41 and 42 (**Figure 5.4**), and notice the Results sidebar.

```
frontDoor.lock()
frontDoor.unlock()
```

Again, just as you closed and opened the door with the appropriate methods, locking and unlocking the door produced similar results in the Results sidebar. Things appear to be working as designed. However, notice a couple of odd things about the Door class.

For instance, ask yourself: Can you lock an open door? Shouldn't a door have to be closed before it's locked? And what if you tell the frontDoor object to close the door when it's already closed (or conversely, tell the frontDoor object to open the door when it's already open). Should a door creak if it's not going to move?

Let's fix these issues right away with some additional logic. **Figure 5.5** shows a new class, NewDoor, along with revised open, close, lock, and unlock methods that handle the various cases, as well as a new object, newFrontDoor.

In the case of the open method, a check is added for the opened property. If it's false (meaning the door is closed), the door is allowed to be opened; otherwise, you are reminded that the door is already opened. The inverse logic is applied to the close method on line 62.

FIGURE 5.5 Addressing holes in the Door class logic

```
44  class NewDoor {
45      var opened : Bool = false
46      var locked : Bool =  false
47      let width : Int = 32
48      let height : Int = 72
49      let weight : Int = 10
50      let color : String = "Red"
51
52      func open() -> String {
53          if opened == false {
54              opened = true
55              return "C-r-r-e-e-a-k-k... the door is open!"
56          }
57          else {
58              return "The door is already open!"
59          }
60      }
61
62      func close() -> String {
63          if opened == true {
64              opened = false
65              return "C-r-r-e-e-a-k-k... the door is closed!"
66          }
67          else {
68              return "The door is already closed!"
69          }
70      }
71
72      func lock() -> String {
73          if opened == false {
74              locked = true
75              return "C-l-i-c-c-c-k-k... the door is locked!"
76          }
77          else {
78              return "You cannot lock an open door!"
79          }
80      }
81
82      func unlock() -> String {
83          if opened == false {
84              locked = false
85              return "C-l-i-c-c-c-k-k... the door is unlocked!"
86          }
87          else {
88              return "You cannot unlock an open door!"
89          }
90      }
91  }
92
93  let newFrontDoor = NewDoor()
94
95  newFrontDoor.close()
96  newFrontDoor.open()
97
98  newFrontDoor.lock()
99  newFrontDoor.unlock()
```

Results panel:
```
NewDoor
"C-r-r-e-e-a-k-k... the door is open!"

"The door is already closed!"

"You cannot lock an open door!"

"You cannot unlock an open door!"

NewDoor

"The door is already closed!"
"C-r-r-e-e-a-k-k... the door is open!"

"You cannot lock an open door!"
"You cannot unlock an open door!"
```

```
class NewDoor {
    var opened : Bool = false
    var locked : Bool = false
    let width : Int = 32
    let height : Int = 72
    let weight : Int = 10
    let color : String = "Red"

    func open() -> String {
        if opened == false {
            opened = true
            return "C-r-r-e-e-a-k-k-k... the door is open!"
        }
        else {
```

```swift
            return "The door is already open!"
        }
    }

    func close() -> String {
        if opened == true {
            opened = false
            return "C-r-r-e-e-a-k-k-k... the door is closed!"
        }
        else {
            return "The door is already closed!"
        }
    }

    func lock() -> String {
        if opened == false {
            locked = true
            return "C-l-i-c-c-c-k-k... the door is locked!"
        }
        else {
            return "You cannot lock an open door!"
        }
    }

    func unlock() -> String {
        if opened == false {
            locked = false
            return "C-l-i-c-c-c-k-k... the door is unlocked!"
        }
        else {
            return "You cannot unlock an open door!"
        }
    }
}

let newFrontDoor = NewDoor()

newFrontDoor.close()
newFrontDoor.open()

newFrontDoor.lock()
newFrontDoor.unlock()
```

FIGURE 5.6 Examining the properties of the newFrontDoor object

```
93  let newFrontDoor = NewDoor()               NewDoor
94
95  newFrontDoor.close()                        "The door is already closed!"
96  newFrontDoor.open()                         "C-r-r-e-e-a-k-k... the door is open!"
97
98  newFrontDoor.lock()                         "You cannot lock an open door!"
99  newFrontDoor.unlock()                       "You cannot unlock an open door!"
100
101 newFrontDoor.locked                         false
102 newFrontDoor.opened                         true
103
104 newFrontDoor.width                          32
105 newFrontDoor.height                         72
106 newFrontDoor.weight                         10
107
```

Likewise, the lock and unlock methods are adapted to check for the opened property. If the door is open, you are reminded that you can neither lock nor unlock the door. You can clearly see the Results sidebar showing the altered output based on the additions in the methods. Feel free to experiment with changing the order of the close, open, lock, and unlock methods on lines 95 through 99 in your playground file.

The only hole left in this logic is locking a door that is locked, or unlocking a door that is unlocked. I'll leave that as an exercise for you to solve.

EXAMINING THE PROPERTIES

Up to this point, we've ignored the other properties of the newFrontDoor object. They are accessible, however, by using the dot notation you've used thus far to call the methods.

Lines 101 through 106 in **Figure 5.6** demonstrate how to access the individual properties, with the results showing in the Results sidebar.

```
newFrontDoor.locked
newFrontDoor.opened

newFrontDoor.width
newFrontDoor.height
newFrontDoor.weight
```

DOOR DIVERSITY

The NewDoor class has proven to be quite clever. Thanks to the added code, the class can open, close, lock, and unlock, and can do so only when appropriate.

However, one thing you cannot currently do is create a door with a different size, weight, or color. Every door object that is created has the same values for the properties. That's because those properties are set to specific values when the object is instantiated (scroll back to lines 47 through 50 of your playground file as a reminder). Those properties also happen to be constants, meaning that their values cannot change once the object is created, so no matter what door you create, you always get the same size, height, and color. A little boring, isn't it?

FIGURE 5.7 Creating your very own init method

```
     ┌──────────────────────────────────────────────────────────────┐
     │ ⊞ │ < │ > │ ▣ Chapter 5                                        │
     ├──────────────────────────────────────────────────────────────┤
44   │ class NewDoor {                                                │
45   │     var opened : Bool = false                                  │
46   │     var locked : Bool =  false                                 │
47   │     let width : Int                                            │
48   │     let height : Int                                           │
49   │     let weight : Int                                           │
50   │     let color : String                                         │
51   │                                                                │
52   │     init(width : Int = 32, height : Int = 72, weight : Int = 10, color : │
     │         String = "Red") {                                      │
53   │         self.width = width;                                    │
54   │         self.height = height                                   │
55   │         self.weight = weight                                   │
56   │         self.color = color                                     │
57   │     }                                                          │
58   │                                                                │
59   │     func open() -> String {                                    │
60   │         if opened == false {                                   │
61   │             opened = true                                      │
62   │             return "C-r-r-e-e-a-k-k... the door is open!"     NewDoor │
63   │         }                                                      "C-r-r-e-e-a-k-k... the door is open!" │
64   │         else {                                                 │
65   │             return "The door is already open!"                 │
66   │         }                                                      │
67   │     }                                                          │
68   │                                                                │
69   │     func close() -> String {                                   │
70   │         if opened == true {                                    │
71   │             opened = false                                     │
72   │             return "C-r-r-e-e-a-k-k... the door is closed!"     │
73   │         }                                                      │
74   │         else {                                                 "The door is already closed!" │
75   │             return "The door is already closed!"               │
```

How can you change this? You could change the constants to variables by changing the let keywords to var keywords. Doing so would allow you to change the properties using dot notation, like so:

```
newFrontDoor.width = 36
newFrontDoor.height = 80
```

This approach would certainly work; however, it feels "wrong" to change a door's dimensions after it has already been instantiated. After all, when you purchase a door at your local hardware store, its size and weight are already determined. These properties should be set at the time the door is created and remain immutable (unchangeable) for the lifetime of the object. So how do you do this?

The answer is a special method known as init, which initializes an object. Up to this point, you haven't actually written an init method; you've just let Swift do the initialization for you. This method seems like a natural and proper place to allow the user to specify alternate values for these properties.

Swift thinks so, too, and actually allows you to create your own init method with your own parameter list. This is a great way to set up an object to your own liking, and that's exactly what is happening in lines 52 through 57 in **Figure 5.7**. Type the init method in your playground file.

```
init(width : Int = 32, height : Int = 72, weight : Int = 10, color :
→ String = "Red") {
    self.width = width
    self.height = height
    self.weight = weight
    self.color = color
}
```

This init method takes four parameters corresponding to the four properties on lines 47 through 50. In Figure 5.7, the default values have been removed from those lines. Instead, they are now part of the default parameter values in the init method's declaration (remember that I discussed default parameters earlier in the book). As a result, you no longer need to initialize the properties on lines 47 through 50. Go ahead and remove these initialization values in your playground file too.

A new keyword is used on lines 53 through 56: self. This keyword is Swift's way of letting an object refer to itself. Using the self keyword is particularly important in this example, because the parameter names in the init method (line 52) match exactly to the property names in the class (lines 53–57). Without self, the following statements would not only be ambiguous, they would cause a Swift compiler error:

```
width = width
height = height
weight = weight
color = color
```

The self keyword explicitly points out that it is the property of the instantiated object receiving the assignment.

If you've kept a sharp eye, you may be asking how the properties width, height, weight, and color, which are declared as constants with the let keyword, can be assigned values if they are constants. You are witnessing an exception to the rule that constants cannot change. Swift allows constant properties of a class to be assigned values at initialization time—but not after. Once the value of an object's constant property has been set in the init method, it cannot be changed later.

Swift also insists that all variables and constants in a class be initialized when the init method has completed. Failure to do this will result in an error: "Return from initializer without initializing all stored properties." You can view this behavior by removing the = false from line 45 or line 46.

One other note: The keyword func does not precede the init method name. Swift gives special consideration to functions that begin with init, as you'll see soon.

With the new init method in place, you can now create another object from the NewDoor class, this time with your very own dimensions.

Line 115 in **Figure 5.8** shows how to instantiate a second NewDoor object with the parameter list defined in your new init method. Notice that the parameter names are being used to explicitly show which values go with which parameters. This is a small but important difference between functions and methods. In methods, parameter names are automatically promoted to external parameter names. As a result, you must specify the names for parameters when creating new objects.

```
let newBackDoor = NewDoor(width: 36, height: 80, weight: 20, color: "Green")
```

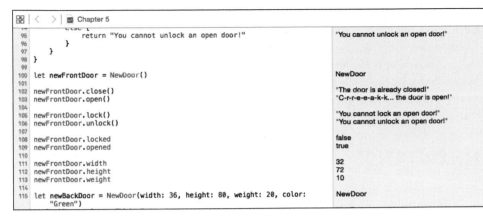

FIGURE 5.8 Exercising the new **init** method with additional parameters

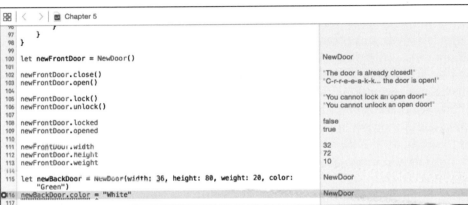

FIGURE 5.9 Attempting to change the color of the **newBackDoor** object

PAINTING THE DOOR

Let's revisit the properties of the NewDoor class. You can assume that once a door is created, its dimensions and weight are fixed, but the color can change. You can paint the door a different color, for example.

Attempting to change the color of the newBackDoor object, however, results in an error, as shown on line 116 of **Figure 5.9**.

```
newBackDoor.color = "White"
```

Can you spot the reason for the error? Look back to line 50 in your playground file for the definition of the color property in the NewDoor class:

```
let color : String
```

Changing the let keyword to var on line 50 removes the error and allows you to change the color of the newBackDoor object, or any object of type NewDoor. Remember to consider which properties should be constants and which should be variables when creating your classes.

You've just seen how classes are created in Swift. Using just a single, compact class, you modeled both the attributes and behavior of a door. How cool was that!

The NewDoor class exercise should also give you an appreciation of just how the modeling process works. When you create a class to model something, you must think about its properties and behaviors, as well as any constraints, and let them guide your design.

INHERITANCE

Another important principle of OOP is the idea of *inheritance* (and no, I'm not talking about your rich uncle's estate). Inheritance allows one class to obtain the attributes and behaviors of another class while bringing its own unique attributes and behaviors to the mix.

It helps to think of inheritance in terms of genealogy and genetics. As an individual, you are the product of your parents' genetics. You inherited one or more of their traits, including possibly their name, yet you remain a unique individual with your own properties (height, weight, eye color, and so on) and behaviors (diet, exercise habits, and so on). Likewise, your children will inherit certain properties and behaviors from you and your parents, yet retain their own.

Inheritance also creates a *hierarchy*. Just as you have parents, your children have you as a parent, and eventually they may become parents. This connection also applies to objects and the classes from which they derive.

There are two terms that you should know that exist in OOP parlance: *superclass* and *subclass*. A class that is derived from another class is known as a *subclass* of that class. The other class from which the subclass is derived is known as the *superclass*. **Figure 5.10** clarifies this relationship.

Inheritance is a neat concept in OOP because it allows you to compartmentalize functionality into a specific class, which can then flow down to subclasses without code duplication.

Recall earlier when you were asked to look around the room you are in to select an object for modeling. We used the door for our class, but if you had chosen a window, how different would that class have been from the Door class you created?

Looking at the Door class in your playground file, you'll come to realize that it has every property and behavior that a window has. Both open and close; both can lock and unlock; and both have dimensions, weight, and color. But is a window a door? Of course not. So what makes a window different from a door?

Well, for one thing, you would consider walking through an open door, but you likely wouldn't walk through an open window. Also, a door might have a door handle and a doorknob; a window doesn't.

Based on that small difference, how can you use inheritance to model both a door and a window in such a way that they share a common set of properties and behaviors yet retain the distinctions that make them uniquely what they are?

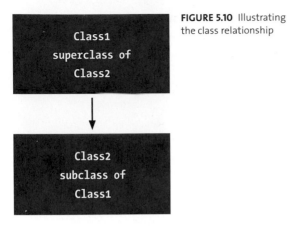

FIGURE 5.10 Illustrating the class relationship

Class1
superclass of
Class2

Class2
subclass of
Class1

MODELING THE BASE CLASS

In OOP parlance, a *base class* is considered the most basic class from where all other classes derive. A base class does not inherit from any other class; it's essentially a root, or anchor, class. In Swift, any class that does not derive from a superclass is known as a base class.

In thinking about the door/window class, you can create a base class that captures most of what currently exists in the Door class. Then you can create two new subclasses: one for doors and one for windows.

The quickest way to achieve this would be to rename the Door class to something else. Thinking about class names is important, and in this case, you want a name that can fit both a door and a window. Let's choose Portal for the new class name. After all, windows and doors are portals, right?

Select and copy lines 44 through 98 (the NewDoor class), and paste it at the very bottom of your playground file at line 118. Once it's pasted, change the class name from NewDoor to Portal on line 118.

Now that you've added the new class Portal, notice that references to the word "door" on lines 136, 139, 146, 149, 156, 159, 166, and 169 seem out of place. The quickest way to handle that is to create a new name property, pass that in the init method, and then use Swift's string interpolation to embed the property name in the string constants. You can see the changes in their entirety in **Figure 5.11**; go ahead and change your playground file accordingly.

```
class Portal {
    var opened : Bool = false
    var locked : Bool = false
    let width : Int
    let height : Int
    let weight : Int
    let name : String
    var color : String
```

```
init(name : String, width : Int = 32, height : Int = 72, weight :
→ Int = 10, color : String = "Red") {
    self.name = name
    self.width = width
    self.height = height
    self.weight = weight
    self.color = color
}

func open() -> String {
    if opened == false {
        opened = true
        return "C-r-r-e-e-a-k-k-k... the \(name) is open!"
    }
    else {
        return "The \(name) is already open!"
    }
}

func close() -> String {
    if opened == true {
        opened = false
        return "C-r-r-e-e-a-k-k-k... the \(name) is closed!"
    }
    else {
        return "The \(name) is already closed!"
    }
}

func lock() -> String {
    if opened == false {
        locked = true
        return "C-l-i-c-c-c-k-k... the \(name) is locked!"
    }
    else {
        return "You cannot lock an open \(name)!"
    }
}
```

```
118  class Portal {
119      var opened : Bool = false;
120      var locked : Bool = false;
121      let width : Int
122      let height : Int
123      let weight : Int
124      let name : String
125      var color : String
126
127      init(name : String, width : Int = 32, height : Int = 32, weight :
             Int = 10, color : String = "Red") {
128          self.name = name
129          self.width = width
130          self.height = height
131          self.weight = weight
132          self.color = color
133      }
134
135      func open() -> String {
136          if opened == false {
137              opened = true
138              return "C-r-r-e-e-a-k-k... the \(name) is open!"      (2 times)
                                                                         (2 times)
139          }
140          else {
141              return "The \(name) is already open!"
142          }
143      }
144
145      func close() -> String {
146          if opened == true {
147              opened = false
148              return "C-r-r-e-e-a-k-k... the \(name) is closed!"
149          }
150          else {
151              return "The \(name) is already closed!"              (2 times)
152          }
153      }
154
155      func lock() -> String {
156          if opened == false {
157              locked = true
158              return "C-l-i-c-c-k-k... the \(name) is locked!"
159          }
160          else {
161              return "You cannot lock an open \(name)!"            (2 times)
162          }
163      }
164
165      func unlock() -> String {
166          if opened == false {
167              locked = false
168              return "C-l-i-c-c-k-k... the \(name) is unlocked!"
169          }
170          else {
171              return "You cannot unlock an open \(name)!"          (2 times)
172          }
```

FIGURE 5.11 The Portal class adjusted with the new name property

```
        func unlock() -> String {
            if opened == false {
                locked = false
                return "C-l-i-c-c-c-k-k... the \(name) is unlocked!"
            }
            else {
                return "You cannot unlock an open \(name)!"
            }
        }
    }
```

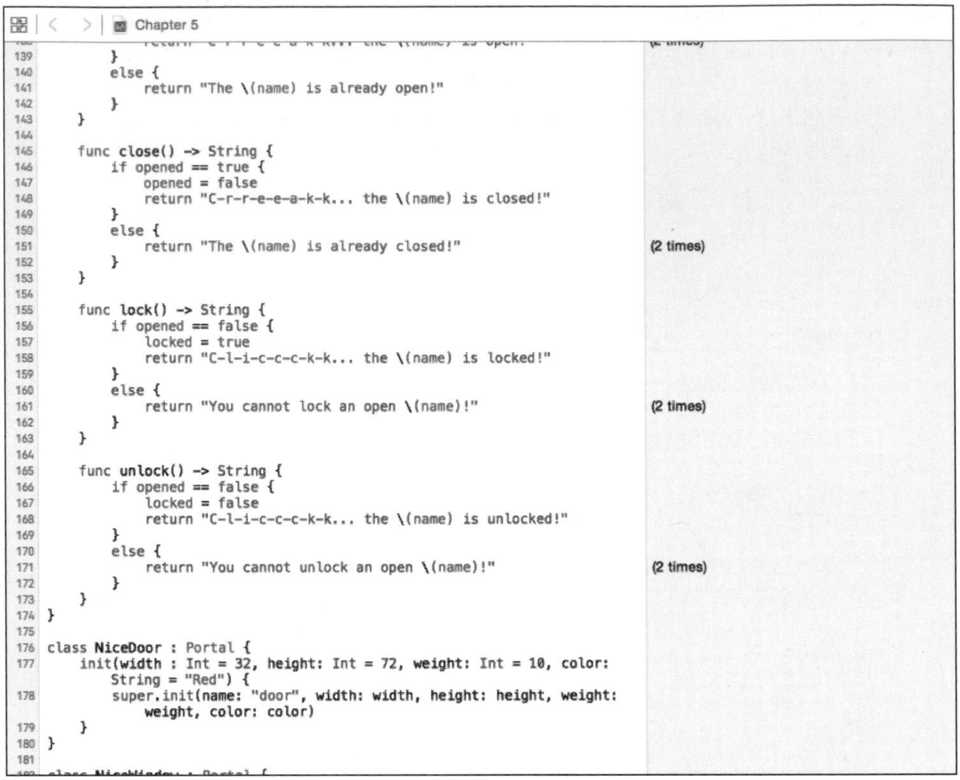

FIGURE 5.12 The addition of the NiceDoor and NiceWindow classes

```
139          }
140          else {
141              return "The \(name) is already open!"
142          }
143      }
144
145      func close() -> String {
146          if opened == true {
147              opened = false
148              return "C-r-r-e-e-a-k-k... the \(name) is closed!"
149          }
150          else {
151              return "The \(name) is already closed!"            (2 times)
152          }
153      }
154
155      func lock() -> String {
156          if opened == false {
157              locked = true
158              return "C-l-i-c-c-c-k-k... the \(name) is locked!"
159          }
160          else {
161              return "You cannot lock an open \(name)!"          (2 times)
162          }
163      }
164
165      func unlock() -> String {
166          if opened == false {
167              locked = false
168              return "C-l-i-c-c-c-k-k... the \(name) is unlocked!"
169          }
170          else {
171              return "You cannot unlock an open \(name)!"        (2 times)
172          }
173      }
174  }
175
176  class NiceDoor : Portal {
177      init(width : Int = 32, height: Int = 72, weight: Int = 10, color:
               String = "Red") {
178          super.init(name: "door", width: width, height: height, weight:
                   weight, color: color)
179      }
180  }
181
182  class NiceWindow : Portal {
```

Notice the addition of the name property on line 124, as well as the name parameter in the init method on line 127 and the assignment on line 128. This allows you to pass an appropriate string to identify the type of object. Also, the word "door" in the string literals has been replaced everywhere with \(name), allowing the printed string to properly identify the object.

The new Portal class looks good so far. Now you'll create the replacement classes to represent the door and window.

CREATING THE SUBCLASSES

You'll create two new classes: NiceDoor and NiceWindow. Both of these classes will be subclasses of the Portal class. Take your time and type in lines 176 through 186 in **Figure 5.12** into your playground window.

```
class NiceDoor : Portal {
    init(width : Int = 32, height : Int = 72, weight : Int = 10, color :
    → String = "Red") {
        super.init(name: "door", width: width, height: height, weight:
        → weight, color: color)
    }
}


class NiceWindow : Portal {
    init(width : Int = 48, height : Int = 48, weight : Int = 5, color :
    → String = "Blue") {
        super.init(name: "window", width: width, height: height, weight:
        → weight, color: color)
    }
}
```

On line 176 is the definition of the NiceDoor class. Notice that the class name is followed by a colon, and then the name of the superclass, Portal. This is how classes in Swift specify the class they wish to inherit from.

Line 177 shows the definition of the init method for the NiceDoor class. Notice that this method is identical to the init method of the Portal class, even down to the default parameter values for the parameters. The reason for this duplication becomes apparent when you look at line 178 and its special syntax.

There you'll notice a new keyword: super. Somewhat related to the self keyword mentioned earlier, super actually refers to the superclass. In our case, the superclass is the Portal class. What follows the keyword is the familiar dot notation and the name of the method to call in the superclass: init.

It is common and expected practice to call the superclass's init method first, giving the superclass the opportunity to initialize itself. In this case, you're passing named parameters, including the new name parameter. Since this is the NiceDoor class, the string "door" is passed, along with the width, height, weight, and color. Since the superclass, Portal, contains the properties for these values, you need to make sure its init method is called.

Lines 182 through 186 show the definition of the NiceWindow class, which looks almost identical to the NiceDoor class. It too derives from the Portal class, but it has width, height, and weight defaults that make sense for a window. The name also reflects this class and gives the string "window" to the superclass's init method.

FIGURE 5.13 Instantiating the NiceDoor and NiceWindow classes

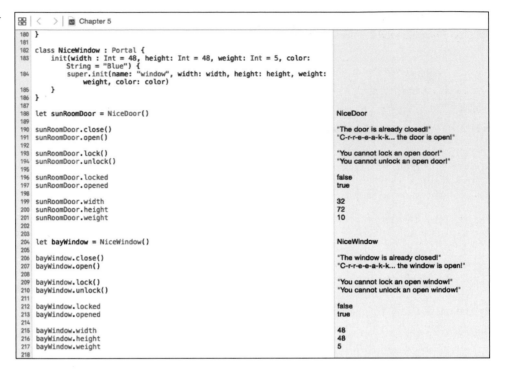

INSTANTIATING THE SUBCLASS

With the new NiceDoor and NiceWindow classes created, now you'll exercise them. **Figure 5.13** shows the earlier code where the frontDoor object was created—keep that code in place. Also notice that the Results sidebar shows the same results even though you've changed the class hierarchy and Door is now subclassed from Portal.

Type in lines 188 through 217 in Figure 5.13, which create two new objects: sunRoomDoor and bayWindow.

```
let sunRoomDoor = NiceDoor()

sunRoomDoor.close()
sunRoomDoor.open()

sunRoomDoor.lock()
sunRoomDoor.unlock()
```

```
sunRoomDoor.locked
sunRoomDoor.opened

sunRoomDoor.width
sunRoomDoor.height
sunRoomDoor.weight
let bayWindow = NiceWindow()

bayWindow.close()
bayWindow.open()

bayWindow.lock()
bayWindow.unlock()

bayWindow.locked
bayWindow.opened

bayWindow.width
bayWindow.height
bayWindow.weight
```

These objects are instantiated from the NiceDoor and NiceWindow class, respectively, and those in turn are subclassed from Portal. The Results sidebar shows the objects being manipulated, which confirms that the code in the Portal superclass is being exercised appropriately.

SECURING THE DOOR

The NiceDoor class can be instantiated to provide a door object that will unlock and lock the door intelligently, but what if you want to add a combination lock? Before such a door can be unlocked, a security code needs to be entered. If the code is wrong, unlocking the door fails. If the code is correct, the door is unlocked and all is well.

This secure door class will require a secret combination code to unlock the door. The combination can be any series of numbers or letters, but for our purposes, you'll define the secret combination with four numbers: 6809. The user of the class will be able to instantiate the object with a personal combination. Then, upon invoking the unlock method on the class, either it will return that the door is unlocked (because the user passed the correct code) or it will indicate that the door remains locked due to an incorrect code.

FIGURE 5.14

The CombinationDoor
class

```
     ┌─────┬─────────────────────────────────────────────────────────────────────────────┐
     │ 🏠 │ ‹  › │ 📄 Chapter 5                                                            │
     ├─────┴─────────────────────────────────────────────────────────────────────────────┤
219  │ class CombinationDoor : NiceDoor {                                                  │
220  │     var combinationCode : String?                                                   │
221  │                                                                                     │
222  │     override func lock() -> String {                                                 │
223  │         return "This method is not valid for a combination door!"    "This method is not valid for a combination door!"
224  │     }                                                                               │
225  │                                                                                     │
226  │     override func unlock() -> String {                                               │
227  │         return "This method is not valid for a combination door!"    "This method is not valid for a combination door!"
228  │     }                                                                               │
229  │                                                                                     │
230  │     func lock(combinationCode : String) -> String {                                 │
231  │         if opened == false {                                                        │
232  │             if locked == true {                                                     │
233  │                 return "The \(name) is already locked!"                             │
234  │             }                                                                       │
235  │             self.combinationCode = combinationCode               CombinationDoor    │
236  │             locked = true                                        CombinationDoor    │
237  │             return "C-l-i-c-c-c-k-k... the \(name) is locked!"    "C-l-i-c-c-c-k-k... the door is locked!"
238  │         }                                                                           │
239  │         else {                                                                      │
240  │             return "You cannot lock an open \(name)"                                │
241  │         }                                                                           │
242  │     }                                                                               │
243  │                                                                                     │
244  │     func unlock(combinationCode : String) -> String {                               │
245  │         if opened == false {                                                        │
246  │             if locked == false {                                                    │
247  │                 return "The \(name) is already unlocked!"        "The door is already unlocked!"
248  │             }                                                                       │
249  │             else {                                                                  │
250  │                 if self.combinationCode != combinationCode {                        │
251  │                     return "Wrong code... the \(name) is still locked!"    "Wrong code... the door is still locked!"
252  │                 }                                                                   │
253  │             }                                                                       │
254  │             locked = false                                       CombinationDoor    │
255  │             return "C-l-i-c-c-c-k-k... the \(name) is unlocked!"  "C-l-i-c-c-c-k-k... the door is unlocked!"
256  │         }                                                                           │
257  │         else {                                                                      │
258  │             return "You cannot unlock an open \(name)"                              │
259  │         }                                                                           │
260  │     }                                                                               │
261  │ }                                                                                   │
262  │                                                                                     │
263  │ let securityDoor = CombinationDoor()                             CombinationDoor    │
264  │                                                                                     │
     └─────────────────────────────────────────────────────────────────────────────────┘
```

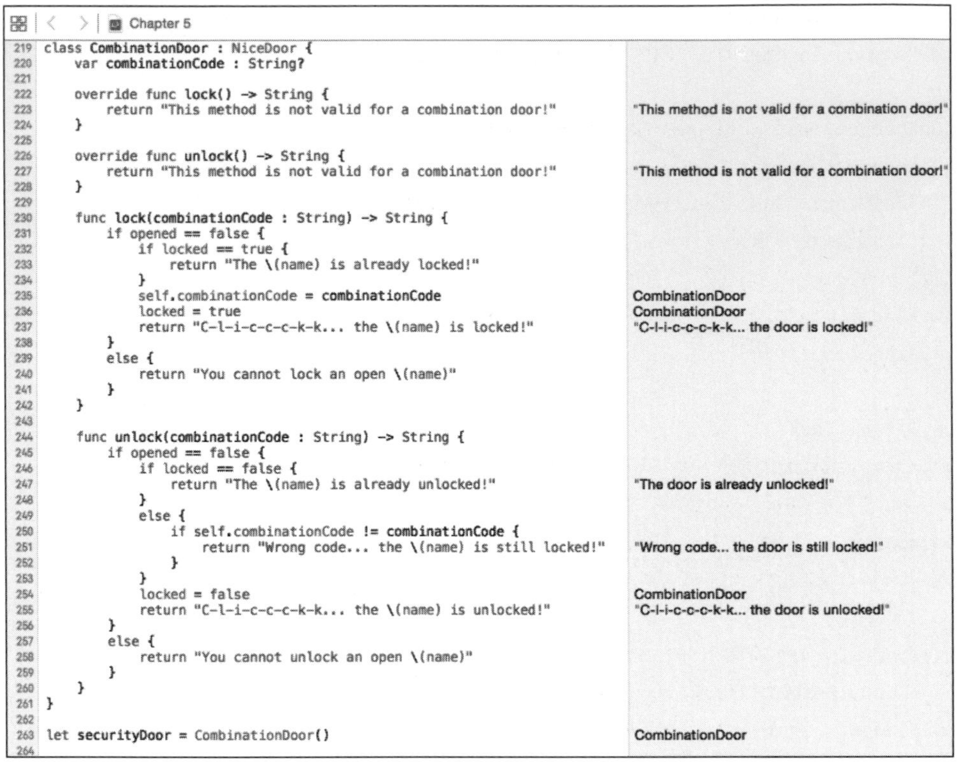

You could add this functionality into the existing NiceDoor class, but how much fun would that be? Instead, create a new class, CombinationDoor, which will be a subclass of NiceDoor. The CombinationDoor class will inherit all the properties and methods of NiceDoor and add the combination lock ability.

Figure 5.14 shows the newly created class on lines 219 through 263.

```
class CombinationDoor : NiceDoor {
    var combinationCode : String?

    override func lock() -> String {
        return "This method is not valid for a combination door!"
    }

    override func unlock() -> String {
        return "This method is not valid for a combination door!"
    }

    func lock(combinationCode : String) -> String {
        if opened == false {
```

```
            if locked == true {
                return "The \(name) is already locked!"
            }
            self.combinationCode = combinationCode
            locked = true
            return "C-l-i-c-c-c-k-k... the \(name) is locked!"
        }
        else {
            return "You cannot lock an open \(name)!"
        }
    }


    func unlock(combinationCode : String) -> String {
        if opened == false {
            if locked == false {
                return "The \(name) is already unlocked!"
            }
            else {
                if self.combinationCode != combinationCode {
                    return "Wrong code.... the \(name) is still locked!"
                }
            }
            locked = false
            return "C-l-i-c-c-c-k-k... the \(name) is unlocked!"
        }
        else {
            return "You cannot unlock an open \(name)!"
        }
    }
}


let securityDoor = CombinationDoor()
```

The new class has a new property, combinationCode, defined on line 220. This is an
optional String property. Remember optionals? I discussed them very early in the book.
They are normal types that can have nil as a value. In this case, there is no explicit initialization, so the combinationCode is presumed to be nil. Defining this property means that you
can defer its initialization to an actual value until later. Combined with the state of the door
being closed at initialization time (see line 119), this is a sensible setting.

Now turn your attention to the lock and unlock methods starting on line 222. A security door with a combination lock like this one cannot just unlock when told—it first has to verify that the security code passed to the method by the user matches its internal code. Only if they are the same does the door unlock. Therefore, creating new methods in the CombinationDoor subclass is necessary to disallow wanton unlocking; otherwise, the superclass's implementation would happily unlock the door when told, no matter what the combinationCode was set to.

The override keyword gives you the ability to create a method of the same name in a subclass. Swift requires that a subclass that redefines a similarly named method and parameter signature in any superclass use this keyword to indicate the intent to override that method. We do not intend to call the superclass's implementation of these methods either.

Lines 230 through 260 hold the new lock and unlock methods. They use the same names as their superclass counterparts but also take a String parameter. In the case of the lock method, a combination code is passed and saved in the property combinationCode, and the door is locked. Notice that you are duplicating the same logic in the non-parameterized methods of the superclass to determine whether the door is closed before you attempt to lock it.

The unlock method is a little larger than the lock method due to the extra logic that must be evaluated. It too takes a String parameter: the combination code to use when unlocking. On line 250, a check is made between the property combinationCode and the passed code. If the passed combination code is incorrect, a message is returned indicating that the code is wrong, and the door remains locked.

If the combination code is correct, the unlock method sets the locked property to false on line 254, and returns the message that the door is unlocked.

On line 263 a shiny new security door object is instantiated. By default it's closed and unlocked, ready for you to interact with it.

So far, you have created the new CombinationDoor class and have instantiated the securityDoor object from it. You've followed the code and you understand how the methods inside your new superclass override the same named methods above. Now it's time to unlock the door!

USING THE RIGHT COMBINATION

With the securityDoor object created on line 263, let's see how the new locking and unlocking works. Lines 265 through 288 are intended to flex and demonstrate the CombinationDoor and its superclasses. I'll go over them one by one.

Lines 266 through 270 of **Figure 5.15** show the values of the properties—including the combinationCode property, which is set to nil as discussed earlier. On line 273, you attempt to unlock the door only to learn in the Results sidebar that this method no longer works. The same message appears on line 276 when the lock method is invoked.

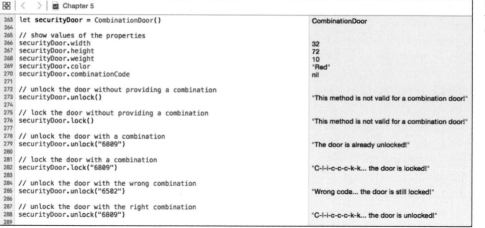

```
263  let securityDoor = CombinationDoor()              CombinationDoor
264
265  // show values of the properties
266  securityDoor.width                                32
267  securityDoor.height                               72
268  securityDoor.weight                               10
269  securityDoor.color                                "Red"
270  securityDoor.combinationCode                      nil
271
272  // unlock the door without providing a combination
273  securityDoor.unlock()                             "This method is not valid for a combination door!"
274
275  // lock the door without providing a combination
276  securityDoor.lock()                               "This method is not valid for a combination door!"
277
278  // unlock the door with a combination
279  securityDoor.unlock("6809")                       "The door is already unlocked!"
280
281  // lock the door with a combination
282  securityDoor.lock("6809")                         "C-l-i-c-c-c-k-k... the door is locked!"
283
284  // unlock the door with the wrong combination
285  securityDoor.unlock("6502")                       "Wrong code... the door is still locked!"
286
287  // unlock the door with the right combination
288  securityDoor.unlock("6809")                       "C-l-i-c-c-c-k-k... the door is unlocked!"
289
```

FIGURE 5.15 Testing the CombinationDoor class

```
// show values of the properties
securityDoor.width
securityDoor.height
securityDoor.weight
securityDoor.color
securityDoor.combinationCode

// unlock the door without providing a combination
securityDoor.unlock()

// lock the door without providing a combination
securityDoor.lock()

// unlock the door with a combination
securityDoor.unlock("6809")
// lock the door with a combination
securityDoor.lock("6809")

// unlock the door with the wrong combination
securityDoor.unlock("6502")

// unlock the door with the right combination
securityDoor.unlock("6809")
```

FIGURE 5.16

An example of conve-
nience initializers in
the Tractor class

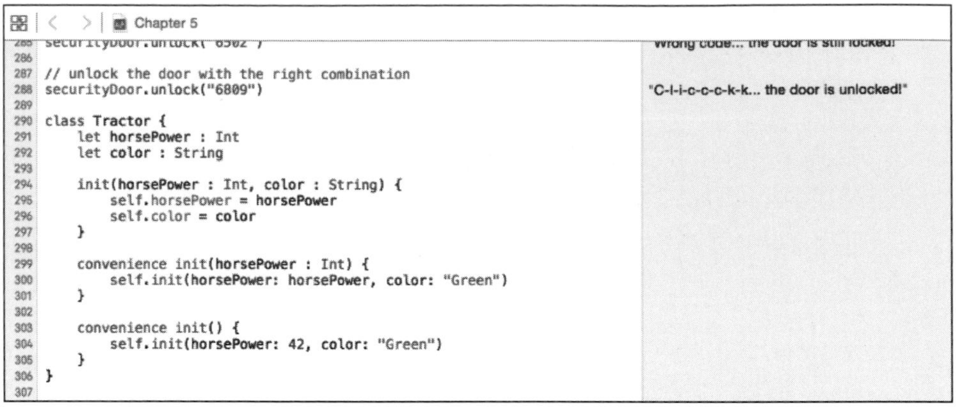

```
⊞  <  >  | 🖥 Chapter 5
285  securityDoor.unlock("6582")                              Wrong code... the door is still locked!
286
287  // unlock the door with the right combination
288  securityDoor.unlock("6809")                              "C-l-i-c-c-c-k-k... the door is unlocked!"
289
290  class Tractor {
291      let horsePower : Int
292      let color : String
293
294      init(horsePower : Int, color : String) {
295          self.horsePower = horsePower
296          self.color = color
297      }
298
299      convenience init(horsePower : Int) {
300          self.init(horsePower: horsePower, color: "Green")
301      }
302
303      convenience init() {
304          self.init(horsePower: 42, color: "Green")
305      }
306  }
307
```

Next, on line 279, the unlock method with the combination parameter is used, but the Results sidebar indicates that the door is already unlocked; this is a good sign, and shows that the logic behind the door code is working.

The door is successfully locked on line 282 with a security code of 6809. With this door locked, an attempt is made to unlock it on line 285 with a different security code—that attempt fails, and the door remains locked. Finally, on line 288 the unlock method is again called with the right combination, and the door unlocks.

Now that you've spent some time going over the ins and outs of classes, subclasses, and inheritance, let's spend a little time diving deeper into the convenience initializers.

CONVENIENCE INITIALIZERS

So far, I've touched lightly on the init method, which is the method that is called when a class is instantiated in Swift. You've seen several init methods already for the classes that you explored in this chapter. In the case of the Door class, no explicit init method was needed, because the properties for that class were assigned default values inside the class itself. Both the NewDoor and NiceDoor classes had init methods along with parameters that had default values assigned to them.

Sometimes, when designing a class, you may want to have a mix of different init meth-ods. For instance, one init method might assume some defaults, whereas another might require the passing of additional parameters. Ultimately, these initializers all funnel to a single init method known as the *designated initializer*. This is typically the init method with the most parameters.

Swift has a special designation for these types of initialization methods. They are known as *convenience initializers*.

Let's explore the concept of convenience initializers by looking at tractors, which come in various sizes for different jobs. I've created a Tractor class defined on lines 290 through 306 in **Figure 5.16**. Type in the code, and let's take a look.

```
class Tractor {
    let horsePower : Int
    let color : String

    init(horsePower : Int, color : String) {
        self.horsePower = horsePower
        self.color = color
    }

    convenience init(horsePower : Int) {
        self.init(horsePower: horsePower, color: "Green")
    }

    convenience init() {
        self.init(horsePower: 42, color: "Green")
    }
}
```

The Tractor class looks somewhat similar to the other classes you've studied in this chapter. It has properties at the top, followed by a number of methods. The properties are the horsepower (an Int) and a color (a String).

On line 294 is the designated initializer. It is the init method that contains the most parameters. Each parameter represents one property in the class, and lines 295 and 296 contain the assignments for those properties. If you wanted to instantiate an object of this class, you could call this method with two parameters of your choosing.

Line 299 contains a second init method, prefaced with the keyword convenience. This is a convenience initializer. It's convenient because you can save some typing when instantiating an object from this method. Note that it contains one fewer parameter than the designated initializer: The color parameter is not passed but is assumed to be the value "Green".

This convenience initializer calls self.init on line 300. The initializer being called here is the designated initializer defined on line 294, which sets the two available properties.

Another convenience initializer is defined on line 303. This init method takes no parameters. Instead, it assumes that the tractor being created is a 42-horsepower tractor with green paint. If that's the kind of tractor you want, you can save yourself some typing by instantiating a Tractor object with this initializer.

Let's create a few tractors, shall we? Enter the following code, starting on line 308.

```
let myBigTractor = Tractor()
let myBiggerTractor = Tractor(horsePower: 71)
let myYardTractor = Tractor(horsePower: 16, color : "Orange")
```

FIGURE 5.17 Creating
tractors with the
Tractor class

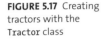

```
        ⟨  ⟩    Chapter 5
289
290   class Tractor {
291       let horsePower : Int
292       let color : String
293
294       init(horsePower : Int, color : String) {
295           self.horsePower = horsePower
296           self.color = color
297       }
298
299       convenience init(horsePower : Int) {
300           self.init(horsePower: horsePower, color: "Green")
301       }
302
303       convenience init() {
304           self.init(horsePower: 42, color: "Green")
305       }
306   }
307
308   let myBigTractor = Tractor()                                    Tractor
309   let myBiggerTractor = Tractor(horsePower: 71)                   Tractor
310   let myYardTractor = Tractor(horsePower: 16, color: "Orange")    Tractor
311
```

Line 308 of **Figure 5.17** calls the convenience initializer that sets up all the parameters for us. You can expect a 42-horsepower tractor in the standard green color.

Likewise on line 309, you are calling one of the convenience initializers that sets the tractor color to green automatically. Finally on line 310, the third tractor is called with the designated initializer, forcing you to pass all the parameters explicitly.

Convenience initializers are certainly convenient. You can create a number of them to aid in the creation of an object, and they all funnel into the designated initializer, which is ultimately responsible for initializing all the properties of the object.

There's more to discuss regarding initializers, but I'll save that for a later time. Instead, let's turn our attention to two other useful Swift language features used for data organization: enumerations and structures.

ENUMERATIONS

Enumerations allow you to specify a group of related names with the intent of referencing those names in your coding. Enumerations are often used in conjunction with classes but are useful anywhere. Their roots are in the C language, but they are much more flexible and powerful in Swift. Enumerations have the following basic form:

```
enum enumerationName {
    // constant definitions
}
```

Since tractors have been on the agenda for the last few examples, here's an example of using an enumeration to represent the different types of fuel for any number of vehicles:

```
enum FuelType {

    case Gasoline
    case Diesel
    case Biodiesel
    case Electric
    case NaturalGas

}
```

In this code snippet, the case keyword is used to define each enumeration member. The member becomes associated with the enumeration name (FuelType) and accessible via dot notation, as you'll see shortly.

For added convenience, multiple enumeration members can be placed on a single line, like so:

```
enum FuelType {
    case Gasoline, Diesel, Biodiesel, Electric, NaturalGas
}
```

And simple mappings in enumerations can be achieved with a feature known as *raw values*:

```
enum FuelType : String {
  case Gasoline = "89 octane"
  case Diesel = "sulphur free"
  case Biodiesel = "vegetable oil"
  case Electric = "30 amps"
  case NaturalGas = "coalbed methane"
}
```

These values can then be extracted using rawValue:

```
let fuelCharacteristic = FuelType.Gasoline.rawValue
```

That's pretty robust for a seemingly simple construct!

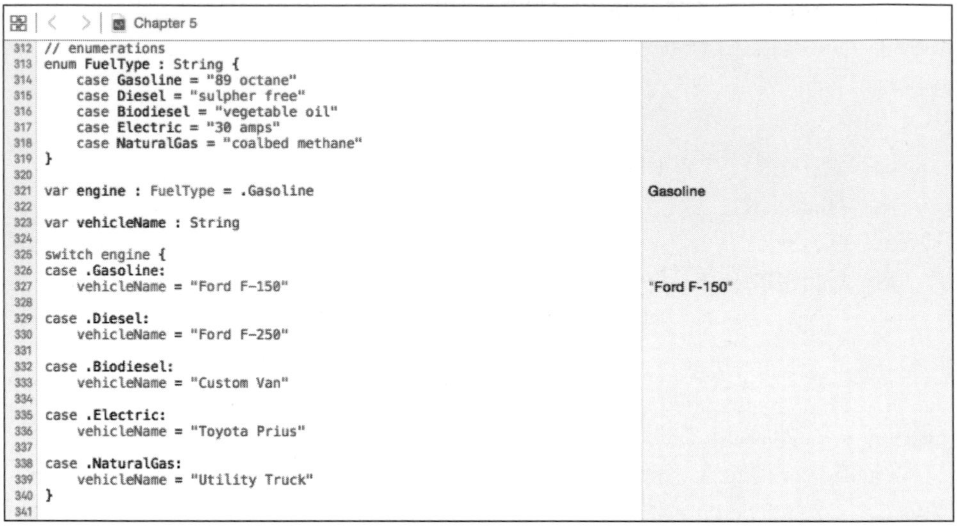

FIGURE 5.18
Creating and using
an enumeration

```
    ⊞  <  >  🖪 Chapter 5
312  // enumerations
313  enum FuelType : String {
314      case Gasoline = "89 octane"
315      case Diesel = "sulpher free"
316      case Biodiesel = "vegetable oil"
317      case Electric = "30 amps"
318      case NaturalGas = "coalbed methane"
319  }
320
321  var engine : FuelType = .Gasoline                    Gasoline
322
323  var vehicleName : String
324
325  switch engine {
326  case .Gasoline:
327      vehicleName = "Ford F-150"                       "Ford F-150"
328
329  case .Diesel:
330      vehicleName = "Ford F-250"
331
332  case .Biodiesel:
333      vehicleName = "Custom Van"
334
335  case .Electric:
336      vehicleName = "Toyota Prius"
337
338  case .NaturalGas:
339      vehicleName = "Utility Truck"
340  }
341
```

Once an enumeration is defined, any of its members can be assigned to a variable and used in your code quite naturally. **Figure 5.18** shows this technique.

```
// enumerations
enum FuelType : String {
    case Gasoline = "89 octane"
    case Diesel = "sulphur free"
    case Biodiesel = "vegetable oil"
    case Electric = "30 amps"
    case NaturalGas = "coalbed methane"
}

var engine : FuelType = .Gasoline

var vehicleName : String

switch engine {
case .Gasoline:
    vehicleName = "Ford F-150"

case .Diesel:
    vehicleName = "Ford F-250"
```

```
case .Biodiesel:
    vehicleName = "Custom Van"

case .Electric:
    vehicleName = "Toyota Prius"

case .NaturalGas:
    vehicleName = "Utility Truck"
}
```

```
print("Vehicle \(vehicleName) takes \(engine.rawValue)")
```

The enumeration defined on lines 313 through 319 shows the different fuel types. On line 321, the variable engine is declared as an enumeration and assigned the value Gasoline. Note that the dot preceding the value is a shorthanded dot notation. Because you are being explicit about declaring the variable as a type of FuelType, Swift assumes that Gasoline is part of that enumeration, so an explicit reference is not needed. You could have typed the following:

```
var engine : FuelType = FuelType.Gasoline
```

The more complete reference would have worked as well, but the extra typing is unnecessary.

On lines 325 through 340, a switch statement is used to traverse all the possibilities in the FuelType enumeration, with a type of vehicle being printed depending on the value of the engine variable.

If you're familiar with enumerations in C, you know that internally the compiler assigns a number to each enumeration value, and that any reference to that enumeration value actually decomposes into a number. This is not so in Swift. Enumeration values remain their actual label names internally.

STRUCTURAL INTEGRITY

Classes are pretty powerful constructs in Swift for representing objects of various kinds, but the language also offers choices for organizing data in similar ways: *structures*.

If you're familiar with C or one of its variants, you'll recognize structures immediately. They are organizational constructs for holding data, and they look and feel like classes in several ways, including how they are created:

```
struct structureName {
    // variable and constant definitions
}
```

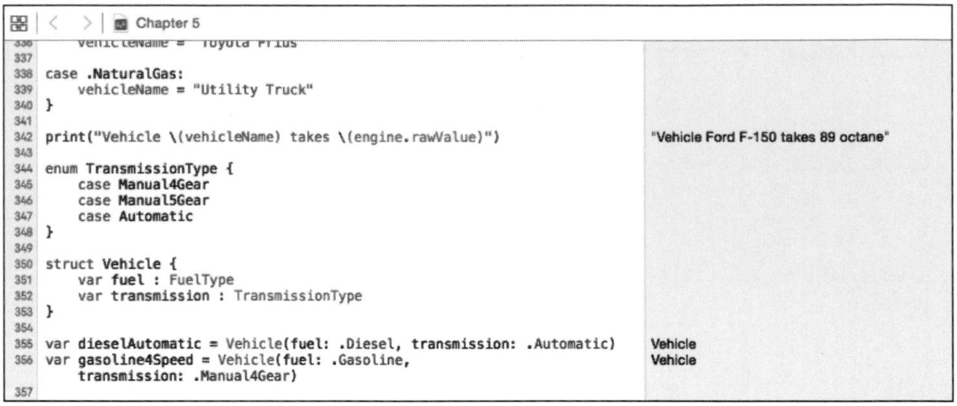

FIGURE 5.19 Creating a
Vehicle structure and
initializing it

```
                                            Chapter 5
336     vehicleName = "Toyota Prius"
337
338  case .NaturalGas:
339     vehicleName = "Utility Truck"
340  }
341
342  print("Vehicle \(vehicleName) takes \(engine.rawValue)")        "Vehicle Ford F-150 takes 89 octane"
343
344  enum TransmissionType {
345     case Manual4Gear
346     case Manual5Gear
347     case Automatic
348  }
349
350  struct Vehicle {
351     var fuel : FuelType
352     var transmission : TransmissionType
353  }
354
355  var dieselAutomatic = Vehicle(fuel: .Diesel, transmission: .Automatic)   Vehicle
356  var gasoline4Speed = Vehicle(fuel: .Gasoline,                            Vehicle
            transmission: .Manual4Gear)
357
```

Lines 344 to 356 of **Figure 5.19** combine an enumeration and a structure. The Vehicle
structure, defined on lines 350 through 353, has two members to represent the type of fuel
and type of transmission. Lines 355 and 356 demonstrate how to create variables representing the structure.

```
enum TransmissionType {
    case Manual4Gear
    case Manual5Gear
    case Automatic
}


struct Vehicle {
    var fuel : FuelType
    var transmission : TransmissionType
}


var dieselAutomatic = Vehicle(fuel: .Diesel, transmission: .Automatic)
var gasoline4Speed = Vehicle(fuel: .Gasoline, transmission: .Manual4Gear)
```

In the C language, structures are very useful for organizing and aggregating related data
because there are no such things as classes. In Swift, structures take on this same behavior,
but they can also include methods. This makes structures almost the same as classes, but
with some notable differences.

Whereas classes can establish hierarchy through inheritance, structures have no notion
of subclassing. Also, structures are copied in their entirety when being assigned from one
variable to the next; classes are *referenced* and not copied between variables.

VALUE TYPES VS. REFERENCE TYPES

```
⊞  ‹  ›  ▣ Chapter 5

344  enum TransmissionType {
345      case Manual4Gear
346      case Manual5Gear
347      case Automatic
348  }
349
350  struct Vehicle {
351      var fuel : FuelType
352      var transmission : TransmissionType
353  }
354
355  var dieselAutomatic = Vehicle(fuel: .Diesel, transmission: .Automatic)     Vehicle
356  var gasoline4Speed = Vehicle(fuel: .Gasoline,                              Vehicle
         transmission: .Manual4Gear)
357
358  // ****************************
359  // value type vs reference type
360  // ****************************
361
362  // In Swift, structures are value types
363  struct Structure {
364      var copyVar : Int = 10
365  }
366
367  var struct1 = Structure() //struct1 created                               Structure
368  var struct2 = struct1 // struct2 is a copy of struct1                     Structure
369  struct2.copyVar = 20 // change struct2's copyVar                          Structure
370  struct1.copyVar // struct1's copyVar                                      10
371  struct2.copyVar // struct2's copyVar                                      20
372
373  // In Swift, classes are reference types
374  class Class {
375      var copyVar : Int = 10
376  }
377
378  var class1 = Class() // class1 instantiated                               Class
379  var class2 = class1 // class2 is a reference to class1                    Class
380  class2.copyVar = 20 // change class2's copyVar                            Class
381  class1.copyVar // class1's copyVar                                        20
382  class2.copyVar // class2's copyVar                                        20
383
```

FIGURE 5.20 Value types versus reference types illustrated by structures and classes

A very subtle but important distinction between classes and structures is how they behave when assigned to a variable or constant. Classes in Swift are known as *reference types*. No matter how many variables or constants are assigned to a particular object, they all point to the same object. Each variable or constant holds a reference, and not a copy, of that object.

Structures are completely different. When a structure is assigned to a variable or constant, a *copy* of that structure is made at that point. The same thing happens if a structure is passed as a parameter to a function. This copy behavior makes structures *value types*.

This behavior can be illustrated in your playground by examining the contents of a class or a structure after it has been assigned. Type in the following code, which lands at lines 358 through 382 in **Figure 5.20**.

```
// ****************************
// value type vs reference type
// ****************************

// In Swift, structures are value types
struct Structure {
```

```
    var copyVar : Int = 10
}

var struct1 = Structure() // struct1 created
var struct2 = struct1 // struct2 is a copy of struct1
struct2.copyVar = 20 // change struct2's copyVar
struct1.copyVar // struct1's copyVar
struct2.copyVar // struct2's copyVar

// In Swift, classes are reference types
class Class {
    var copyVar : Int = 10
}

var class1 = Class() // class1 instantiated
var class2 = class1 // class2 is a reference to class1
class2.copyVar = 20 // change class2's copyVar
class1.copyVar // class1's copyVar
class2.copyVar // class2's copyVar
```

On line 363, a simple structure, Structure, with one member, copyVar, is defined. The copyVar member is assigned the value 10 by default. On line 367, a variable named struct1 is assigned an instance of Structure. In the Results sidebar, the value of copyVar is shown as 10, as you would expect.

On line 368, a second variable, struct2, is assigned to the struct1 variable that was just created. At this point struct1 is copied and assigned to struct2; because it is a copy, any change to struct2's copyVar will be independent and not affect struct1's copyVar. This is tested on line 369, where copyVar of struct2 is assigned the value 20.

With that assignment made, both struct1 and struct2's copyVar contents are shown in the Results sidebar. As you would expect from a copy type, copyVar of struct1 remains the initial value, 10, whereas copyVar of struct2 is 20. The values are different, proving that struct1 and struct2 are not references to the same structure—they are completely different, independent copies.

Contrast that behavior to the contrived Class class on line 374. This class looks identical to the structure example with the same variable, copyVar, except it is marked as a class.

Just as in the structure example, a new class is instantiated on line 378 and assigned to class1. On the next line, the variable class2 is assigned to the new class1 variable. At this point a *reference* is made from class2 to class1, which means that both variables are referencing, or pointing to, the exact same object in memory.

To demonstrate this, class2's copyVar is set to 20 on line 380, and then both copyVar variables from class1 and class2 are evaluated on lines 381 and 382. According to the Results sidebar, they are both set to 20, proving that both class1 and class2 point to the same object. Any modification of variables in class1 will immediately affect class2.

This behavior is important to understand, and it should guide your use of classes versus structures. Any type of language construct that is copyable should be thought of as "expensive to use" compared with a referenced construct, because a copy of an object typically consumes more memory than a reference to it. For this reason, structures should be relegated to uses in which small aggregations of data are tightly related, like this example:

```swift
struct Triangle {
    var base : Double
    var height : Double

    func area() -> Double {
        return (0.5 * base) * height
    }
}
```

Here, the structure is organized around the idea of a triangle's measurements of base and height, and a single function that computes the area. Although a class would also work here, a structure fits better for this type of compact representation. Classes are more appropriate for larger, more disparate data organized with a number of different methods.

LOOKING BACK, LOOKING AHEAD

From classes to structures and enumerations, you've covered quite a lot of territory in this chapter. Although we have yet to explore a few intricacies of these Swift constructs, that will come. For now, you have enough of an understanding to begin to exploit these concepts.

I encourage you to practice modeling various types of objects around you and defining them in terms of classes. What are their properties? What are their behaviors? What types of objects are similar? Can they inherit properties and behaviors from other objects?

Now, turn the page and move forward into the next chapter. There, you'll expand your existing Swift knowledge with several additional class-related concepts: protocols and extensions.

Formalizing with Protocols and Extensions

Congratulations on completing a set of milestone topics in the last chapter: classes, structures, and enumerations—your Swift journey through this book is almost halfway finished! Yet you've only scratched the surface of what Swift's object-oriented capabilities are. There's still plenty to explore in this area, and for now, our focus will remain on concepts related to classes and structures.

Two significant features of the Swift language expand the utility and flexibility of classes and structures: protocols and extensions. That material will carry us through this chapter.

FOLLOWING PROTOCOL

Dinner fork versus salad fork. Saying "please" and "yes, sir" or "yes, ma'am." These are behavior examples you learn to apply in certain situations (in this case, eating at a table or addressing someone). Such behaviors are usually taught by a parent and become mannerisms. Essentially, when you employ such behaviors, you are following existing protocols or modes of conduct.

The idea of protocol also extends to Swift, specifically with respect to classes and structures. Protocols enforce a "code of conduct" on classes and structures, making them promise to implement certain methods or properties. This enforcement is mandatory, but only if the class or structure decides to opt in, or *adopt* the protocol.

To illustrate how to use a protocol in Swift, think back to the Portal class in the previous chapter (you might want to review the playground file for that chapter). The Portal class was created when you realized that the Door class and the Window class shared an ability to both lock and unlock. It demonstrated class hierarchy and inheritance principles that are central to OOP.

CLASS OR PROTOCOL?

Inheritance made sense for doors and windows, but what about other unrelated objects that can also be locked and unlocked? A car and a house can both be locked and unlocked, but constructing a class hierarchy that could encapsulate the properties and behaviors of both objects would be unwieldy. They're different enough to make inheritance too much of a reach. That's where protocols come into play.

As you can see on lines 8 through 11 in **Figure 6.1**, a protocol definition looks a lot like a class definition. The basic form of a protocol is:

```
protocol ProtocolName {
    // protocol members
}
```

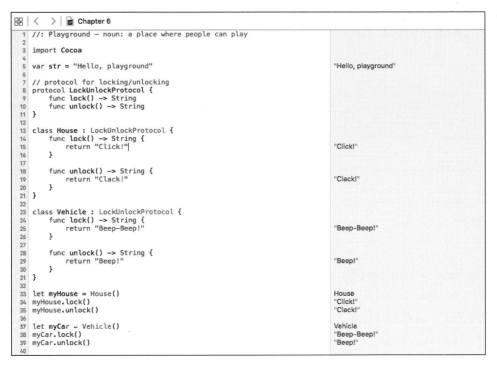

FIGURE 6.1
Demonstrating Swift's protocol feature

```
1  //: Playground - noun: a place where people can play
2
3  import Cocoa
4
5  var str = "Hello, playground"                          "Hello, playground"
6
7  // protocol for locking/unlocking
8  protocol LockUnlockProtocol {
9      func lock() -> String
10     func unlock() -> String
11 }
12
13 class House : LockUnlockProtocol {
14     func lock() -> String {
15         return "Click!"|                               "Click!"
16     }
17
18     func unlock() -> String {
19         return "Clack!"                                "Clack!"
20     }
21 }
22
23 class Vehicle : LockUnlockProtocol {
24     func lock() -> String {
25         return "Beep-Beep!"                            "Beep-Beep!"
26     }
27
28     func unlock() -> String {
29         return "Beep!"                                 "Beep!"
30     }
31 }
32
33 let myHouse = House()                                  House
34 myHouse.lock()                                         "Click!"
35 myHouse.unlock()                                       "Clack!"
36
37 let myCar = Vehicle()                                  Vehicle
38 myCar.lock()                                           "Beep-Beep!"
39 myCar.unlock()                                         "Beep!"
40
```

Start up Xcode, and create a playground named **Chapter 6**. Type the following code into your playground file on line 7 (Figure 6.1):

```
// protocol for locking/unlocking
protocol LockUnlockProtocol {
    func lock() -> String
    func unlock() -> String
}


class House : LockUnlockProtocol {
    func lock() -> String {
        return "Click!"
    }

    func unlock() -> String {
        return "Clack!"
    }
}
```

```
class Vehicle : LockUnlockProtocol {
    func lock() -> String {
        return "Beep-Beep!"
    }

    func unlock() -> String {
        return "Beep!"
    }
}

let myHouse = House()
myHouse.lock()
myHouse.unlock()

let myCar = Vehicle()
myCar.lock()
myCar.unlock()
```

On lines 9 and 10, two functions are declared: lock and unlock. Both take no parameters and return a String type. What might look strange is that the body of the function is missing, but that's the point of a protocol. It lists the method signatures a class must adopt.

To clarify, look at line 13. This is a regular class declaration, but notice what follows the colon: the name of the protocol. This looks a lot like inheritance, as you saw in the last chapter, but in this case, a protocol follows, not a superclass name.

Lines 14 and 18 show the definition of the lock and unlock methods in the House class. Those same methods exist in the Vehicle class on lines 24 and 28, except the result returned is different (locking a house sounds different than locking a vehicle).

Lines 33 through 39 show the declaration of constants of type House and Vehicle, and the subsequent calls to lock and unlock both via the methods dictated by the LockUnlockProtocol.

```
37  let myCar = Vehicle()                                    Vehicle
38  myCar.lock()                                             "Beep-Beep!"
39  myCar.unlock()                                           "Beep!"
40
41  // new lock/unlock protocol with locked variable
42  protocol NewLockUnlockProtocol {
43      var locked : Bool { get set }
44      func lock() -> String
45      func unlock() -> String
46  }
47
48  class Safe : NewLockUnlockProtocol {
49      var locked : Bool = false
50
51      func lock() -> String {
52          locked = true                                    Safe
53          return "Ding!"                                   "Ding!"
54      }
55
56      func unlock() -> String {
57          locked = false                                   Safe
58          return "Dong!"                                   "Dong!"
59      }
60  }
61
62  class Gate : NewLockUnlockProtocol {
63      var locked : Bool = false
64
65      func lock() -> String {
66          locked = true                                    Gate
67          return "Clink!"                                  "Clink!"
68      }
69
70      func unlock() -> String {
71          locked = false                                   Gate
72          return "Clonk!"                                  "Clonk!"
73      }
74  }
75
76  let mySafe = Safe()                                      Safe
77  mySafe.lock()                                            "Ding!"
78  mySafe.unlock()                                          "Dong!"
79
80  let myGate = Gate()                                      Gate
81  myGate.lock()                                            "Clink!"
82  myGate.unlock()                                          "Clonk!"
83
```

FIGURE 6.2 Adding a variable to a protocol definition

MORE THAN JUST METHODS

Swift protocols can work with more than just methods. Variable declarations can even be dictated to the adopters of protocols. Recall in Chapter 5 that a variable, locked, was used to track the lock status? This makes a great candidate for enhancing the previous example.

Type the following code starting on line 41 (**Figure 6.2**):

```
// new lock/unlock protocol with locked variable
protocol NewLockUnlockProtocol {
    var locked : Bool { get set }
    func lock() -> String
    func unlock() -> String
}

class Safe : NewLockUnlockProtocol {
    var locked : Bool = false
```

```
        func lock() -> String {
            locked = true
            return "Ding!"
        }

        func unlock() -> String {
            locked = false
            return "Dong!"
        }
    }

    class Gate : NewLockUnlockProtocol {
        var locked : Bool = false

        func lock() -> String {
            locked = true
            return "Clink!"
        }

        func unlock() -> String {
            locked = false
            return "Clonk!"
        }
    }

    let mySafe = Safe()
    mySafe.lock()
    mySafe.unlock()

    let myGate = Gate()
    myGate.lock()
    myGate.unlock()
```

A new protocol, NewLockUnlockProtocol, is created on lines 42 through 46. It's nearly identical to the previous protocol except for the addition of line 43:

```
var locked : Bool { get set }
```

Within the context of a protocol, a variable can be designated as mandatory by adding the familiar var keyword, the name of the variable, and the type following a colon. What is new is the { get set } that follows the type.

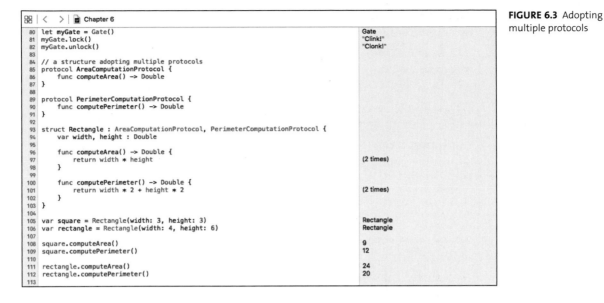

FIGURE 6.3 Adopting multiple protocols

```
80  let myGate = Gate()                                                 Gate
81  myGate.lock()                                                       "Clink!"
82  myGate.unlock()                                                     "Clonk!"
83
84  // a structure adopting multiple protocols
85  protocol AreaComputationProtocol {
86      func computeArea() -> Double
87  }
88
89  protocol PerimeterComputationProtocol {
90      func computePerimeter() -> Double
91  }
92
93  struct Rectangle : AreaComputationProtocol, PerimeterComputationProtocol {
94      var width, height : Double
95
96      func computeArea() -> Double {
97          return width * height                                       (2 times)
98      }
99
100     func computePerimeter() -> Double {
101         return width * 2 + height * 2                               (2 times)
102     }
103 }
104
105 var square = Rectangle(width: 3, height: 3)                          Rectangle
106 var rectangle = Rectangle(width: 4, height: 6)                       Rectangle
107
108 square.computeArea()                                                9
109 square.computePerimeter()                                           12
110
111 rectangle.computeArea()                                             24
112 rectangle.computePerimeter()                                        20
113
```

Both get and set are special qualifiers that force the protocol adopter to consider the mutability of the variable. With both get and set present, the resulting locked declaration in any adopting class or structure must declare it with the var keyword, indicating mutability. With only get present, the adopting class or structure can be declared with either the let or var keyword.

ADOPTING MULTIPLE PROTOCOLS

Swift allows a class or structure to adopt more than one protocol; this flexibility allows you to refactor your work into separate protocols for better organization. Take, for instance, the task of finding the area of a geometric shape as well as the perimeter. The area is the measurement of the space within the bounds of the shape, whereas the perimeter is the measurement of the length of all the sides.

If you consider the computation of the area and perimeter as methods declared in separate protocols, they can be adopted by a variety of structures that represent different shapes. Type the following code starting on line 84 (**Figure 6.3**):

```
// a structure adopting multiple protocols
protocol AreaComputationProtocol {
    func computeArea() -> Double
}

protocol PerimeterComputationProtocol {
    func computePerimeter() -> Double
}
```

```swift
struct Rectangle : AreaComputationProtocol, PerimeterComputationProtocol {
    var width, height : Double

    func computeArea() -> Double {
        return width * height
    }

    func computePerimeter() -> Double {
        return width * 2 + height * 2
    }
}

var square = Rectangle(width: 3, height: 3)
var rectangle = Rectangle(width: 4, height: 6)

square.computeArea()
square.computePerimeter()

rectangle.computeArea()
rectangle.computePerimeter()
```

Lines 85 through 91 show the two new protocols, each requiring the creation of a single function. On line 93, the Rectangle structure shows the multiple adoption syntax. Each protocol is separated by a comma. Since both protocols are specified, the methods and variables of both must be adopted. In this case, only the functions computeArea and computePerimeter are necessary for adoption by the Rectangle structure.

Lines 105 and 106 show the declaration of two variables: One is a square (which is a special case of a rectangle), and the other is a rectangle. Both create an instance of the Rectangle structure with the width and height parameters; the Results sidebar confirms their creation.

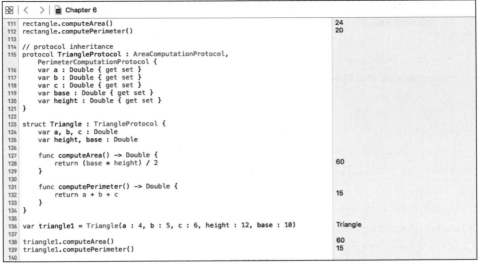

FIGURE 6.4
Demonstrating
protocol inheritance

```
     ⊞ | ‹ › | 🖹 Chapter 6
111  rectangle.computeArea()                                           24
112  rectangle.computePerimeter()                                      20
113
114  // protocol inheritance
115  protocol TriangleProtocol : AreaComputationProtocol,
         PerimeterComputationProtocol {
116      var a : Double { get set }
117      var b : Double { get set }
118      var c : Double { get set }
119      var base : Double { get set }
120      var height : Double { get set }
121  }
122
123  struct Triangle : TriangleProtocol {
124      var a, b, c : Double
125      var height, base : Double
126
127      func computeArea() -> Double {
128          return (base * height) / 2                                 60
129      }
130
131      func computePerimeter() -> Double {
132          return a + b + c                                           15
133      }
134  }
135
136  var triangle1 = Triangle(a : 4, b : 5, c : 6, height : 12, base : 10)   Triangle
137
138  triangle1.computeArea()                                           60
139  triangle1.computePerimeter()                                      15
140
```

PROTOCOLS CAN INHERIT, TOO

It may come as a surprise, but just as classes can inherit from each other, protocols can as well. Protocol inheritance allows you to build on basic protocols and extend them with either new method or variable requirements.

Type the following code beginning on line 114 (**Figure 6.4**):

```
// protocol inheritance
protocol TriangleProtocol : AreaComputationProtocol,
→ PerimeterComputationProtocol {
    var a : Double { get set }
    var b : Double { get set }
    var c : Double { get set }
    var base : Double { get set }
    var height : Double { get set }
}

struct Triangle : TriangleProtocol {
    var a, b, c : Double
    var height, base : Double
```

```
    func computeArea() -> Double {
        return (base * height) / 2
    }

    func computePerimeter() -> Double {
        return a + b + c
    }
}

var triangle1 = Triangle(a : 4, b : 5, c : 6, height : 12, base : 10)

triangle1.computeArea()
triangle1.computePerimeter()
```

Line 115 shows the TriangleProtocol definition, followed by the names of the two protocols it inherits: AreaComputationProtocol and PerimeterComputationProtocol. In addition to adopting these two protocols, TriangleProtocol also enforces the addition of five helpful variables for computing both the area and the perimeter of a triangle. Note that each variable has both the get and set qualifiers specified.

On line 123, a new structure, Triangle, is defined that adheres to the TriangleProtocol. By adhering to that protocol, the Triangle structure must also adhere to AreaComputationProtocol and PerimeterComputationProtocol. Those methods are defined on lines 127 through 133. Lines 124 and 125 create the additional variables, which are required by the TriangleProtocol definition.

Line 136 creates an instance of the Triangle structure, aptly named triangle1, along with the initialization of the parameters. Lines 138 and 139 show the result of calling the computation methods, and you can verify the results in the Results sidebar.

DELEGATION

One specific use for Swift's protocols is an important programming design pattern known as *delegation*. Delegation allows one class or structure to concede work or even decision making to another class or structure. When you delegate a task to someone, you expect that person to do the task and report back the status to you; it's very much the same idea in Swift. Other classes can be delegates, performing work on behalf of your class, and protocols are perfect for this. Delegation can also be used to query, or ask, another class or structure whether or not something is permissible.

```
141  // delegation via protocol
142  protocol VendingMachineProtocol {
143      var coinInserted : Bool { get set }
144      func shouldVend() -> Bool
145  }
146
147  class Vendor : VendingMachineProtocol {
148      var coinInserted : Bool = false
149
150      func shouldVend() -> Bool {
151          if coinInserted == true {
152              coinInserted = false                    (2 times)
153              return true                             (2 times)
154          }
155          return false                                (2 times)
156      }
157  }
158
159  class ColaMachine {
160      var vendor : VendingMachineProtocol
161
162      init(vendor : VendingMachineProtocol) {
163          self.vendor = vendor
164      }
165
166      func insertCoin() {
167          vendor.coinInserted = true                  (2 times)
168      }
169
170      func pressColaButton() -> String {
171          if vendor.shouldVend() == true {
172              return "Here's a Cola!"                 "Here's a Cola!"
173          }
174          else {
175              return "You must insert a coin!"        (2 times)
176          }
177      }
178
179      func pressRootBeerButton() -> String {
180          if vendor.shouldVend() == true {
181              return "Here's a Root Beer!"
182          }
183          else {
184              return "You must insert a coin!"
185          }
186      }
187  }
188
189  var vendingMachine = ColaMachine(vendor : Vendor())     ColaMachine
190
191  vendingMachine.pressColaButton()                        "You must insert a coin!"
192  vendingMachine.insertCoin()                             ColaMachine
193  vendingMachine.pressColaButton()                        "Here's a Cola!"
194  vendingMachine.pressColaButton()                        "You must insert a coin!"
195
```

FIGURE 6.5 Using a protocol for delegation

Begin typing the following code on line 141 (**Figure 6.5**). This snippet demonstrates delegation by modeling a vending machine, which takes a coin and vends an item:

```
// delegation via protocol
protocol VendingMachineProtocol {
    var coinInserted : Bool { get set }
    func shouldVend() -> Bool
}

class Vendor : VendingMachineProtocol {
    var coinInserted : Bool = false

    func shouldVend() -> Bool {
        if coinInserted == true {
            coinInserted = false
            return true
```

```
            }
            return false
        }
    }

    class ColaMachine {
        var vendor : VendingMachineProtocol

        init(vendor : VendingMachineProtocol) {
            self.vendor = vendor
        }

        func insertCoin() {
            vendor.coinInserted = true
        }

        func pressColaButton() -> String {
            if vendor.shouldVend() == true {
                return "Here's a Cola!"
            }
            else {
                return "You must insert a coin!"
            }
        }

        func pressRootBeerButton() -> String {
            if vendor.shouldVend() == true {
                return "Here's a Root Beer!"
            }
            else {
                return "You must insert a coin!"
            }
        }
    }
```

```
var vendingMachine = ColaMachine(vendor : Vendor())

vendingMachine.pressColaButton()
vendingMachine.insertCoin()
vendingMachine.pressColaButton()
vendingMachine.pressColaButton()
```

Lines 142 through 145 define the protocol, VendingMachineProtocol, with a Bool variable and a method. The variable is set to true to indicate that a coin is inserted, or false if not. The method returns a Bool indicating whether or not an item should be vended.

Lines 147 through 157 define a new class, Vendor, which adheres to the VendingMachineProtocol. It creates the coinInserted variable that the protocol dictates, as well as the shouldVend method. The logic is simple: If a coin has been inserted, clear the coinInserted variable and return true, indicating that an item should be vended; otherwise, no coin has been inserted—return false to prevent an item from vending.

Lines 159 through 187 define the ColaMachine class, which holds an object that adheres to the VendingMachineProtocol protocol. The init method on line 162 takes that object and assigns it to the self.vendor variable on line 163. This vendor object will act on behalf of your class to determine whether it is appropriate to vend an item.

A convenient method, insertCoin, is defined on lines 166 through 168, and simply sets the vendor object's coinInserted variable to true when called.

Two other methods, pressColaButton and pressRootBeerButton, call the vendor's delegate method shouldVend to determine whether to return a vended item (a cola or a root beer) or to remind the user gently to insert a coin.

Finally, a new vendingMachine variable is created on line 189, and its methods called on lines 191 through 194 to demonstrate that the class works as expected. Figure 6.5 shows the results in the Results sidebar.

EXTENDING WITH EXTENSIONS

In the previous chapter, you were introduced to subclassing as a means of extending a Swift class through inheritance. Inheritance via subclassing is a time-tested way of extending an existing class, and it works well for modeling and solving problems in object-oriented languages.

However, alternatives to subclassing in Swift still allow you to extend the functionality of a class without inheritance. Such an approach can be useful when you want to extend, and not fundamentally create, a new class structure. Subclassing is also limited to classes and does not work on structures.

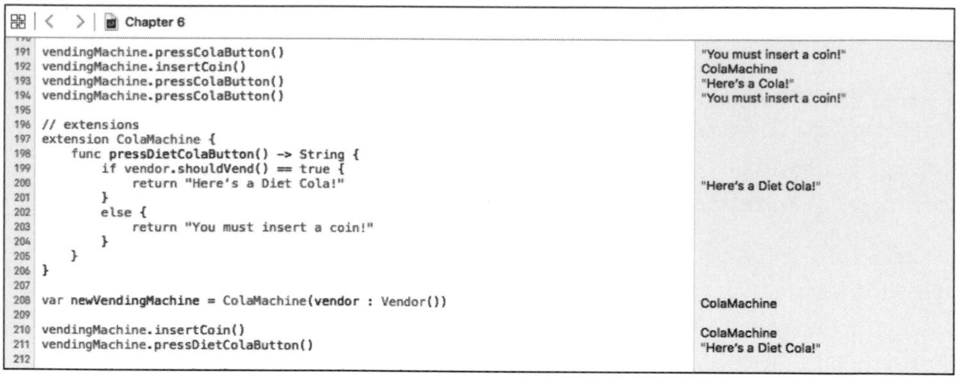

FIGURE 6.6 Extending
the ColaMachine class
with an extension

```
                                                                    "You must insert a coin!"
191  vendingMachine.pressColaButton()
192  vendingMachine.insertCoin()                                    ColaMachine
193  vendingMachine.pressColaButton()                               "Here's a Cola!"
194  vendingMachine.pressColaButton()                               "You must insert a coin!"
195
196  // extensions
197  extension ColaMachine {
198      func pressDietColaButton() -> String {
199          if vendor.shouldVend() == true {
200              return "Here's a Diet Cola!"                        "Here's a Diet Cola!"
201          }
202          else {
203              return "You must insert a coin!"
204          }
205      }
206  }
207
208  var newVendingMachine = ColaMachine(vendor : Vendor())          ColaMachine
209
210  vendingMachine.insertCoin()                                     ColaMachine
211  vendingMachine.pressDietColaButton()                            "Here's a Diet Cola!"
212
```

On the other hand, *extensions* allow you to expand and extend the behavior and functionality of classes, structures, and even basic types in a non-invasive and straightforward manner. Swift's extensions are analogous to Objective-C categories but are much more powerful.

In true Swift form, the basic form of an extension looks similar to a class or protocol declaration:

```
extension className {
    // extension methods
}
```

In the case of an extension, the keyword is followed by the name of the class or structure that will be extended. Let's start by extending the class you just worked with: the ColaMachine class. Right now, the class contains methods to vend colas and root beers. Let's extend the class to also vend diet colas. Type the following code starting on line 196 (**Figure 6.6**):

```
// extensions
extension ColaMachine {
    func pressDietColaButton() -> String {
        if vendor.shouldVend() == true {
            return "Here's a Diet Cola!"
        }
        else {
            return "You must insert a coin!"
        }
    }
}

var newVendingMachine = ColaMachine(vendor : Vendor())

vendingMachine.insertCoin()
vendingMachine.pressDietColaButton()
```

```
202              else {
203                  return "You must insert a coin!"
204              }
205          }
206      }
207
208      var newVendingMachine = ColaMachine(vendor : Vendor())      ColaMachine
209
210      vendingMachine.insertCoin()                                  ColaMachine
211      vendingMachine.pressDietColaButton()                         "Here's a Diet Cola!"
212
213      // extending Int to handle memory size designations
214      extension Int {
215          var kb : Int { return self * 1_024 }                    4,096
216          var mb : Int { return self * 1_024 * 1_024 }            8,388,608
217          var gb : Int { return self * 1_024 * 1_024 * 1_024 }    2,147,483,648
218      }
219
220      var x : Int = 4.kb                                           4,096
221      var y = 8.mb                                                 8,388,608
222      var z = 2.gb                                                 2,147,483,648
223
```

FIGURE 6.7 Using extensions to extend the Int type

Line 197 in Figure 6.6 shows the start of the extension of the ColaMachine class. Following that is the new method, pressDietColaButton, on lines 198 through 205, which mirrors similar methods in the definition of the ColaMachine class earlier in the playground.

A new vending machine object is instantiated on line 208, and the new extension method is called on lines 210 and 211. The Results sidebar shows the results of that code.

You may be asking, "Why create an extension when I could have simply added the function to the ColaMachine class?" In this case, you could have certainly done that, but as you build your apps in Swift, you'll find yourself relying on third-party classes, and you may not necessarily have access to the source code. Using extensions is a great way to add features to a class defined elsewhere, even when the class's source code is not available.

EXTENDING BASIC TYPES

Bringing additional functionality to classes via extensions is one thing, but extending types is something entirely different. Swift's extensions allow you to enhance standard types such as Double and String to make them more powerful and easier to use.

MEGABYTES AND GIGABYTES

Let's start out by extending the most common of the basic Swift types: the ubiquitous integer (Int). Type the following code starting on line 213 to convert an Int to kilobytes (kb), megabytes (mb), or gigabytes (gb) (**Figure 6.7**):

```
// extending Int to handle memory size designations
extension Int {
    var kb : Int { return self * 1_024 }
    var mb : Int { return self * 1_024 * 1_024 }
    var gb : Int { return self * 1_024 * 1_024 * 1_024 }
}

var x : Int = 4.kb
var y = 8.mb
var z = 2.gb
```

FIGURE 6.8 Using extensions on the Double type

```
     ⊞ |  <   > |  🖻 Chapter 6
212
213   // extending Int to handle memory size designations
214   extension Int {
215       var kb : Int { return self * 1_024 }                          4,096
216       var mb : Int { return self * 1_024 * 1_024 }                  8,388,608
217       var gb :  Int { return self * 1_024 * 1_024 * 1_024 }         2,147,483,648
218   }
219
220   var x : Int = 4.kb                                                4,096
221   var y = 8.mb                                                      8,388,608
222   var z = 2.gb                                                      2,147,483,648
223
224   // extending Double to handle temperature conversions
225   extension Double {
226       var F : Double { return self }                                80.4
227       var C : Double { return (((self - 32.0) * 5.0) / 9.0) }       26.8888888888889
228       var K : Double { return (((self - 32.0) / 1.8) + 273.15) }    300.038888888889
229   }
230
231   var temperatureF = 80.4.F                                         80.4
232   var temperatureC = temperatureF.C                                26.8888888888889
233   var temperatureK = temperatureF.K                                300.038888888889
```

This extension demonstrates a feature known as *computed properties*. Unlike class inheritance, extensions prevent the addition of regular (or stored) properties from their base class, but computed properties are very much allowed. Computed properties are just that: Their values are derived from computations and take on the following form:

var *propertyName* : *type* { *code* }

On lines 215 through 217, the extension to the Int type takes care of conversions for kilobytes, megabytes, and gigabytes by performing simple math on the value of the type, represented by the keyword self.

The declared variables on lines 220 through 222 are assigned values appended with the now familiar dot notation and the appropriate symbol (kb, mb, or gb).

Computed properties follow the syntax of a property instead of a method, so you don't append parentheses () to the computed property's name. The name itself is all that is required.

WHAT'S THE TEMPERATURE?

Let's extend the Double type to handle computations for three types of temperature units: F for degrees Fahrenheit, C for degrees Celsius, and K for degrees Kelvin. Type the following code starting on line 224 (**Figure 6.8**):

```
// extending Double to handle temperature conversions
extension Double {
    var F : Double { return self }
    var C : Double { return (((self - 32.0) * 5.0) / 9.0) }
    var K : Double { return (((self - 32.0) / 1.8) + 273.15) }
}

var temperatureF = 80.4.F
var temperatureC = temperatureF.C
var temperatureK = temperatureF.K
```

```
226      var F : Double { return self }                              80.4
227      var C : Double { return (((self - 32.0) * 5.0) / 9.0) }     26.8888888888889
228      var K : Double { return (((self - 32.0) / 1.8) + 273.15) }  300.038888888889
229  }
230
231  var temperatureF = 80.4.F                                        80.4
232  var temperatureC = temperatureF.C                                26.8888888888889
233  var temperatureK = temperatureF.K                                300.038888888889
234
235  // extending String with functions
236  extension String {
237      func prependString(value : String) -> String {
238          return value + self                                      "prefixx"
239      }
240
241      func appendString(value : String) -> String {
242          return self + value                                      "ypostfix"
243      }
244  }
245
246  "x".prependString("prefix")                                      "prefixx"
247  "y".appendString("postfix")                                      "ypostfix"
248
```

FIGURE 6.9 Using methods to extend the String type

This looks a lot like the Int extensions I just discussed. Computed properties are once again used to extend the Double type.

In Figure 6.8, the variables lines 231 through 233 are assigned values appended with the recurring dot notation and the symbol F, C, or K. The results can be confirmed by looking at the Results sidebar in Figure 6.8.

Computed properties are quite handy in giving new functionality and utility to even the most elementary types, but there's a bonus: Extensions can extend a type with functions too!

BEFORE OR AFTER?

Since I've been picking on Int and Double, let's show the String type a little love. Type the following code starting on line 235 to use extensions and add two methods: prepend and append (**Figure 6.9**):

```
// extending String with functions
extension String {
    func prependString(value : String) -> String {
        return value + self
    }

    func appendString(value : String) -> String {
        return self + value
    }
}

"x".prependString("prefix")
"y".appendString("postfix")
```

FIGURE 6.10 Using a mutating method on the Int class

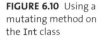

```
       ▦  <  >   ▣ Chapter 6
245
246    "x".prependString("prefix")                              "prefixx"
247    "y".appendString("postfix")                              "ypostfix"
248
249    // extensions with mutating instance methods
250    extension Int {
251        mutating func triple() {
252            self = self * 3                                   9
253        }
254    }
255
256    var trip = 3                                              3
257    trip.triple()                                            9
258
259    extension String {
260        mutating func decorate() {
261            self = "*** " + self + " ***"                     "*** decorate this ***"
262        }
263    }
264
265    var testString = "decorate this"                         "decorate this"
266    testString.decorate()                                    "*** decorate this ***"
267
```

Lines 237 through 243 define two methods that create a new string by combining a literal string such as `"prefix"` with the passed-in `String` object. Again, the `self` keyword is used to reference the value. In the case of the prepend method, `self` is being added to the passed value parameter. For the append method, `self` comes before `value`.

Lines 246 and 247 demonstrate using the new methods. In both cases, the `"x"` or `"y"` string literal calls the method, which itself takes a single parameter, with the results appearing in the Results sidebar.

IT'S MUTATING!

Up to this point, all the extension examples have returned some variant of `self`: Depending on the type, there's `self` appended with a string, `self` prepended with a string, `self` multiplied by a number, and so on. The result can be captured in a constant or variable, as I showed on lines 231 through 233 in Figure 6.9.

What if you want to change the value of `self` instead of simply returning some variation of it? Swift allows this by specifying a method as *mutating*. A mutating method in an extension allows the actual object to be changed.

Type the following code starting on line 249 to create such a mutating method on the `Int` type (**Figure 6.10**):

```
// extensions with mutating instance methods
extension Int {
    mutating func triple() {
        self = self * 3
    }
}
```

```
var trip = 3
trip.triple()

extension String {
    mutating func decorate() {
        self = "*** " + self + " ***"
    }
}

var testString = "decorate this"
testString.decorate()
```

On line 251, the `mutating` keyword is used before the function definition. This keyword is required when creating a mutating method; if it is omitted, the Swift compiler will throw an error on line 252 when it attempts to assign a value to `self`.

The `triple` function simply takes the value and multiplies it by three. This is done on line 252, where `self` is assigned to itself times three. This is the essence of a mutating method: `self` appears on the left side of the equal sign, indicating that it will be modified.

On line 256, a variable named `trip` is created and assigned the value 3. Following that is a call to the `triple` method, which triples the value. The Results sidebar shows the value changing from 3 to 9.

Likewise, on line 260, a mutating function is defined for the `String` type. Line 261 sets `self` to be bounded by asterisks in the decorate method. Lines 265 and 266 demonstrate the creation of a string variable that calls the decorate method. Once again, the Results sidebar reveals that the method indeed works.

Remember, mutating methods are all about change—modifying the actual value of the extended class. They cannot work on constants since, by definition, a constant is immutable, and attempting to call a mutating method on a constant will result in a Swift compiler error.

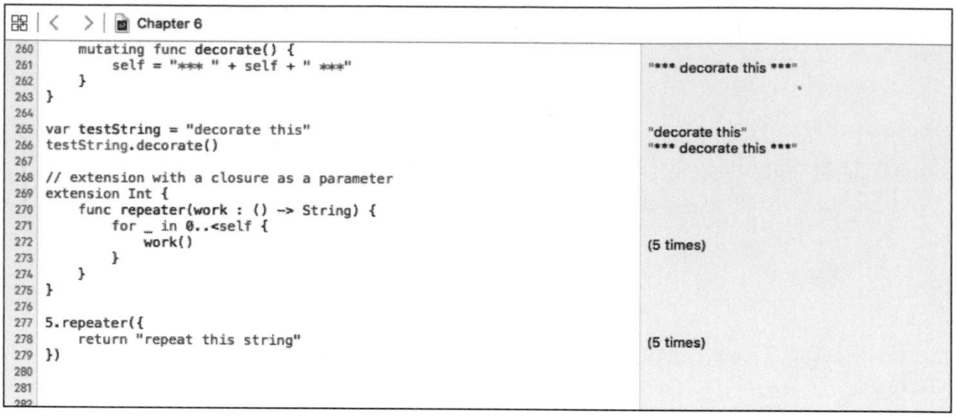

FIGURE 6.11 Using a closure in an extension

```
260    mutating func decorate() {
261        self = "*** " + self + " ***"          "*** decorate this ***"
262    }
263 }
264
265 var testString = "decorate this"                "decorate this"
266 testString.decorate()                           "*** decorate this ***"
267
268 // extension with a closure as a parameter
269 extension Int {
270    func repeater(work : () -> String) {
271        for _ in 0..<self {
272            work()
273        }                                        (5 times)
274    }
275 }
276
277 5.repeater({
278    return "repeat this string"
279 })                                              (5 times)
280
281
282
```

USING CLOSURES IN EXTENSIONS

Closures are blocks of code that can be passed around just like variables in Swift. You can pass a closure as a parameter to an extension on the Int type to make a useful repeating feature. Type the following code starting on line 268 (**Figure 6.11**):

```
// extension with a closure as a parameter
extension Int {
    func repeater(work : () -> String) {
        for _ in 0..<self {
            work()
        }
    }
}


5.repeater({
    return "repeat this string"
})
```

Line 269 shows that this is clearly an extension on the Int type. For repeatable tasks, an integer is the right type choice (a Double wouldn't work well since you cannot repeat something 3.153 times, for example).

In line 270, you're using a function named repeater to extend Int, but the parameter is interesting:

```
work: () - > String
```

This is the simplest form of a closure declaration, a block of code that takes nothing as a parameter and returns a String as a result. The name of the parameter is work.

```
260     mutating func decorate() {            "*** decorate this ***"
261         self = "*** " + self + " ***"
262     }
263 }
264
265 var testString = "decorate this"          "decorate this"
266 testString.decorate()                     "*** decorate this ***"
267
268 // extension with a closure as a parameter
269 extension Int {
270     func repeater(work : () -> String) {
271         for _ in 0..<self {
272             work()                        (5 times)
273         }
274     }
275 }
276
277 5.repeater({
278     return "repeat this string"           (5 times)              ◉◉

            repeat this string


279 })
280
```

FIGURE 6.12 Clicking the circle shows the Timeline pane in your playground

In lines 271 through 273, a simple for-in loop iterates over the closure, which is called the number of times equal to the value of self. What may be new to you is the underscore (_) in the place where you might expect a variable. This is a great feature of the Swift language; essentially, it's a "don't care" symbol that tells Swift to disregard any use of a variable. In this case, you don't need to use a variable to iterate through the loop, because the loop variable is not used anywhere in the for-in loop.

The code on lines 277 through 279 uses the repeater method on the integer literal 5. The "repeat this string" string is returned from the passed closure.

Remember, to view the results, click the round circle next to the output in the Results sidebar and then click the multiline icon (**Figure 6.12**).

SUMMARY

It's been another whirlwind chapter, hasn't it? You've taken in a lot, so feel free to go back and review all the code examples. And of course take some time to experiment with your playground file to get a good grounding on the concepts.

Now is also a good time for a break as you leave this section and start the next one. Although you still have more features of the Swift language to cover, next you'll start learning how to write an app or two. Delving into writing a full-fledged program is a great way to learn Swift. And there's no better way to start than by learning the ins and outs of Xcode, Apple's incredible development environment.

SECTION II

Developing with Swift

Welcome to the second half of the book! Over the last six chapters, you spent time learning important aspects of the Swift language. Even though you didn't explore every aspect of the language, you did cover the basics as well as some of Swift's intermediate features. Now it's time for you to begin to build upon your newly gained knowledge.

Since you've made it this far, you should now consider yourself a graduate of sorts—no more playgrounds or simple examples for you in the next few chapters. You're moving on to full-fledged development and debugging of Swift applications using Xcode.

- Chapter 7, Working with Xcode
- Chapter 8, Making a Better App
- Chapter 9, Going Mobile with Swift
- Chapter 10, Becoming an Expert
- Chapter 11, Heading Downhill

CHAPTER 7

Working with Xcode

As Apple's hallmark software development platform for Mac and iOS app creation, Xcode is the tool that virtually every Swift developer needs to know and use in order to make the most of the language. Up to now, you have had very light interaction with Xcode—specifically when creating your playgrounds. But Xcode is so much more, as you'll soon learn. It can do a lot to help you hone your Swift skills and make the best apps possible.

Xcode is an *integrated development environment* (IDE). Essentially, it's a system of integrated components that make writing, debugging, and testing software easier. The major components of any modern IDE are:

- Compiler—Turns your human-readable source code into processor-specific executable code that can run on your computer
- Debugger—Helps you find problems in your code when things aren't working correctly
- Editor—Lets you edit your code
- Project manager—Helps you organize your software project's tens (or even hundreds) of files
- Test subsystem—Facilitates testing (an always-important aspect of software development)
- Profiling and analyzing tools—Helps you inspect your code while it's running to determine how well it performs, uses resources, and so on

Xcode contains all these components and more. We'll touch on most of these throughout the remainder of the book. But first a little history lesson.

XCODE'S PEDIGREE

At the time of this writing, Xcode is in its seventh major release. That's quite an achievement for a single IDE. Because it is an Apple product, Xcode has exclusively focused on building software for Apple products. It uses the Objective-C programming language, as well as C and C++.

Xcode 1.0 was released in the fall of 2003. Based on Apple's earlier IDE, Project Builder, Xcode 1.0 was Apple's foray into a single development platform that would become the basis for its growing line of Macintosh computers.

It wasn't until Xcode 3.1 that support for iPhone OS (now iOS) came into being. By that time, additional debugging and inspection tools were made available, embodied in a powerful application known as Instruments. It was also the version that heralded a powerful compiler technology that is ubiquitous in Xcode today: the LLVM compiler system.

Xcode 6 introduced support for Apple's new Swift language alongside Objective-C. Now with Xcode 7, Swift continues to evolve, and you can expect Apple to continue to develop and enhance both the language and the development tools for some time.

CREATING YOUR FIRST SWIFT PROJECT

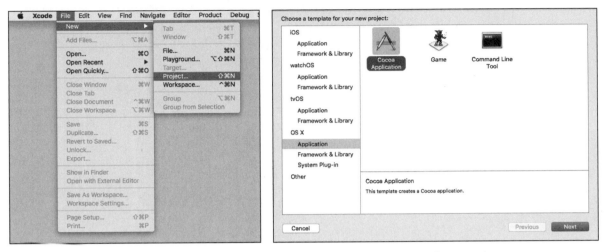

FIGURE 7.1 Xcode 7's File menu

FIGURE 7.2 Select a new project template in Xcode.

Let's start by taking a tour of Xcode. If you haven't already launched Xcode 7, do so now. Choose File > New > Project, as shown in **Figure 7.1**.

Previously, you used the Playground menu item to create a new playground. This time, you're creating a new project.

What is an Xcode project? It's a file package that contains references to all the code source files and resources that make up an application. The project file essentially manages all these files for you and makes certain that the Swift compiler does the right thing with them.

When you choose the Project menu item, a new Xcode window appears along with a drop-down sheet. Here you are prompted to select a project template (**Figure 7.2**).

Two major groups are available for project creation: iOS and OS X. If you are writing an iOS app, you would normally select an item from the first group.

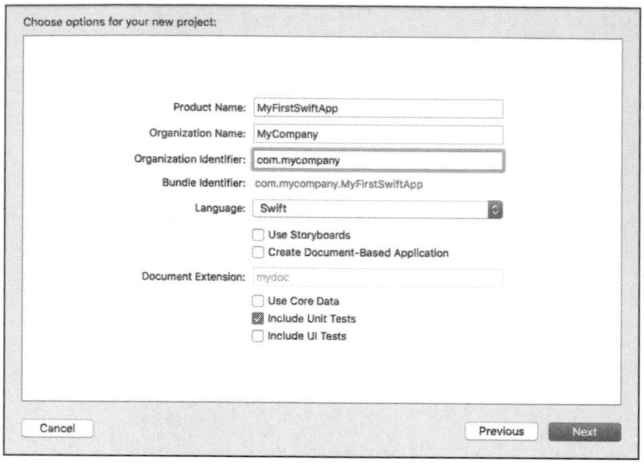

FIGURE 7.3 Options for the new project

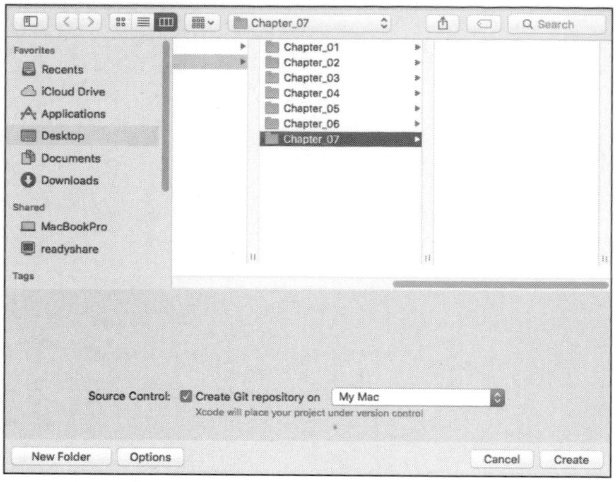

FIGURE 7.4 The project save dialog. Navigate to a location on your Mac in which to save the project.

Choose OS X as the project template. Specifically, select the Application item, select Cocoa Application in the template chooser, and then click Next. In the dialog that appears, you can set the project's options (**Figure 7.3**).

If your organization name is different than what appears in Figure 7.3, you can simply ignore it for now. More importantly, ensure that Product Name is set to MyFirstSwiftApp and that Language is set to Swift and not Objective-C. You can leave the remaining options selected as they appear in Figure 7.3. Click Next.

Another dialog appears, prompting you to save the project. **Figure 7.4** shows where your project will be saved. You can choose any convenient location. Feel free to leave the Create Git Repository option selected (if it is already); however, we won't be worrying about source control. Once you have selected a place to save the project, click Create.

Congratulations! You've taken your first step toward creating your first Swift app on your Mac.

DIVING DOWN

Now that you've created your project, you're ready to dive into the details. The project window may seem daunting and intimidating at first. Don't worry. I'll show you the ins and outs of this window and how you can use it to manage your Swift development.

The project window is composed of five major areas, four of which you see now:

■ The **toolbar**, which runs along the top, is where you can quickly see the name of your project file and obtain the status of any compilations or other work going on in Xcode.

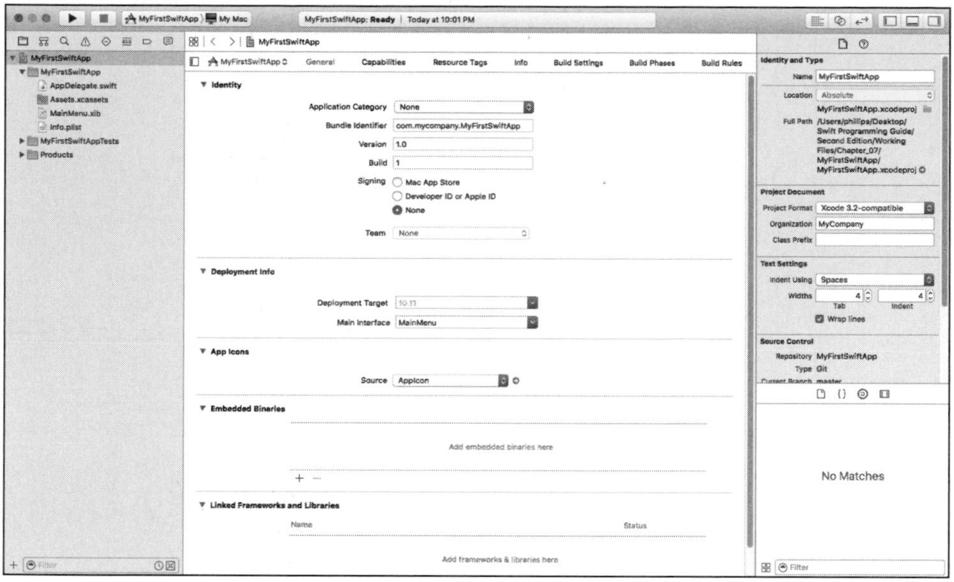

FIGURE 7.5 Setting up the target

- The **navigator area** falls along the left side of the window. It arranges all the files in your project in a hierarchical fashion, allowing you to organize and browse according to your liking. You'll refer to the navigator area quite a bit when working with your project.

- On the right side of the project window is the **utilities area**. This area is automatically populated with information about the currently selected file in the navigator area. It's also a place where you can set information about various resources that compose your application.

- The **debug area** rests at the bottom of the project window. It is currently hidden from your view, but we'll look at it soon. As you might expect, this is where you interact with the debugger to fix issues in your code.

- The **editor area** is where you will spend most of your time interacting with Xcode. You'll edit your source code in this area. It is also the largest and centermost area of the project window, allowing you to focus on your code.

At the moment, the editor area doesn't contain source code, but instead shows the general panel related to your application. You can ignore many of these settings for the purposes of learning Swift, but you should understand the correlation between the navigator area and this panel.

In the navigator area, the topmost selected item is the name of your project. When this is selected, the editor area shows the content shown in **Figure 7.5**. A subpane of the editor area shows your project, MyFirstSwiftApp, as well as two targets. A *target* in Xcode is a destination of sorts. It's an entity that is expected to be "built" or "made." Your application, MyFirstSwiftApp, is a target and is currently selected. A second target, in our case MyFirstSwiftAppTests, is automatically created for an application project such as this. It allows you to write tests that help fortify and strengthen your code.

FIGURE 7.6 Selecting the AppDelegate.swift source file from the navigator area

FIGURE 7.7 The AppDelegate.swift code in the editor area

INTERACTING WITH THE PROJECT WINDOW

Go to the navigator area on the left side of the window (Figure 7.5), and locate the file named AppDelegate.swift. Xcode expects all Swift source files to have the *.swift* extension, so this should become familiar to you over time.

In the navigator area, single-click the AppDelegate.swift source file (**Figure 7.6**). Doing so will show the code in **Figure 7.7**.

The code in Figure 7.7 should look somewhat familiar to you. It has comments on lines 1 through 7 and a class definition starting at line 12. The rest looks strange and new. Not to worry; I'll explain it to you shortly.

What you are looking at is the entry point to a Mac OS X application written in Swift—specifically, the method applicationDidFinishLaunching, which is a member function of the AppDelegate class. This is the first method in your code that will be called after the application has started up.

The comment in the method directs you to insert code to initialize your application. A second method, applicationWillTerminate, is called when the application is terminating.

Both of these methods are wrapped in the AppDelegate class, which is the class that OS X applications are expected to implement (and indeed, this class is automatically created for you).

Also note that the editor area provides visual clues about your source code: Comments are colored in green, and Swift keywords are in blue. This coloring gives you immediate, at-a-glance cues as to how your source code is composed. The colors are actually configurable by going to the Xcode > Preferences menu and selecting the Fonts & Colors toolbar button. (I'll leave that as an exercise for you to play with.)

For clarity, let's review the code in the AppDelegate.swift file line by line.

The comments in lines 1 through 7 indicate the vintage of the file as well as the author and company to whom it belongs.

Line 9 shows the import statement:

```
import Cocoa
```

The import keyword tells the Swift compiler to import other software components into your project. In this case, that component is Cocoa. Cocoa is the name of Apple's vast framework of classes that make up the OS X experience. You'll be learning a bit about these frameworks throughout the remainder of the book.

Line 11 is a special attribute type that tells the Swift compiler to generate code specifically for starting the application. You can safely ignore it.

Line 12 is a now-familiar class definition. Named AppDelegate, it inherits from a base class named NSObject. This is a historical class that has its roots in Objective-C. This is followed by NSApplicationDelegate, which is a protocol.

```
class AppDelegate: NSObject, NSApplicationDelegate {
```

Line 14 should look somewhat familiar. It's a declaration for a variable named window of type NSWindow. The strange-looking preface, @IBOutlet weak, is a special attribute that identifies this variable as an outlet to a UI element (you'll see this a bit later). The exclamation mark following the type NSWindow is a special character related to optionals (remember that those were discussed in the beginning of the book). I'll get into the actual meaning of the ! operator later. For now, just ignore it.

```
@IBOutlet weak var window: NSWindow!
```

Lines 17 through 23 are the member methods of the AppDelegate class defined by the Cocoa framework. In both cases, the methods are passed the following parameter:

```
aNotification: NSNotification
```

Notifications are special objects used to pass information between classes in Cocoa; a notification is an instantiated object of the NSNotification class passed into both methods when they are called. As you become more familiar with programming in Swift in environments such as iOS and Mac OS X, you will see notifications in a lot of places. They are part of a larger design philosophy that allows your application to be aware of object life cycles and other events.

That completes the tour of the AppDelegate.swift source file. It's short, sweet, and automatically generated by Xcode when it creates an app. Think of it as a boilerplate, or template, for you to start your project with.

FIGURE 7.8
The window of your
first Swift application

IT'S ALIVE!

You may find it difficult to believe, but even with this minimal source file, you actually have a runnable application. This is one of Xcode's many great features: You can get off the ground running with minimal effort. To convince you of just how neat this is, choose Product > Run to start the compilation process. In short order, you'll see a window like the one in **Figure 7.8**.

You've just run your first Swift app! The window appears with the name of the app, MyFirstSwiftApp, advertised in the window title bar. It's something to show for your minimal work, but as a blank window, it's not that impressive. That's because you haven't done anything to the project yet, but you'll get to that soon enough.

As a running app, MyFirstSwiftApp takes a prominent position in your Dock with a rather generic icon. You can also move the window around and resize it by dragging its lower-right corner. That's a lot of functionality you get "for free."

This is cool, but it's ultimately a means to an end—you want to build something useful. After all, that's what learning Swift is all about.

Next you'll make some alterations, so quit the new app by pressing Command-Q (be sure the app has window focus so that the keystroke is sent to MyFirstSwiftApp).

PIQUING YOUR INTEREST

An empty window isn't something that gets you excited, but what can you put there? That depends on what you want to build.

An earlier chapter touched on interest rate calculations. The idea worked OK in the REPL, but the user interface wasn't the best. Who wants to type code to get the answer when they can point and click?

A simple interest calculator is a perfect fit for your first real Swift app, and the user interface should be simple to craft. I'll do a quick inventory of the user interface elements you need to make this app work; but first, the core problem you're trying to solve is computing simple interest on a loan.

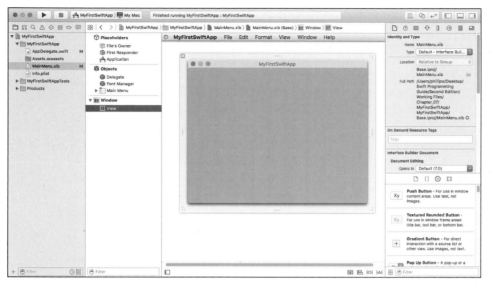

FIGURE 7.9 Selecting `MainMenu.xib` from the navigator area

To do that, you need to think about the inputs (what the user will type in) and the outputs (what the calculation will yield).

- Inputs—Simple interest requires three inputs: a loan amount, a period of time (or term), and an interest rate.

- Outputs The result of the calculation is a single output: the total amount of the loan over the term at the given interest rate.

If you take a quick inventory of how the user interface (or UI, as I'll call it from now on) looks, you'll need three input fields and an output field. You'll also need a button the user can click to perform the calculation.

Now that you know what you need, you can start building. Before you get to that, however, now is a good time to address the screen real-estate issue of Xcode.

MAKING ROOM

Xcode gives you all the tools you need to create your user interface; in fact, it already created the window for you, as you saw when you ran the app. That window is hiding in a file named `MainMenu.xib`. Locate that file in the navigator area (it's under the group folder named MyFirstSwiftApp), and click it.

The editor area changes to look something like **Figure 7.9**.

The AppDelegate.swift code goes away, and the editor area's contents change to an inner pane and what looks like a partial window. Just above the window is the menu bar for the app. By clicking the `MainMenu.xib` file, the editor area changed to accommodate the view of the window. The editor area is context sensitive, showing the content you want to edit.

FIGURE 7.10 Xcode allows you to collapse areas (A) and use the entire screen (B) to maximize your workspace.

FIGURE 7.11 The Push Button UI element

FIGURE 7.12 The window with the Push Button UI element placed

If you're working on a Mac with a smaller screen, you may not be able to see the entire editor area. To help maximize your screen real estate while working with large content, Xcode gives you some options.

In the upper-right corner of the Xcode window are three buttons (identified as A in **Figure 7.10**) you can click to reclaim areas of the Xcode window. These buttons expand or collapse various areas of the Xcode window. Be aware that the area you collapse might be needed for subsequent work, so use these carefully. Of course, you can click the icon again to bring the areas back if you need to.

You can also click the green button on the top left of the window (identified as B in Figure 7.10) to put Xcode into full-screen mode and utilize the entire area of your monitor.

Whichever method you choose, have the entire window visible in the Xcode editor area and ensure that the utilities area on the right of the Xcode window is still visible—you will need access to it shortly.

BUILDING THE UI

Now the fun begins! You can start building your application's window with the appropriate UI elements. Start by looking at the lower-right corner of the Xcode window (the utilities area). There you'll see a table of UI elements you can scroll through. This is the "palette" of goodies you can use in your apps.

BUTTON UP!

Let's start with the Push Button element (**Figure 7.11**). Locate it, and drag it onto the window in the editor area.

When dragging the button in the area inside the app window, Xcode places helpful perforated guidelines indicating when the button is centered in the window, as well as appropriate edge boundaries that conform to Apple's user interface guidelines. Don't worry about being too exact with placement—just position the button in the bottom of your app window (**Figure 7.12**).

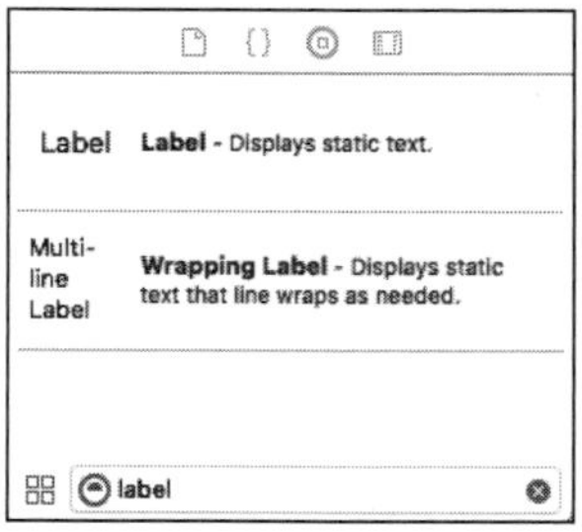

FIGURE 7.13 Using the search field to locate a specific UI element (in this case, "Label")

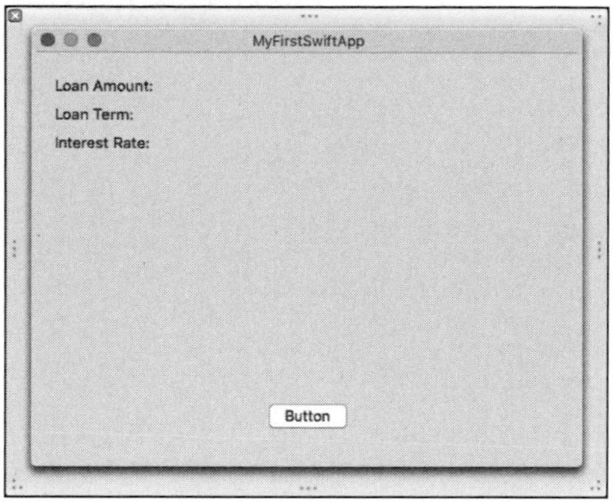

FIGURE 7.14 The window populated with the labels

LABELS, LABELS, LABELS

Labels are special noneditable text fields used to hold textual information. In this app, they will guide the user to type specific information in editable text fields.

To find the Label UI element, you can scroll through the element library in the utilities area until you find "Label," but a quicker way is to use the search field. Doing so gets you right to that element (**Figure 7.13**).

Two types of labels are available: single-line and multi-line (also known as a wrapping label). The latter is convenient if you need labels to span multiple lines for larger descriptions. For this app, a single-line label is all that's needed.

Drag the label from the utilities area into the window in the editor area. Notice the placement in **Figure 7.14**. Again, don't worry about getting it exactly right; just place it in the general area. Double-click the "Label" text to highlight it, and type the following to replace the text:

Loan Amount:

The label field's width automatically expands to accommodate the additional text.

Drag two more labels to the window, and position them underneath the first label. Again, refer to Figure 7.14 for general placement, and be sure to use Xcode's perforated guides to line things up. Give the additional two labels the following text:

Loan Term:

Interest Rate:

Next we'll bring the editable text fields into view.

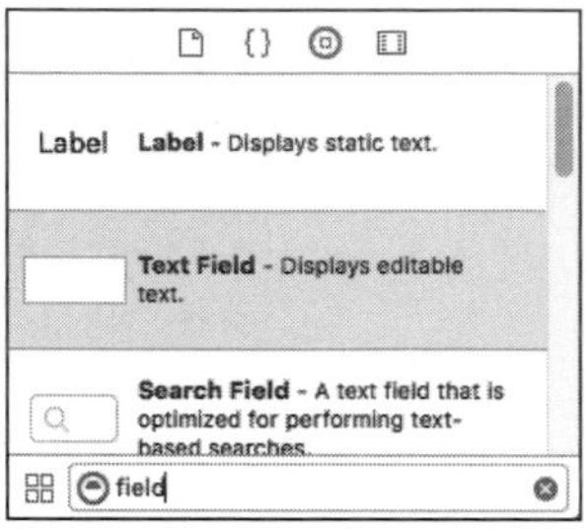

FIGURE 7.15 The text field in the UI element library

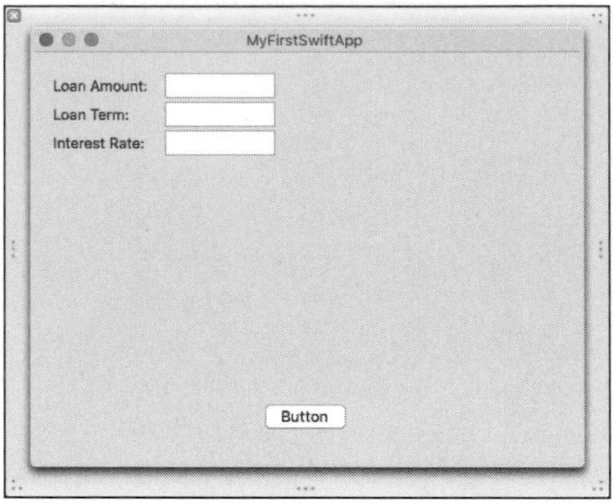

FIGURE 7.16 The window now has a button, three labels, and three text fields.

INPUT'S THE KEY

By now you should be getting the rhythm of the UI element library: Find the appropriate type of control in the list and drag it to the window. This is part of the process of building a user interface. There's one more set of elements to bring into the window: text fields.

A text field is similar to a label, but it is editable. Text fields are where your user interacts with the app. In this case, you need three, corresponding to the three labels you just created.

Using the search field below the UI element library, search for "field" (**Figure 7.15**). Once you've located the element, drag it into the window, aligning the text field to the right of the label. Repeat the process twice more, aligning the text field with the labels as in **Figure 7.16**.

Note that the text fields are "taller" than their companion labels. As you place them on the window and move them around, Xcode will use layout guides to suggest a proper vertical spacing. This is a convenient feature, and you should position the labels' vertical spacing so they line up horizontally with their corresponding text field.

TIDYING UP

You are almost finished with the user interface and will soon move on to the fun stuff—coding the logic in Swift. However, you have a few more things to do before moving on to the next phase.

RENAME THE BUTTON TITLE

The name of the button is "Button," which obviously isn't intuitive. Double-click the button, and rename it **Calculate**.

ADD A RESULT LABEL

The app needs to communicate the result of the calculation, and this is best done using a label. Drag a Label object from the UI element library over to the window, and insert it between the Interest Rate text field and the button. Double-click this label, and set its name to **RESULT**.

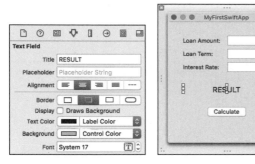

FIGURE 7.17 The Attributes inspector pane

FIGURE 7.18 The app's window is complete and ready to go.

To make the label stand out, click the Attributes inspector icon in the utilities area, and change the Font setting from System Regular to System 17 to increase its size (**Figure 7.17**). Also, click the second icon from the left in the Alignment set so that the label is centered in the text field. Use the mouse cursor to expand the width of the label to accommodate the text better if need be.

OPTIMIZE THE WINDOW SIZE

The default window size is a little large for our app. Take this opportunity to reposition the UI elements so that the real estate is better utilized. Then click the lower-right corner of the window and drag inward until an optimal size is reached. **Figure 7.18** shows the desired result. Again, don't worry about getting your window exactly right—just go through the exercise to understand the process.

TAKE IT FOR A QUICK SPIN

Now that the window is set up properly, choose Product > Run to run the application. You should be able to interact with the three text fields and click the Calculate button. Of course, nothing of interest happens, because there's Swift code to write! That's coming next.

CLASS TIME

Recall that in Chapter 5, Swift's class concept was introduced. The idea behind the class is to create reusable models of real-world and even abstract concepts. It also helps organize your code logically. A huge benefit is that a Swift class can be easily added into one or more of your projects, providing you with instant functionality.

Creating a Swift class to handle interest calculations is a good approach here. So how do you do this? Up to now, you've used a playground to write your class code. Here, playgrounds aren't applicable. Instead, you must create a class file.

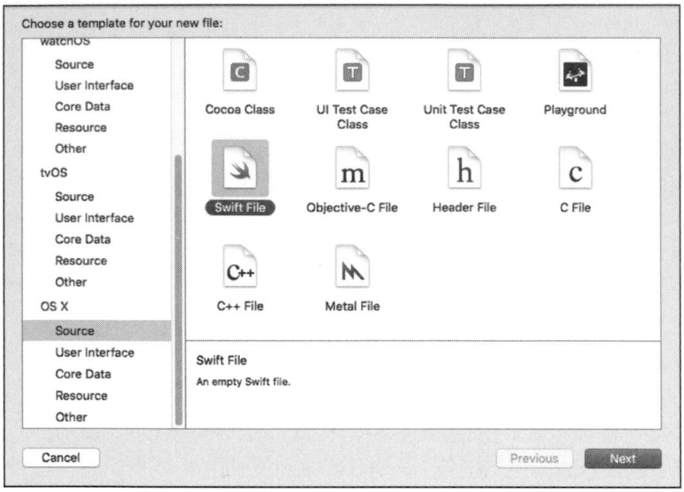

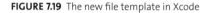

FIGURE 7.19 The new file template in Xcode

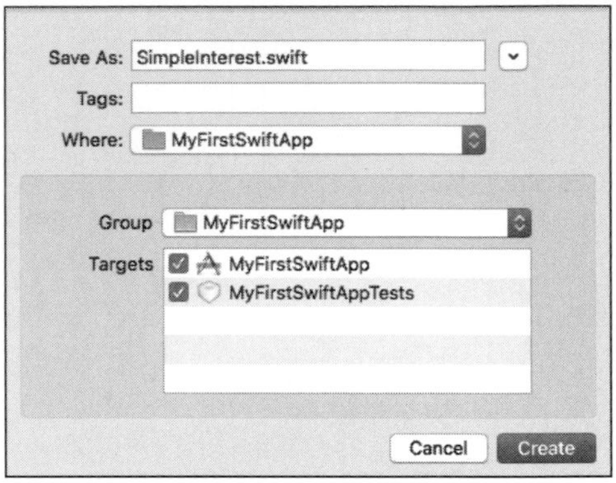

FIGURE 7.20 The file creation dialog

Choose File > New > File. The new file template dialog appears (**Figure 7.19**).

Here you have the opportunity to create many different file types. The file types are grouped by platform (for example, iOS and OS X). Since this is an OS X app and you're creating a Swift class, select the Source option on the left, click Swift File on the right, and click Next. You'll be prompted to save the newly created file via the file save dialog in **Figure 7.20**. Name the file **SimpleInterest.swift**.

You can select which targets the file will be associated with. `MyFirstSwiftApp` is already selected; go ahead and select the `MyFirstSwiftAppTests` target as well.

Xcode creates the file and gives it the extension .swift. It also adds the file in the navigator area. The editor area is updated to show the contents of the file, which contains a set of comments and an `import` statement. Below that line is where you can start building your class.

You wrote a simple interest calculation closure in Chapter 4. For this new class, `SimpleInterest`, you'll promote that to a method. Type in the following lines of code at the end of the newly created class file:

```
class SimpleInterest {
    func calculate(loanAmount : Double, var interestRate :
    → Double, years : Int) -> Double {
        interestRate = interestRate / 100.0
        let interest = Double(years) * interestRate * loanAmount

        return loanAmount + interest
    }
}
```

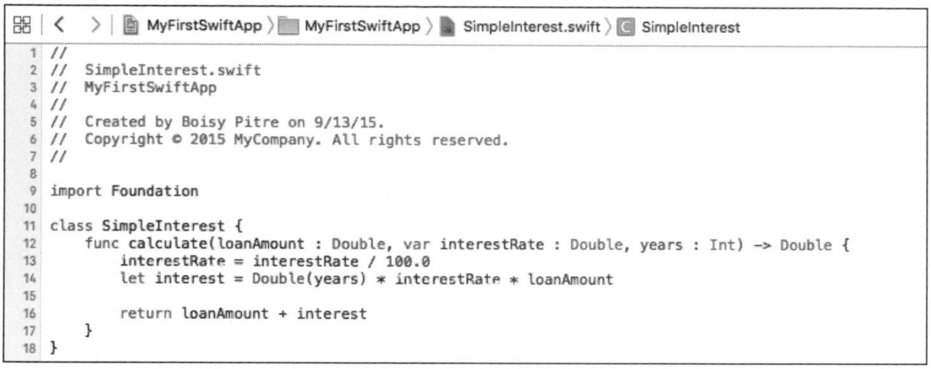

FIGURE 7.21

The SimpleInterest
class as it appears in
the editor

```
     MyFirstSwiftApp  >  MyFirstSwiftApp  >  SimpleInterest.swift  >  C SimpleInterest
1  //
2  //  SimpleInterest.swift
3  //  MyFirstSwiftApp
4  //
5  //  Created by Boisy Pitre on 9/13/15.
6  //  Copyright © 2015 MyCompany. All rights reserved.
7  //
8
9  import Foundation
10
11 class SimpleInterest {
12     func calculate(loanAmount : Double, var interestRate : Double, years : Int) -> Double {
13         interestRate = interestRate / 100.0
14         let interest = Double(years) * interestRate * loanAmount
15
16         return loanAmount + interest
17     }
18 }
```

This should look familiar to you: a method that takes a loan amount, an interest rate, and a term (in years), and returns the value of the loan after the term (**Figure 7.21**).

Now turn your attention to the AppDelegate.swift file by clicking its name in the navigator area. Just below line 9 (the import Cocoa statement), replace subsequent lines with the following code:

```
@NSApplicationMain
class AppDelegate: NSObject, NSApplicationDelegate {

    @IBOutlet weak var window : NSWindow!

    @IBOutlet weak var loanAmountField : NSTextField!
    @IBOutlet weak var interestRateField : NSTextField!
    @IBOutlet weak var yearsField : NSTextField!
    @IBOutlet weak var resultsField : NSTextField!

    var simpleInterestCalculator : SimpleInterest = SimpleInterest()

    func applicationDidFinishLaunching(aNotification: NSNotification) {
        // Insert code here to initialize your application
    }

    func applicationWillTerminate(aNotification: NSNotification) {
        // Insert code here to tear down your application
    }

    @IBAction func buttonClicked(sender : NSButton) {
        var result : Double
```

FIGURE 7.22 The code as it appears in the editor area of Xcode

```
      ⊞  <  >  │  📄 MyFirstSwiftApp  ▶  📁 MyFirstSwiftApp  ▶  📄 AppDelegate.swift  ▶  Ⓒ AppDelegate
  1   //
  2   //  AppDelegate.swift
  3   //  MyFirstSwiftApp
  4   //
  5   //  Created by Boisy Pitre on 9/12/15.
  6   //  Copyright © 2015 MyCompany. All rights reserved.
  7   //
  8
  9   import Cocoa
 10
 11   @NSApplicationMain
 12   class AppDelegate: NSObject, NSApplicationDelegate {
 13
 14       @IBOutlet weak var window : NSWindow!
 15
 16       @IBOutlet weak var loanAmountField : NSTextField!
 17       @IBOutlet weak var interestRateField : NSTextField!
 18       @IBOutlet weak var yearsField : NSTextField!
 19       @IBOutlet weak var resultsField : NSTextField!
 20
 21       var simpleInterestCalculator : SimpleInterest = SimpleInterest()
 22
 23       func applicationDidFinishLaunching(aNotification: NSNotification) {
 24           // Insert code here to initialize your application
 25       }
 26
 27       func applicationWillTerminate(aNotification: NSNotification) {
 28           // Insert code here to tear down your application
 29       }
 30
 31       @IBAction func buttonClicked(sender : NSButton) {
 32           var result : Double
 33
 34           result = simpleInterestCalculator.calculate(loanAmountField.doubleValue,
 35               interestRate: interestRateField.doubleValue, years:yearsField.integerValue)
 36           self.resultsField.stringValue = result.description
 37       }
 38   }
```

```
result = simpleInterestCalculator.calculate
   →  (loanAmountField.doubleValue, interestRate:
   →  interestRateField.doubleValue, years:yearsField.integerValue)

   self.resultsField.stringValue = result.description
   }
}
```

Let's go through the code line by line, referring to the line numbers in **Figure 7.22**.

I discussed lines 9 through 14 earlier, but I deferred the discussion of the exclamation mark (!) at the end of line 14. Now four additional variables, declared on lines 16 through 19, also have the exclamation mark appended.

So what is this exclamation mark? It is known as an *implicitly unwrapped optional* and is used when, among other things, you are declaring a variable. So what's an implicitly unwrapped optional?

Remember that I discussed optionals in Chapter 1. An optional is a special type that indicates that a variable can either hold a value or be nil. Accessing a variable whose value is nil is not something the Swift runtime is fond of, so as a Swift programmer, you must always be cognizant of your variables' values, especially when they *could* be nil.

Declaring a variable as an implicitly unwrapped optional is effectively telling the Swift compiler that you are promising that this variable will never be accessed when its value is nil. It is a contract you are making with the compiler, and you are obliged to keep it. If you don't, and the variable is accessed while nil, a runtime error will occur and your app will stop.

I have more to talk about regarding optionals, especially the idea of *unwrapping* them, but I'll save that for a little later. For now, let's continue stepping through the code.

Still looking at lines 16 through 19, these variables are marked with @IBOutlet. This special keyword is an advertisement to the compiler that the variables are *outlets* to actual user interface elements. You'll notice that the names of these four variables correspond to the text fields and labels you created earlier on the window. You'll "hook these up" in just a bit.

On line 21 is a variable declaration for an object named simpleInterestCalculator of type SimpleInterest. This, of course, is the SimpleInterest class you created a short while ago. The object is instantiated right there on the line so that it's ready to use.

You may be surprised that the two methods on lines 23 and 27 haven't changed— they're still empty. It's not a problem, because the code on lines 31 through 37 is where everything happens.

The *action method*, buttonClicked, is a special method that is called when the user interacts with a UI element. Recall that you created a Calculate button on the window— this is the method that will be called when that button is clicked.

Action methods are prefaced with the @IBAction keyword, which is a big hint to you and the Swift compiler.

The method takes as a parameter the sender, or caller. This is a reference to the NSButton object that is clicked. Even though you don't reference that parameter in this method, you still need to have it present in the parameter list.

This method also doesn't have a return type, implying that it returns nothing.

What it does do is declare a Double variable named result and assign it to the return of the simpleInterestCalculator object's calculate method, passing in three parameters: loanAmountField.doubleValue, interestRateField.doubleValue, and yearsField.integerValue.

These three parameters reference the NSTextField objects you created earlier on the window. Since the contents of these text fields will return strings, you use the doubleValue and integerValue methods on them to provide numeric types that are necessary to do the math in the SimpleInterest class.

The result of the calculation is a Double, but it must be converted to a String to be assigned to the resultsField:

```
self.resultsField.stringValue = result.description
```

The description method is a special method available on a Swift class. It allows that class to return a String representation of its data. Here, the Double variable result is returning the String representation of its number, the result of the simple interest calculation. The resulting string is assigned to the contents of the results field.

Run the app by choosing Product > Run, and type in some values in each of the fields. Click the Calculate button. Did anything happen? Did you get a result?

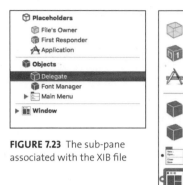

FIGURE 7.23 The sub-pane associated with the XIB file

FIGURE 7.24 Click the Document Outline button to hide or show more detail about the interface.

FIGURE 7.25 The connection dialog prior to connections being made

HOOKING IT UP

Clicking the Calculate button ended up in disappointment—nothing happened. That's because you still have some work to do.

The `@IBOutlet` and `@IBAction` tags are cues both to the compiler and to you, the developer. When you see these tags in the editor area, you'll also notice a small circle just to the left of the corresponding line number. That hollow circle indicates whether your outlets and actions are *connected*.

Connecting your outlets and actions to the user interface is a critical step in making the app complete and working. It's what ties the user interface to the code you write. Without these connections, the user interface doesn't have the "backing" it needs to perform the work.

You can hook up outlets and actions in several ways in Xcode. Here's one way you'll use: In the navigator area, click the `MainMenu.xib` file. The editor area shows the window with the fields you assembled earlier. To the left of the window is a sub-pane showing several sections: Placeholders, Objects, and Window. Select the object named Delegate (**Figure 7.23**). Note that you may have to click the icon highlighted in **Figure 7.24** to show the document outline area in full.

The Delegate object here is an instantiated reference to the source code in AppDelegate.swift that you just reviewed. Inside the XIB file is a stored, serialized instance of this object that will be automatically created and instantiated by the runtime environment when the app is launched. Because of this, all of this object's outlets and actions are available for connecting to the UI.

Right-click Delegate. A HUD window (known as a heads-up display window because of its transparent property) appears (**Figure 7.25**). You can see the list of outlets and actions for the app delegate. Two are already connected: `window` (which connects to the window object) and `delegate`. You need to connect the rest:

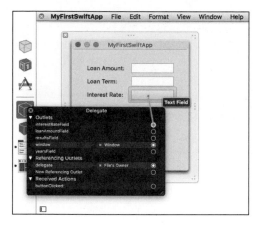

FIGURE 7.26 The act of connecting an outlet to its corresponding UI element

FIGURE 7.27 Your first Swift app running correctly!

- `interestRateField`—Outlet to the Interest Rate text field
- `loanAmountField`—Outlet to the Loan Amount text field
- `yearsField`—Outlet to the Loan Term text field
- `resultsField`—Outlet to the Result text field
- `buttonClicked`—Action to the Calculate button

Click the circle on the right of the HUD window for each outlet and action, and begin dragging. A line appears. Drag the line to the Calculate button UI element on the window, and the connection will be made (**Figure 7.26**).

Once all four outlets and the actions have been connected, rerun the app. This time, input the values in **Figure 7.27**, and click the Calculate button. If everything is hooked up correctly, you'll see the result field change to 13125.0, or $13,125. If you don't get the correct answer, or you get no answer at all, double-check that you have made the proper outlet and action connections.

YOU MADE AN APP!

Sure it's simple, but it works. You wrote your very own Swift app. And it was easy. As you saw, Xcode's environment made it a cinch to create the basic skeleton of the app. All you needed to do was add some UI elements, write code to perform actions, capture values from those elements, and connect the code and the elements. That's the basic idea behind any application.

There's still more Swift to learn, and more that can be done with your new app. You'll do that, and more, in the next chapter.

Making a Better App

You may have heard the saying "The last 20 percent of a task takes 80 percent of the effort." That axiom certainly rings true for software development. Oftentimes as a developer, you'll expend most of your energy on getting the final touches of your application just right. It's what makes the difference between a good app and a great app.

IT'S THE LITTLE THINGS

The simple interest calculator you began working on in the last chapter is an example of such a process. Although it is definitely functional, it could use some additional tender loving care. Let's dive into making this nice little app better, and at the same time, dive deeper into Swift.

SHOW ME THE MONEY

In the simple interest app, the result is not shown as a dollar amount, which is an obvious deficiency. The default representation of a Double using the description method is to show the number in plain decimal representation. This is fine in most cases, but for applications that deal with money, it's a bit bland.

How can you spice this up? One idea would be to build a string that prefaces the number with a dollar sign ($), but what about the numbers after the decimal place? Representing change in cents is customary, with two numbers following the decimal point. We'll have to think about how to do that.

Also, if the amount is greater than $999.99, adding a comma for the thousands place would be nice (for example, $11,311.33 instead of $11313.33).

Beyond that, we're only thinking in terms of U.S. dollars (assuming you're in the U.S., of course). What if this app will be used in other countries with other currencies? Their format for money can be entirely different, even using commas instead of decimal points.

As you can see, solving this problem can get out of hand fairly quickly, depending on how accurately you want to convey the visual representation of a financial amount.

You're in luck, because Cocoa provides something known as a *formatter*. A formatter is a special class that understands how to format data in a specific way. There are date formatters and number formatters, for instance, and you can even create your own formatters for reuse in your apps.

The class NSNumberFormatter is what we're interested in. It is actually a subclass of NSFormatter, which is the base class for all formatter classes. NSNumberFormatter can accommodate a handsome number of numeric formats, including currency, which is perfect for this application. Not only that, it handles formatting in a number of different localizations, so users in the United Kingdom or Spain, for example, will see the result formatted in a style customary for their locale.

How do you use this class? More importantly, how can you easily integrate it into the existing code? Recall Swift's extension language feature, which was discussed in Chapter 6. Extensions would make an excellent candidate for adding functionality to the Double type, and that's exactly what is done in **Figure 8.1**.

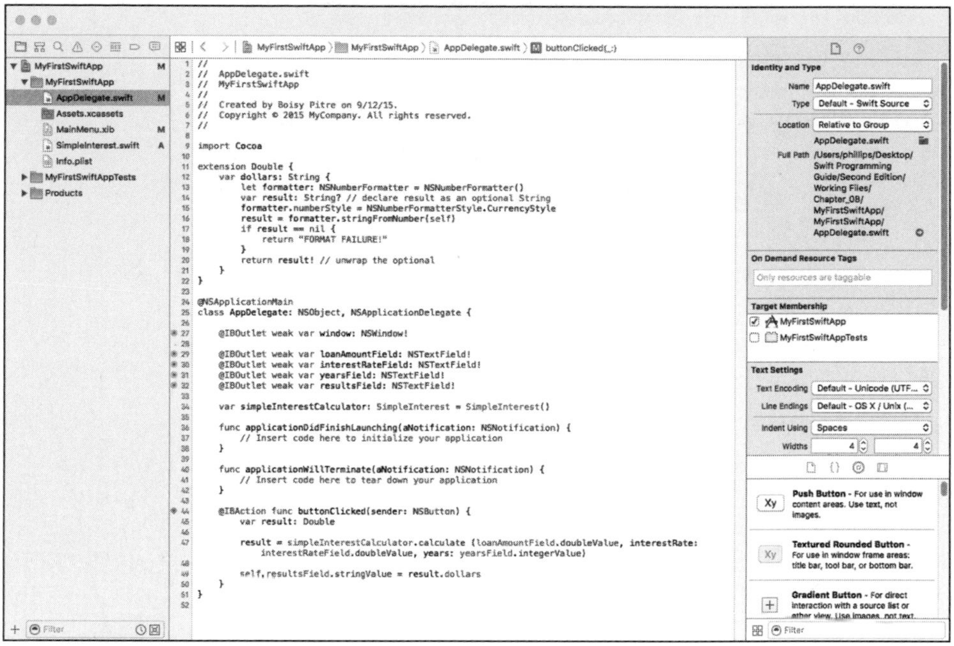

FIGURE 8.1
The Double type is extendable, just like any other Swift class.

Be sure that Xcode is running and that your MyFirstSwiftApp project is loaded, and then replace all the existing code after the line import Cocoa with the following code:

```swift
extension Double {
    var dollars: String {
        let formatter: NSNumberFormatter = NSNumberFormatter()
        var result: String? // declare result as an optional String
        formatter.numberStyle = NSNumberFormatterStyle.CurrencyStyle
        result = formatter.stringFromNumber(self)
        if result == nil {
            return "FORMAT FAILURE!"
        }
        return result! // unwrap the optional
    }
}

@NSApplicationMain
class AppDelegate: NSObject, NSApplicationDelegate {

    @IBOutlet weak var window: NSWindow!
```

```
@IBOutlet weak var loanAmountField: NSTextField!
@IBOutlet weak var interestRateField: NSTextField!
@IBOutlet weak var yearsField: NSTextField!
@IBOutlet weak var resultsField: NSTextField!

var simpleInterestCalculator: SimpleInterest = SimpleInterest()

func applicationDidFinishLaunching(aNotification: NSNotification) {
    // Insert code here to initialize your application
}

func applicationWillTerminate(aNotification: NSNotification) {
    // Insert code here to tear down your application
}

@IBAction func buttonClicked(sender: NSButton) {
    var result: Double

    result = simpleInterestCalculator.calculate
    → (loanAmountField.doubleValue, interestRate:
    → interestRateField.doubleValue, years: yearsField.integerValue)

    self.resultsField.stringValue = result.dollars
}
}
```

The extension to the Double type adds a computed property aptly named dollars, which returns a type of String and uses NSNumberFormatter. A variable of that type, named formatter, is declared, as well as a variable named result of type String? (there's that question mark again!). The formatter object has a numberStyle property, which is set to NSNumberFormatterStyle.CurrencyStyle since you want to format for currency. Finally, you call the formatter's stringFromNumber method, passing self (the value of the Double) and getting back a String that holds the formatted text. The variable result is then checked against nil, and if true, a failure message is returned, else result is returned with a conspicuous syntax:

```
return result!
```

So what's going on here? What's all of this nil checking? Enough suspense! Let's unravel these mysterious symbols that keep appearing in Swift. I'll digress for just a bit to explain this core concept of Swift. Then I'll get right back to the code.

REMEMBER THE OPTIONAL?

Optionals were covered in Chapter 2. They extend types in such a way that variables declared as optionals can either contain a reference to an object of that type, or they can contain `nil` (or a nonexistent reference).

The declaration of the `result` variable of type `String?` is your way of telling Swift that the result might contain an assignment to a legitimate string, or it might contain `nil`. In fact, as declared earlier without an assignment, `result` is automatically assigned to `nil` at that point.

That result is declared in this way because of the `NSNumberFormatter`'s `stringFromNumber` method return type. Its return type is `String?` and not just `String`. Therefore, the variable that captures the returned object must be of the same type.

You may be wondering, Why would `stringFromNumber` return an optional? Why not just return a `String` without the appended optional marker (?) and be done with it? The reason is that there may be cases where the method fails to do the conversion. One such example is looking at `NSNumberFormatter`'s converse method, `numberFromString`, which takes a `String` value and converts it to a number. Passing `"33"` or `"145"` to this method would return a numeric type, but a string with a non-numeric character such as `"3X4"` would fail—it is not a number, and as such it cannot be converted into numeric form from a `String`. In that case, `numberFromString` would return `nil`.

Methods in Swift's Cocoa classes that return an optional type are letting you know that they *may* return `nil` and that you should be aware of the possibility.

UNWRAPPING OPTIONALS

In Swift, variables of optional types come presented like a gift: in nice, shiny wrapping paper. To extract the value held in a variable of an optional type, you must "unwrap" it. The act of unwrapping converts a type into a variable whose value cannot be nil. But be careful! If the value of the variable's value is `nil`, unwrapping it will cause a runtime error. Swift does not take kindly to unwrapping an optional whose value is `nil`.

That's where the exclamation mark comes in. It's short syntax for telling Swift "Hey, unwrap this optional now!" You (the developer) need to ensure that the value of the variable is not `nil` to prevent the aforementioned runtime error.

In the previous code example, checking for the result being `nil` and returning an alternative string value is your way of handling the case where the `stringFromNumber` method *might* return `nil`.

As you go along, you'll see more examples of this safety checking. It's all part of Swift's emphasis on safe coding.

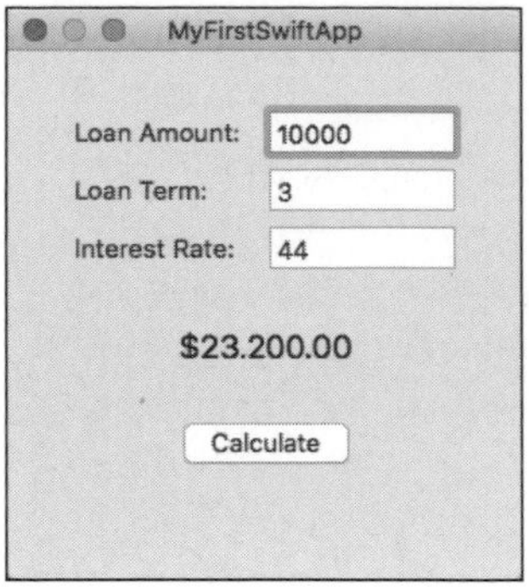

FIGURE 8.2
The NSNumberFormatter
showing the currency
format

LOOKING BETTER

The final change in the example code is the addition of the computed property reference
on this line:

```
self.resultsField.stringValue = result.dollars
```

Adding this invokes the computed property created in the extension on the Double type,
completing the feature addition in the application.

To see the code in action, tell Xcode to run the application via the Product > Run menu.
Figure 8.2 shows the application running with the new code in place and the result shown
formatted for the U.S. currency locale (your formatting may be different depending on your
locale settings).

FORMATTING: A DIFFERENT TECHNIQUE

While the result looks great, you still have two text fields that could use some face-lifting
too: the loan amount and interest rate.

Like the result field, the loan amount is a monetary figure, and you should represent
the contents of that field as such. The same goes for the Interest Rate field. Having the user
type $20,000 for the loan amount, for example, as well as 6.25% for the interest rate would
clarify the meanings of these fields.

Instead of doing this in code, however, you're going to use Xcode to facilitate the process. You will still use your new friend, NSNumberFormatter, to perform the job, just in a
different way.

DISCOVERING IN XCODE

As you use Xcode, you will begin to discover the cornucopia of classes and methods Swift offers. The NSNumberFormatter you used in the example is just one of the many, many classes the Cocoa frameworks grant you access to.

One of Xcode's great features is context-sensitive help right in the editor area. To see this in action, hold down the Option key on your keyboard and hover the mouse pointer over the word NSNumberFormatter on line 13. The pointer changes to a question mark, and a dotted line underscores the word. Click, and a popover appears like the one in **Figure 8.3**.

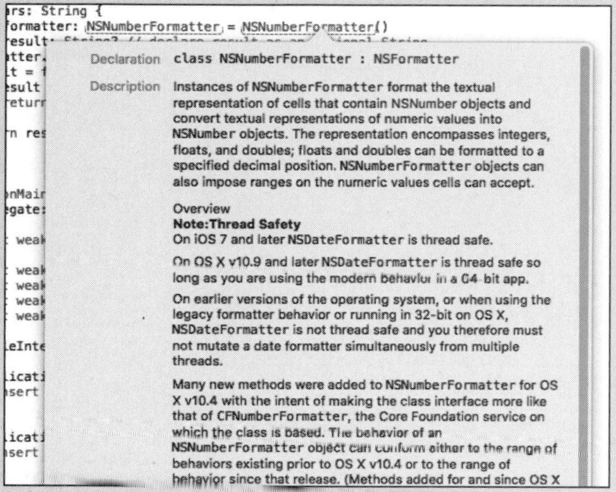

FIGURE 8.3 Context-sensitive help in Xcode

The contents of the window provide the name of the class as well as a clickable link to its superclass, which gives information on that as well. A description and compatibility information are also provided, as well as a link to more complete class documentation. Once you're finished viewing the help information, click outside the help window to dismiss it.

Commit this Option-click keyboard shortcut to memory—you'll find that it comes in handy as you learn Swift and Cocoa.

Another handy feature is to hold down the Command key while hovering the mouse pointer over your source code. Using the NSNumberFormatter again, try this trick. The pointer changes to a hand, and a solid underline appears under the word. Click, and this time the editor area's content changes to show you the Swift class file for the NSNumberFormatter class. Here you are getting the direct scoop on all the variables and methods available to you. This, combined with the documentation available in Xcode, gives you a very comprehensive view of the Cocoa frameworks that are available in Swift.

When you're finished, click the left arrow icon at the top of the main editor view to go back to the file you were previously on.

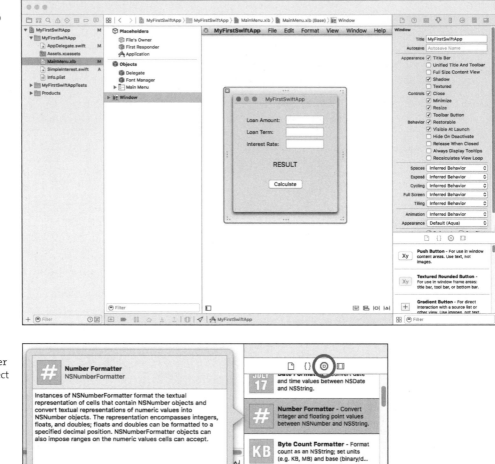

FIGURE 8.4 Bringing the window back into Xcode's editor area

FIGURE 8.5
The NSNumberFormatter object in Xcode's object library

Make sure that the interest calculator window appears in the editor area of Xcode by selecting MainMenu.xib in the navigator area (you may have to click the folder icon in the navigator area toolbar to bring the files into view), and then click the MyFirstSwiftApp window to select it (**Figure 8.4**). This sets the stage for the work you'll do next.

Now, turn your attention to the right side of the Xcode window and down to the object library. Make sure the Object button is selected in the object library toolbar, as shown in **Figure 8.5**. Scroll or use the search field to locate the NSNumberFormatter object. This is the same object you created earlier in the code—now it's available right from Xcode's object list (Figure 8.5).

FIGURE 8.6 The Attributes inspector of the newly created NSNumberFormatter for the Loan Amount text field

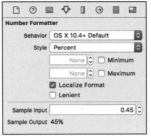

FIGURE 8.7 The Attributes inspector of the newly created NSNumberFormatter for the Interest Rate text field

FIGURE 8.8 The interest calculator application with properly formatted input

FIGURE 8.9 The interest calculator application with properly formatted output

Using your mouse or trackpad, drag the NSNumberFormatter object from the object library into the text field to the right of the Loan Amount label. When you do this, the utility area on the upper-right side automatically switches tabs to show the Attributes inspector. This is where you can set the attributes of the NSNumberFormatter object you just created by dragging onto the text field. Set the Style pop-up menu to Currency (**Figure 8.6**).

Perform the same action again for the interest rate: drag the NSNumberFormatter object from the object library to the text field to the right of the Interest Rate label. This time in the Attributes inspector, choose Percent from the Style pop-up menu (**Figure 8.7**).

Now build and run the application. When the application's window appears, type in a number for the loan amount, and fill in the rest of the fields.

If you're noticing an annoying beep when you try to move away from the Loan Amount text field to enter other data, that's expected. The formatter object is complaining that you aren't entering the data in adherence to the currency format. To get around this, type a dollar sign as the first character of the loan amount. A small bonus: If you didn't type the comma as the thousands separator, the formatter automatically inserts it for you.

The same annoying beep occurs when you move to the Interest Rate field. Just a number won't do—you'll need to append a percent symbol (%) for the formatter to accept your input.

Figure 8.8 shows what everything looks like just prior to clicking the Calculate button; it will also add ".00" if you haven't entered a decimal point. Make sure the text field contents in your app match what's here, and then click the Calculate button.

The result (**Figure 8.9**) looks nice, but isn't it a pain to type in that dollar sign and percentage character? Not only that, but your users probably won't be inclined to type them either, and they will remain puzzled as the app constantly beeps at what seem to be perfectly valid numbers. Sure, you could add some cue, such as an additional label, to prod the user to type in the numbers with the appropriate designators, but that will clutter your window and impede the flow of your app; it also looks strange. There has to be a way for your users to have their cake and eat it too.

FIGURE 8.10
The object tree shows
all your objects in rela-
tion to each other.

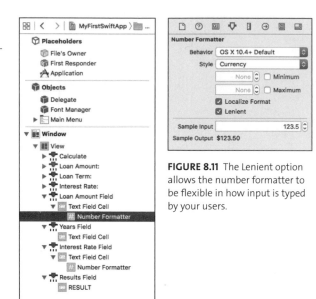

FIGURE 8.11 The Lenient option
allows the number formatter to
be flexible in how input is typed
by your users.

As it turns out, there is. With *input leniency*, your users benefit from the formatter redoing their input to conform to appropriate formatting rules, and they can input the data the way they feel most comfortable.

Quit the app, and then turn on leniency by navigating to the number formatter for both fields in the object tree to the left of the editor area (**Figure 8.10**). This tree is a very convenient and informative view of how all the objects in your `MainMenu.xib` file relate to each other. Finding the formatters here is easy because they fall right underneath the text fields to which they are attached.

Figure 8.11 shows that the Lenient option is selected. Make sure it is selected for both the loan amount and interest rate formatters.

Tell Xcode to run your program again. This time, type any plain number in both the Loan Amount and Interest Rate text fields. Not only are the numbers accepted, but they automatically change to accommodate the formatting rules you've chosen for each field.

As a bonus, the formatters reject any invalid input that doesn't adhere to the formatting rules. For example, you can type an alphabetic character in the text field, but you are not allowed to proceed until it is erased, because a valid number cannot be obtained. The same annoying beep you heard earlier will be repeated as a reminder.

COMPOUNDING

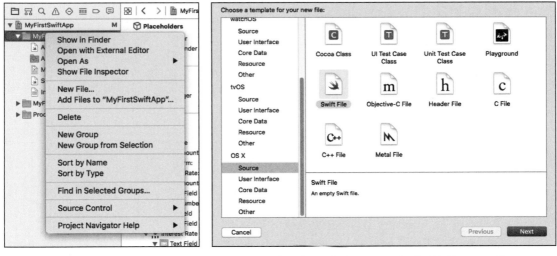

FIGURE 8.12 Right-clicking in the navigator area to add a new file to Xcode

FIGURE 8.13 Select the Swift File option under the OS X Source section.

Given the current state of the interest calculation app, adding compound interest calculation wouldn't be a stretch. After all, the parameters are the same.

In Chapter 4, you reviewed the compound interest calculation. Here it is again:

futureValue = presentValue$(1 + interestRate)^{years}$

Adding a compound interest class seems like the quickest and easiest way to bring the functionality into your app; doing so requires adding a new Swift file. In the last chapter, you chose File > New > File to create a new Swift source file. That will certainly work, but a slightly quicker method will create the file and put it in the right place in your project.

To begin, go to Xcode's navigation area, and look for the folder named MyFirstSwiftApp. Right-click that folder, and choose New File from the shortcut menu (**Figure 8.12**).

In the file template dialog (**Figure 8.13**), select Swift File under the OS X Source section, and click Next.

A new dialog appears asking you to give a name to the class. Type in **CompoundInterest**, and click Next. The file save dialog appears, where you can then select the MyFirstSwiftAppTests checkbox in the Targets area at the bottom. Finally, click the Create button, and the window is dismissed. The new file appears in the navigator area.

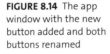

FIGURE 8.14 The app window with the new button added and both buttons renamed

With the new file selected and the editor window in view, type the following code below the import Foundation statement:

```
class CompoundInterest {
    func calculate(loanAmount: Double, var interestRate: Double, years: Int) ->
    → Double {
        interestRate = interestRate / 100.0
        let compoundMultiplier = pow(1.0 + interestRate, Double(years))

        return loanAmount * compoundMultiplier
    }
}
```

The compound interest rate calculation formula used here is the same one that was used in Chapter 4. The method takes the same parameters and returns the same type (Double) as the simple interest calculation method in the SimpleInterest.swift class file.

With this new class file created and part of your Xcode project, turn your attention to the user interface. In the navigation area, click the MainMenu.xib file, and make sure the window is in view in the editor area.

HOOKING THINGS UP

Currently, you have a single button the user clicks to calculate the simple interest. Since you're giving the user an option to calculate compound interest as well, why not create a second button for that calculation?

You could drag a new NSButton object from the object library on the lower-right corner of the Xcode window, but there's a slightly quicker way. Click the Calculate button to select it, and then press Command-D to duplicate it. Align the new button under the current one, double-click it to rename it, and enter **Calculate Compound**. Double-click the top button, and rename it **Calculate Simple**.

You may need to adjust the window size slightly to accommodate the new button, as well as re-center the buttons on the screen. When you're finished, the window should look something like **Figure 8.14**.

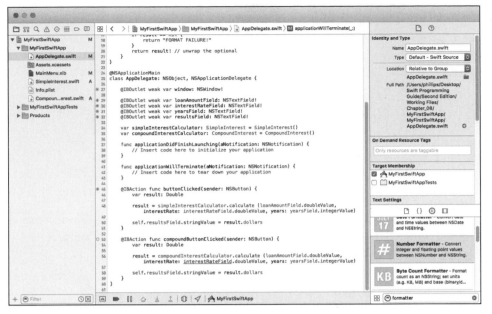

FIGURE 8.15
The contents of the file after adding the new method

With the window up to snuff, next you'll tie the new button to the compound interest class you just created.

Before proceeding, let's review how the current button is connected. Recall that in the last chapter you created a method in the AppDelegate.swift file named buttonClicked. It had a single parameter (an NSButton object reference), did not have a return value, and was tagged with the special @IBAction keyword.

An easy option would be to copy the method and rename it, and then hook up your new button to that. Here are the steps:

Start by copying the code. Select the AppDelegate.swift file in the Xcode navigator area, and then drag to select lines 44 through 50. Choose Edit > Copy to copy the selected code to the copy buffer. Click at the start of line 51 in the editor area, press Return once, and choose Edit > Paste to paste the copied code to that location (**Figure 8.15**).

Now, you need to do some renaming. Double-click the buttonClicked method name on line 52, and rename it **compoundButtonClicked**. Highlight the text simpleInterestCalculator on line 55, and rename it **compoundInterestCalculator**.

Move the cursor just below line 34 (where the simpleInterestCalculator object is declared), and type this line:

```
var compoundInterestCalculator: CompoundInterest = CompoundInterest()
```

With these changes you have successfully created the code necessary to integrate the new compound interest calculator into the application. The only thing left is to tie the action of the compound button calculator to the appropriate action method.

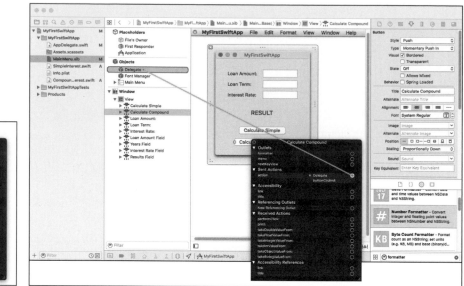

FIGURE 8.16 Break the Calculate Compound button action.

FIGURE 8.17 Connect the selector of the new button to the `compoundButtonClicked` method.

FIGURE 8.18 The window that appears with the compoundButtonClicked method ready to connect

To do that, select `MainMenu.xib` in the navigator area, and bring up the window. Right-click the Calculate Compound button to bring up the connections heads-up display, and then break the existing connection between the `buttonClicked` method and the App Delegate by clicking the ▣ button (**Figure 8.16**).

This connection must be broken because it came along "for the ride" when you duplicated the button earlier. When clicked, the new button should call the `compoundButtonClicked` method instead.

Click the circle to the far right of the selector row in the heads-up window, then drag the generated line over to the Delegate icon just to the left of the editor area (**Figure 8.17**). When you release the mouse button, a new heads-up window appears; select the `compoundButtonClicked` method in that smaller window (**Figure 8.18**). This action binds the new button to the proper action method.

TESTING YOUR WORK

Now you'll put your app through its paces with some real-world data. Run the app in Xcode, and input the following values:

- Loan Amount: $25,000
- Loan Term: 10
- Interest Rate: 8%

Click the Calculate Simple button to calculate simple interest.

If you didn't receive an answer in the result area, be sure to recheck your work and your connections.

If you did get an answer, it should be $45,000. Is it?

I'll wager that instead, you're seeing $25,200. That means everything is wired right, but the calculation is wrong. What's going on?

You've encountered a bug. Don't fret—it happens to even the best of us. Bugs are a fact of life in software development, even with languages as easy to use as Swift. However, you don't have to live with it. Apple has imbued Xcode with a powerful debugging tool that helps you find bugs and terminate them on the spot.

WHEN THINGS GO WRONG

Tracking down bugs can be both frustrating and instructive at the same time. There's nothing quite so exhilarating as finding and fixing a particularly tricky problem in your code. It gives you the satisfaction of knowing that you can troubleshoot problems, and it builds your confidence going forward.

When I encounter a bug, I ask the following questions:

1. What are the symptoms?
2. What changed since the last time it worked (assuming it did work before)?
3. Where should I begin looking to find the root cause?

Let's go over and answer each of these questions for this particular bug:

- Question 1: In this app, the symptom is obvious: The calculation for simple interest is providing an incorrect result.
- Question 2: The simple interest app worked in the last chapter. What changed? You've added NSNumberFormatter objects to the loan amount and interest rate text fields. This certainly warrants some investigation.
- Question 3: Since the result of the calculation is wrong, the first place to start hunting for the bug is in the code where the calculation occurs.

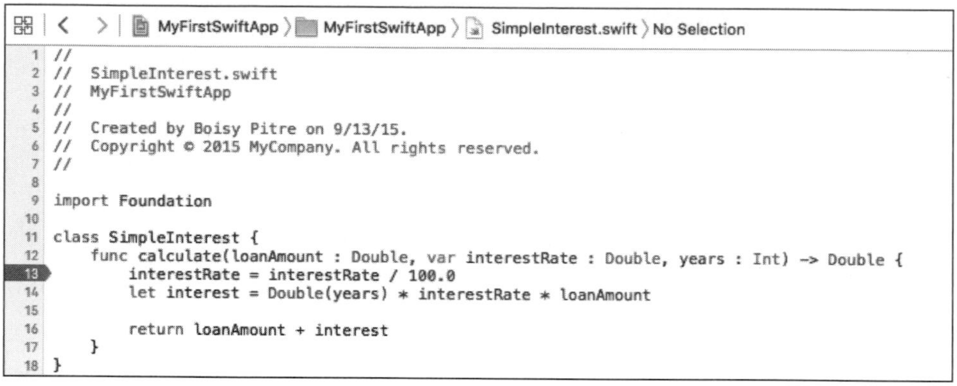

FIGURE 8.19 Setting
a breakpoint in the
calculate method

```
⊞  <  >  |  📄 MyFirstSwiftApp  〉 📁 MyFirstSwiftApp  〉 📄 SimpleInterest.swift  〉 No Selection
 1  //
 2  //  SimpleInterest.swift
 3  //  MyFirstSwiftApp
 4  //
 5  //  Created by Boisy Pitre on 9/13/15.
 6  //  Copyright © 2015 MyCompany. All rights reserved.
 7  //
 8
 9  import Foundation
10
11  class SimpleInterest {
12      func calculate(loanAmount : Double, var interestRate : Double, years : Int) -> Double {
13          interestRate = interestRate / 100.0
14          let interest = Double(years) * interestRate * loanAmount
15
16          return loanAmount + interest
17      }
18  }
```

WHERE'S THE BUG?

The answers to our questions should lead you to the SimpleInterest.swift file since that is the location of the calculation method. Go to the navigator area in Xcode, and select that file so it appears in the editor area.

Looking over the calculate method, everything seems to be in order. The variable interestRate is divided by 100 to yield a number between 0 and 1; it's then multiplied by the loanAmount and the years (cast as a Double from an Int). This is indeed the calculation for simple interest.

Nothing obvious stands out. The formula looks correct, yet the result is wrong. What to do? This sounds like a job for the debugger.

AT THE BREAKING POINT

Intuitively, you understand that code is executed in a linear fashion. After one line of code is executed, the next one is, and the next one, and so on. There are exceptions of course: Threads allow multiple lines of code in the same app to execute on different processor cores at the same time, but we're not concerned with that level of detail here. Analyzing the calculate method in a linear fashion is enough for us.

If there were some way to "break into" the code as it is executing and inspect the variables, you could verify the proper operation of the calculate method and thereby rule it in or out as the problem. And there is just such a way to do that. It's called the *breakpoint*.

Breakpoints are stopping points you can place anywhere in the executable areas of your source code. When Xcode runs your application, it stops when it encounters a breakpoint, affording you the opportunity to inspect the environment: variables, constants, and something called the stack trace.

So where should you set this breakpoint? And how do you do it?

The area directly to the left of your source code in the editor area—where the line numbers appear—is known as the *gutter*. Clicking a line in that gutter creates a breakpoint—a blue arrow (**Figure 8.19**).

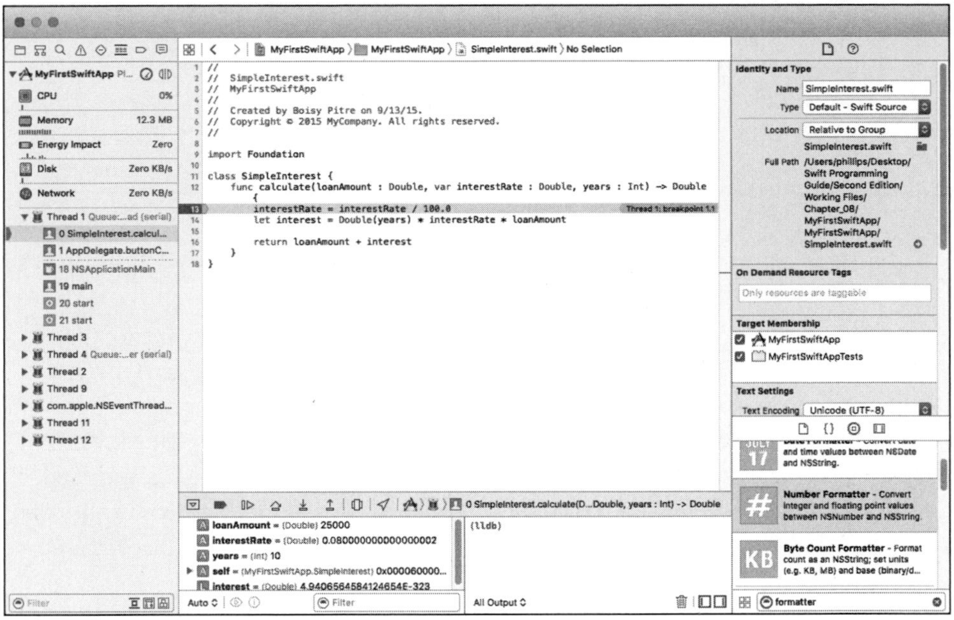

FIGURE 8.20
The breakpoint is
encountered.

For this particular debugging session, click line number 13 in the gutter area to set the breakpoint at the first executable line of the calculate method.

The breakpoint is now set, which means that when you run the program again, it will stop when it encounters this location in the execution path.

Run the app again in Xcode. The app starts, and the window appears. Type in the following values for the fields again:

- Loan Amount: $25,000
- Loan Term: 10
- Interest Rate: 8%

Again, you know the answer should be $45,000, but instead, you're getting $25,200. Click the button to calculate simple interest. As soon as you do, Xcode appears in the forefront of your screen, as in **Figure 8.20**. The breakpoint has been encountered, and line 13 is highlighted. Your app is literally frozen in a state where you can inspect all its values.

In addition to Xcode taking over, a new area appears at the bottom. This is the debug area, and it is composed of a split pane. The left pane shows what appears to be the variable names in the calculate method along with their values. The right pane shows an (lldb) prompt, which is the command-line interface to Apple's debugger, known as LLDB.

The prompt area allows you to type commands directly in the LLDB debugger. You won't be using the command-line version of the debugger in this book, but if you're interested, the Xcode help has documentation on this powerful way to interact with the debugger.

FIGURE 8.21 The debug toolbar allows you to execute control over the Xcode debug process. The Step Over icon is highlighted.

FIGURE 8.22 The updated variables view after stepping over line 13. Note that the `interestRate` value has changed from what it was in Figure 8.20.

Instead, you'll concentrate on the left pane. Notice that the `loanAmount`, `interestRate`, and `years` variables are displayed prominently along with their values. You can see clearly that the values correspond to what you typed earlier in the text fields of the application.

You can instruct Xcode to "step over" the current line, which has not executed yet. Stepping over a line causes its code to run and lands the execution point on the following line. The debug toolbar icons are located just above the debug area. To step over line 13, click the fourth icon from the left (**Figure 8.21**). It is shaped like a triangle, indicating that you are When you click the icon, the green arrow indicator moves to line 14, indicating that it will be executed next. Meanwhile, the code on line 13 (to modify the `interestRate` variable) has executed. You can see that the value in the debug area has changed from .08 to .0008 due to the division by 100.0 (**Figure 8.22**).

This change of the `interestRate` value is certainly interesting. It went from .08 to .0008, and as you can see on line 14, it will be used to calculate the `interest` variable. Remembering back to your math days, .08 is 8%, but .0008 is .08%. You should be asking for a calculation on an 8% interest rate, not .08%.

If you do the math on line 14 to compute the amount of interest with .0008 as the interest rate, you get:

Interest = 10 years × .0008 × $25,000 = $200

And adding the original loan amount of $25,000 to the $200 of interest gives you $25,200, which is what the app is currently showing.

Now consider the formula using the .08 rate:

Interest = 10 years × .08 × $25,000 = $20,000

Adding $20,000 of interest to $25,000 gives you $45,000, which is the right answer. The bug seems to be identified, but let's continue to be sure.

So why did this same method work in the previous chapter? What is different about the application then compared to now?

`NSNumberFormatter` is certainly new. Considering what `NSNumberFormatter`'s percent style does (transforms a number into a percent), it appears that the 8 you typed into the text field was actually transformed into 0.08. This is confirmed in Figure 8.20, where the debug area shows the `interestRate` variable to be 0.08 and not 8.

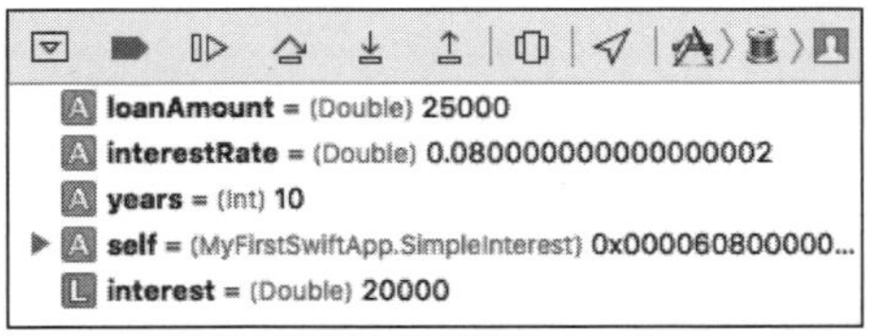

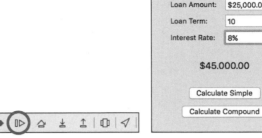

FIGURE 8.23 The interestRate variable reflects the correct number, 0.08.

FIGURE 8.24 The Continue Program Execution button resumes execution of your app.

FIGURE 8.25 The application showing the correct value for simple interest

Prior to adding the formatter, the value of the text field was passed verbatim to the calculate method, and that's why the division by 100.0 was necessary. Now, with the NSNumberFormatter doing its job, the division isn't needed anymore.

The solution to fixing this bug? Simply remove line 13 from the SimpleInterest.swift class. In this case, however, turn line 13 into a comment by placing the // characters at the beginning of the line. This preserves the breakpoint. Notice that when you do this, the Swift compiler instructs Xcode to place a warning on line 12 suggesting that you remove the var for the interestRate parameter. Since that parameter is no longer mutated in the function, it's a good idea to follow the Swift compiler's advice and change the declaration to remove the var keyword.

Run the application again after commenting out line 13, and use the same input values as before. When the breakpoint is encountered, control will be at line 14 (since line 13 is now a comment). Note that in the debug area the value of interestRate is now 0.08, which is what is needed for the calculation result to be accurate.

Step over line 14 by clicking the Step Over icon in the debug toolbar, and look in the debug area for the interest variable. It should be set to 20000, or $20,000 (**Figure 8.23**).

At this point, you should be confident that the application will supply the correct result. Since you are still in the debugger and control is stopped, you can instruct Xcode to let the program continue to run unimpeded. Do so by clicking the Continue Program Execution button on the debug toolbar (**Figure 8.24**).

With the application running at full speed, the result now appears, and you should see a working and accurate simple interest calculation application like the one in **Figure 8.25**.

FIGURE 8.26
The correct compound
interest calculation

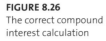

THE CONFOUNDING COMPOUND

You could declare victory here, but the truth is your work is not complete. There is the compound interest calculation. Is it correct also? A quick examination of the source code in the CompoundInterest.swift file shows that the same assumption is made about the interestRate variable on line 13. It too is being divided by 100.

It's a safe bet that you will need to strike that statement as well to ensure that the compound interest calculator is accurate. Go ahead and comment out that line, and then run the same numbers on the compound interest calculator. You should get the answer shown in **Figure 8.26**, which is the correct one. You may encounter one of the breakpoints set earlier in your debugging session. If you do, you can click the breakpoint icon and drag it out of the gutter to remove it, and then click the Continue Program Execution button in the debug toolbar to continue.

THE VALUE OF TESTING

Bugs are sometimes easy to spot and sometimes not so easy. In this case, you obviously needed to check the calculation, but what led you down this path was that the application worked in Chapter 7. Adding the NSNumberFormatter to the text fields broke the calculation, and you were astute enough to notice that the value didn't seem correct.

This demonstrates the complexity of software development and underscores the need for verifiable testing to catch problems like the one you just solved. In testing parlance, the bug you fixed was known as a *regression*. A regression is a failure of something that once worked, and it is one of the worst bugs to deal with. Regressions can sneak up on you because you are lulled into a false sense of security that something that was working one or two versions ago is still working correctly.

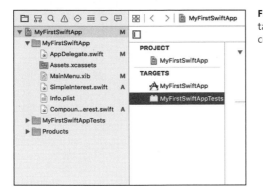

FIGURE 8.27 The `MyFirstSwiftAppTests` target is a unit test target automatically created by Xcode.

THE UNIT TEST

Many different types of tests and testing methodologies are available in software development, but the unit test in particular can be useful. A *unit test* is a very specific, targeted test that verifies one piece of functionality. A unit test can be written to cover one particular method in a class, and there can be many different unit tests for one class. Taken as a whole, a set of unit tests can be used to verify the functionality of a fundamental block of code and ensure that it is working correctly.

Apple emphasizes the use of unit testing right in Xcode. In fact, when you created the Xcode project for your first Swift application, you may have noticed the `MyFirstSwiftAppTests` target right below your application target (**Figure 8.27**).

The navigator area has a group folder named `MyFirstSwiftAppTests` and, underneath that, a Swift source code file named `MyFirstSwiftAppTests.swift`. Without you even asking for it, Xcode created all the infrastructure you need to develop tests for your application.

CRAFTING A TEST

Often when creating unit tests, you'll find yourself asking the question "What tests do I need to write?" The answer to this question depends on the functionality of your application and the pieces and parts that make up the app.

If you examine the interest calculator app, the calculation methods themselves are obviously candidates for unit tests. Testing the accuracy of the calculation method can give you confidence not only that it is correct, but also that it will remain correct if you decide to change it or tweak it later.

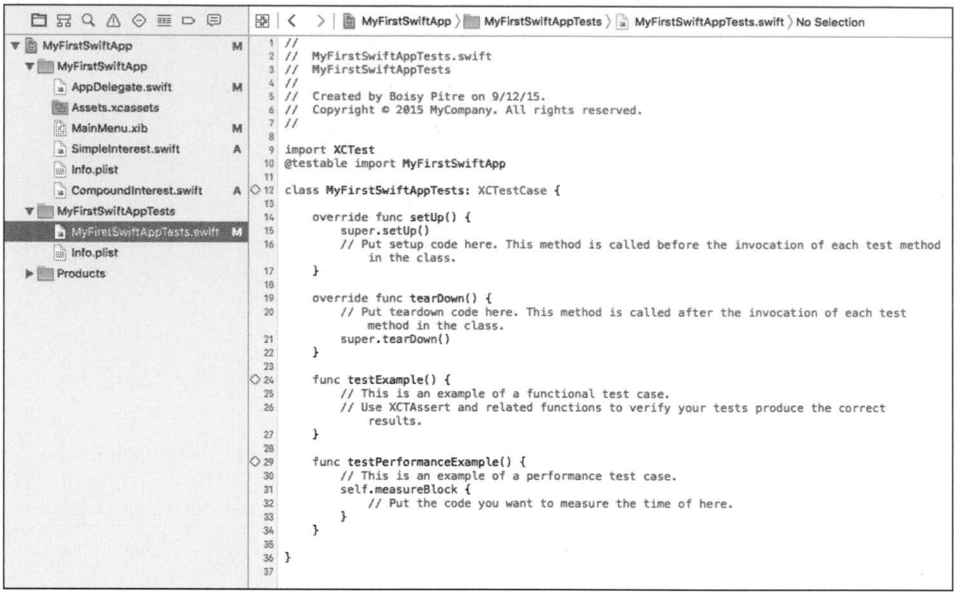

FIGURE 8.28 The unit test file, ready for you to make changes

Let's start by looking at the `MyFirstSwiftAppTests.swift` source file. Locate the source file in the navigator area of Xcode, and then click the file. The editor area changes to show the contents of that file (**Figure 8.28**).

Notice that this is a Swift source file, and it contains a Swift class named `MyFirstSwiftAppTests`. It is a subclass of the `XCTestCase` class, which is a special unit test class that provides a number of helpful features in performing tests.

Next, notice that a number of methods already exist in the class. The first two—`setUp` and `tearDown`—are special methods called when starting and stopping, respectively, the test class. These methods provide entry points for you to create objects that may be needed during the testing process.

Two additional methods—`testExample` and `testPerformanceExample`—are example test methods you can use as a starting point for your own tests.

In the unit test framework, any method that begins with the word "test" is a test method, and it will be called when the unit test runs. You can have one such method, or many. How you structure your unit tests is entirely up to you.

Given that the interest app has two classes, one for simple interest and one for compound interest, creating two test methods probably makes sense. These two methods will test the veracity of the `calculate` methods, ensuring that they are always returning accurate values.

Replace line 12 through the last line in the `MyFirstSwiftAppTests.swift` file with the following code:

```swift
class MyFirstSwiftAppTests: XCTestCase {

    var mySimpleInterestCalculator: SimpleInterest = SimpleInterest()
    var myCompoundInterestCalculator: CompoundInterest = CompoundInterest()

    override func setUp() {
        super.setUp()
        // Put setup code here. This method is called before the invocation of
        → each test method in the class.
    }

    override func tearDown() {
        // Put teardown code here. This method is called after the invocation
        → of each test method in the class.
        super.tearDown()
    }

    func testSimpleInterest() {
        // This is an example of a functional test case.
        var result: Double
        result = mySimpleInterestCalculator.calculate(25_000, interestRate:
        > 0.08, years: 10)
        XCTAssertEqualWithAccuracy(result, 45000, accuracy: 0.1,
        → "Unexpected result: \(result)")
    }

    func testCompoundInterest() {
        // This is an example of a functional test case.
        var result: Double
        result = myCompoundInterestCalculator.calculate(25_000, interestRate:
        → 0.08, years: 10)
        XCTAssertEqualWithAccuracy(result, 53973.12, accuracy: 0.1,
        → "Unexpected result: \(result)")
    }
}
```

The two methods, testSimpleInterest and testCompoundInterest, test the simple and compound interest calculations, respectively. The test involves using the calculate method of each class to verify that the passed loan amount, loan term, and interest rate yield an expected answer.

FIGURE 8.29 The view of the code when the tests have passed

FIGURE 8.29 The view of the code when the tests have passed

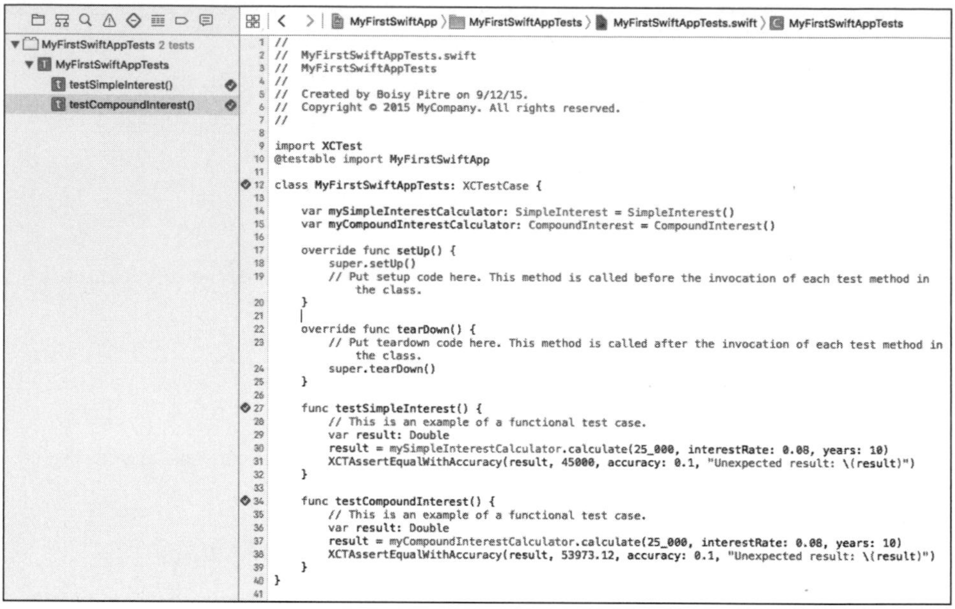

Two objects, mySimpleInterestCalculator and myCompoundInterestCalculator, are instantiated at the top of the MyFirstSwiftAppTests class on lines 14 and 15. These objects are then used in the test methods at lines 30 and 37 to test interest calculation on a 10-year loan for $25,000 at 8% interest—the same values you used earlier to test the app.

For each test method, a variable named result of type Double is defined and assigned to the return value of the calculate method for the respective object. To verify that the test passed, a call to the XCTAssertEqualWithAccuracy function is made. This function takes four parameters: the variable to evaluate, the value that the variable should be, an accuracy factor, and a String that is shown only if the test fails. When dealing with Float or Double types, this particular test function is useful since floating point numbers aren't always exact due to how they are represented in memory. Here, you are indicating that the passed variable and the result can be equal to within 0.1, or 10 cents.

With the source file modified, run the test by choosing Product > Test. The tests run, and the navigator area changes its content to show the results of the two tests. Switch to the test navigator view in the navigator area by clicking the Test Navigator icon (the green diamond-shaped icon). You should see green checkmarks next to the names of each method. You'll also see the same green checkmarks in the gutter next to the source code (**Figure 8.29**).

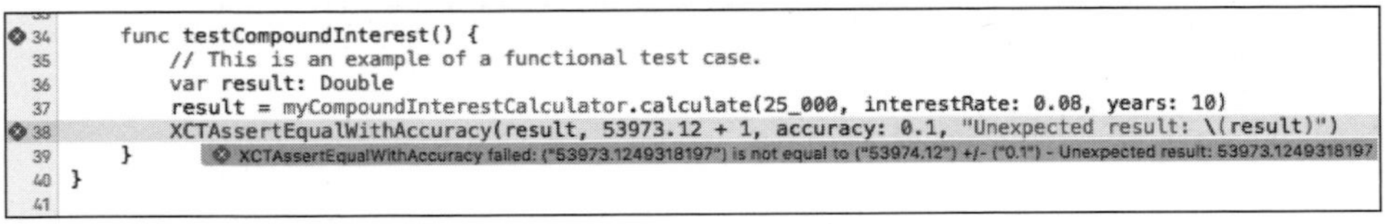

FIGURE 8.30 The result
of a failed test

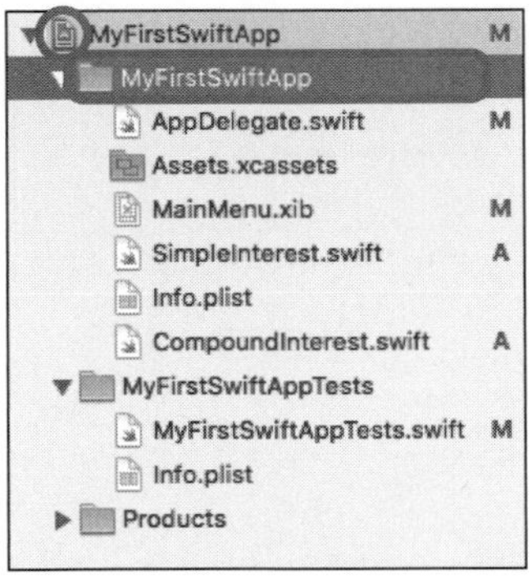

```
34    func testCompoundInterest() {
35        // This is an example of a functional test case.
36        var result: Double
37        result = myCompoundInterestCalculator.calculate(25_000, interestRate: 0.08, years: 10)
38        XCTAssertEqualWithAccuracy(result, 53973.12 + 1, accuracy: 0.1, "Unexpected result: \(result)")
39    }
40 }
41
```
⊗ XCTAssertEqualWithAccuracy failed: ("53973.1249318197") is not equal to ("53974.12") +/- ("0.1") - Unexpected result: 53973.1249318197

FIGURE 8.31 The folder icon shows your
project's files in the navigator area.

WHEN TESTS FAIL

So far the tests pass, but what happens when a failure occurs? Forcing a failure is simple enough—simply change the second parameter in one of the XCTAssertEqualWithAccuracy methods to a completely different value. Try this by changing the value 53973.12 on line 38 to 53973.12 + 1 and rerun the tests. The test fails, and the green checkmark for that method turns into a red X. The test error message is also printed to highlight the details of the error (**Figure 8.30**).

Now that you know how to invoke a failure, you can fix the problem by simply deleting the + 1, and the test will pass again.

One irony of this particular set of unit tests is that it would not have caught the bug you fixed earlier in the chapter; that bug wasn't caused by the calculate method itself, but by the interestRate variable passed into it from the NSNumberFormatter. As the old adage goes, "garbage in, garbage out."

TESTS THAT ALWAYS RUN

Unit tests are only good when you actually run them. So far, you have used the Product > Test menu to invoke the tests each time. What if instead the tests ran every time you actually ran your app? That way, any changes you make to your program can immediately benefit from retesting. Even though you may think the change is harmless and won't introduce bugs, always run your tests prior to building. Here's how to tell Xcode to do this for you automatically:

Select the folder icon in the navigation area, and then click the MyFirstSwiftApp project entry at the top (**Figure 8.31**).

FIGURE 8.32 Select-
ing the target and the
Build Phases tab

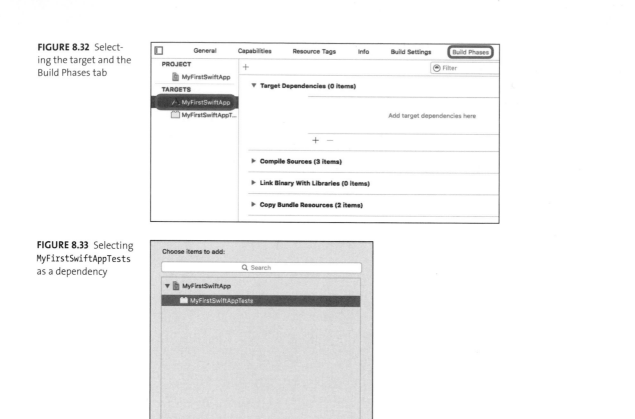

FIGURE 8.33 Selecting
MyFirstSwiftAppTests
as a dependency

In the editor area, click the MyFirstSwiftApp target, and then click the Build Phases tab. Click the disclosure triangle next to the Target Dependencies entry, and then click the Add (+) icon to add a dependency (**Figure 8.32**).

A dialog appears showing MyFirstSwiftAppTests as a potential dependency. Select it, then click the Add button (**Figure 8.33**).

Now you have added the test as a dependency of your application. Every time you build your app, the unit tests build and execute first. If any of the tests fail, your app will not be built, forcing you to address the failed tests before moving on.

WRAPPING UP

Over the last two chapters, you've managed to take the Swift knowledge you've acquired and write a full-fledged application. Not only that, you also used Xcode's debugging environment to find and fix a bug, as well as to write several unit tests to ensure your calculations would always work correctly. That's a lot of work and a big accomplishment!

Take a well-deserved coffee break, and gear up for the next chapter!

CHAPTER 9

Going Mobile with Swift

In the last chapter, you spent some time perfecting your first Swift application for your Mac. Although you were not creating the most complex or demanding app, it was a useful exercise for getting your feet wet with Xcode. You even ventured into debugging and automated testing!

In this chapter, you'll continue with the theme of app development and the Swift language, but this time you'll move away from the desktop and onto the other major Apple platform: iOS. That's right! You'll get some first-hand experience writing a Swift app for the premier mobile platform.

If you don't have an iPhone or iPad, that won't be a problem. You will be playing exclusively in Apple's great iOS simulator environment, so you won't need the actual hardware.

IN YOUR POCKET VS. ON YOUR DESK

The beauty of Swift is that it is agnostic to the platform that you are developing on. Whether it's an app for a notebook or desktop running Mac OS X, the latest iPhone or iPad running iOS, or even watchOS for the Apple Watch and tvOS for Apple TV, Swift just works.

The differences between OS X and iOS are centered on the particular user interfaces (UIs) and the frameworks used to construct those UIs. As you saw with the interest calculator app in the previous chapters, OS X apps have free rein of the desktop; they are window-based apps that can co-exist peacefully on the same screen as other apps.

In the mobile case, screen real estate is limited, and the UI changes from a keyboard and trackpad (or mouse) to a touchscreen with virtual keyboards that come and go as needed.

Apple's Cocoa framework on OS X is known as Cocoa Touch on iOS, aptly named for the expressive, touch-based interaction iPhones and iPads are known for.

In this chapter, you will be introduced to an iOS-based app, written in Swift, that takes into account the differences between the two environments. As usual, I'll introduce some Swift language features for you to study and contemplate. So get yourself a cup of joe or your favorite beverage, and settle in for some more fun!

HOW'S YOUR MEMORY?

The OS X Swift app you perfected in the last chapter was a bit on the serious side. Loan interest calculators are certainly important in the banking business, but they are not most people's idea of fun.

For this next app, you'll use Swift to write something a little more playful.

In 1978, Milton Bradley released Simon, a handheld electronic game. Simon contained four large backlit buttons (the button colors were red, green, yellow, and blue). Simon was a round device, and the four buttons were arranged in a circular pattern.

Simon tested the player's ability to memorize patterns. It would light one of the four buttons at random; the player would then press that button to confirm. After a slight pause, that same button would light up again, followed by another button. The player would press the two buttons in the same order as the lighting sequence. With that round properly completed, Simon would play the sequence again along with an additional button.

The game would continue in this manner, with a new button highlighted at the end of each round. A good player could follow 20 or more lighting sequences, but when the player pressed a button out of order, the game was over.

A game like this makes a perfect candidate to explore a touch-based interactive experience on the iPhone. With Swift in your corner, this will be not only a fun game to write, but an educational one too!

THINKING ABOUT GAMEPLAY

When considering how a game like Simon is played, several elements should guide your understanding of how to develop this in Swift. Let's go through those now.

- Game elements: This particular game has four buttons: red, green, yellow, and blue. Each button is both an input device (can be touched by the user) and an output device (can brighten, or light up). The code will need to process touches as well as brighten and dim each button.

- Randomness: The description of the game includes an element of randomness. The computer decides the order in which to light up the buttons. As the game designer and developer, you will need to employ some type of random number generator to come up with a different sequence for each turn.

- Playability: To make the game interesting, it has to be challenging, perhaps offering different levels of mastery. For this version, the speed at which the computer lights up each button sequentially would certainly affect the degree of difficulty. If each button lights up for a quarter of a second, that would allow the user enough time to observe and learn the pattern. On the other hand, if the button lit up for only one tenth of a second before the next one, the game would be harder to play.

- What it means to "lose": The game has a very specific lose condition: The player presses the wrong button when mimicking the sequence. When this happens, the player should receive some stimulus that indicates the game is lost: a message on the screen or some type of sound.

- What it means to "win": Winning the game would constitute reaching some terminal number of presses without a single error. If that number is too high, winning the game might be nearly impossible. If it is too low, the game will be too easy to defeat.

- Play flow: A game like this is fairly easy to envision from start to finish. The player launches the game, playing until either winning or losing. In either case, a message appears either congratulating or admonishing the player. Once the message is dismissed, the game restarts from the beginning.

DESIGNING THE UI

A game such as this is fairly easy to design from a UI perspective. The screen has four colored buttons, which are touchable elements. To make the game easy to play, the buttons should cover as much of the screen area as possible.

The button arrangement should also facilitate easy and fun gameplay. The easiest way to do that is to arrange the buttons in a 2 x 2 grid so that as the user watches the order in which they light up, everything is in one easy field of view. **Figure 9.1** shows the potential layout of the buttons.

For simplicity, this design will be created on the iPhone; iPads can still run the game, although not in their native resolution.

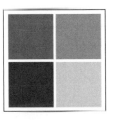

FIGURE 9.1 How the game might look in its simplest form

FIGURE 9.2
The buttons on an
iPhone 5s

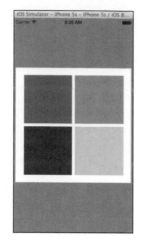

The iPhone aspect ratio is such that the screen is taller than it is wide. This leaves room along the bottom (or top) of the screen for other potential game information. **Figure 9.2** shows how the buttons would look on an iPhone 5s.

Finally, how about a name? Every game or app needs a good name, and this one is no exception. For the fun of it, let's call this game "FollowMe," since the object of the game is to follow the order in which the buttons light up.

CREATING THE PROJECT

You've been through this step before—launching Xcode and creating a new project. This time, however, there's a twist: You'll be creating not an OS X application but an iOS one.

With Xcode running, choose File > New > Project. For this project, select Application under iOS. The template you'll be using is named Single View Application (**Figure 9.3**).

Other application templates are available, including one named Game. Although FollowMe is a game, it's very simple in design and will work just fine as a Single View Application.

Once you've selected the Single View Application template, click Next. In the subsequent window, set the Product Name to **FollowMe**, and ensure that the settings mimic **Figure 9.4**.

Click Next to continue to the Save dialog, and then click Create. You'll see the Xcode window for the new project, as in **Figure 9.5**.

FIGURE 9.3 Selecting the Single View Application template

FIGURE 9.4 Setting the options

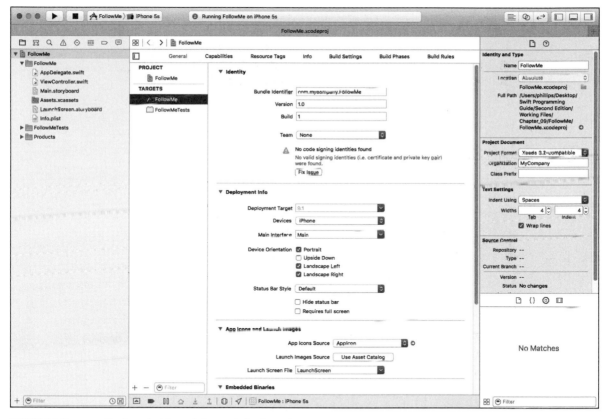

FIGURE 9.5 Your new Xcode project is ready for you to begin work.

BUILDING THE USER INTERFACE

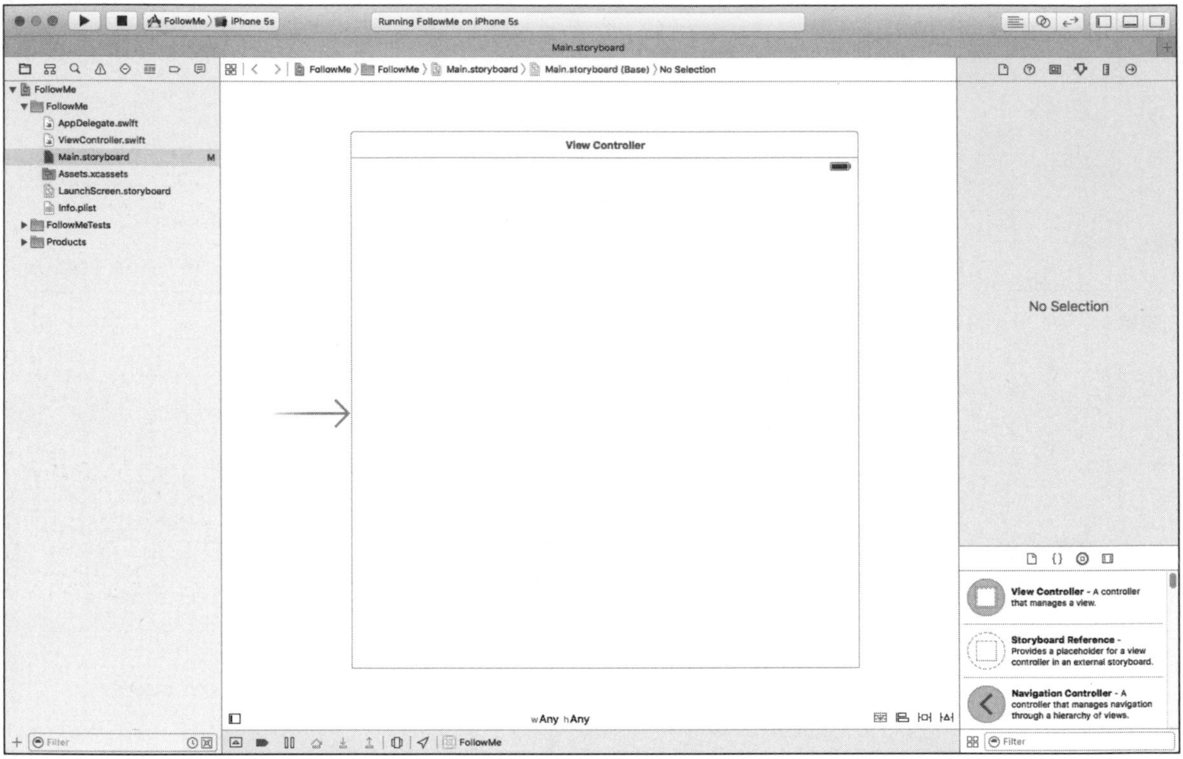

FIGURE 9.6 The editor area showing the view of the storyboard

Now that you have a project, you need to start building the UI. By default, iOS apps have a slightly different method for working with views than what you experienced with the Mac OS X app earlier. Xcode provides a convenient technology named *storyboarding*, which allows you to build your app in a view-by-view approach, similar to how animators would create a series of scenes in a film.

Locate the storyboard file named `Main.storyboard` in the navigator area on the left side of the Xcode window, and click it. The editor area appears, showing the main view of the storyboard (**Figure 9.6**).

This single view is where you'll begin to build the content for the game. If the size of the view looks a little wider than that of an iPhone, that's because it is. It's a 600 x 600 view and is intended to be a generic view space. Xcode defaults to a sizing feature known as Auto Layout. It conveniently adapts the content dynamically to the view irrespective of aspect ratio, and lets designers focus more on the content and less on the layout.

Auto Layout can be complex and can take some time to learn. It is an important part of developing for iOS, and you'll get some minimal exposure to it shortly.

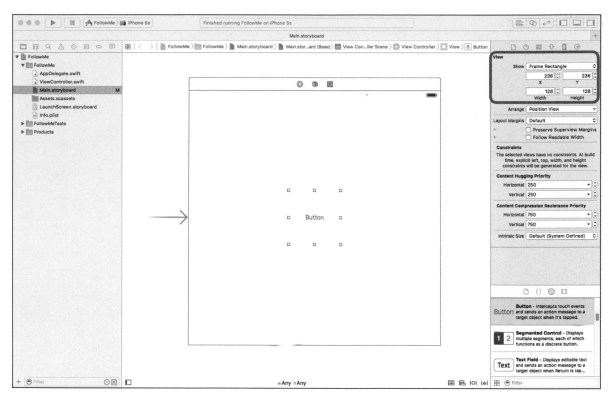

FIGURE 9.7 Creating the first button

CREATING THE BUTTONS

Given how the game will work, Cocoa Touch's UIButton object is the best choice for the user interface object. UIButton objects can have their background color modified, and, as a bonus, they also accept touch input.

Start by locating the Button object in the object library. Drag a single button into the view, and then navigate to the Size inspector at the top of the utility area to change the size to 128 x 128 (**Figure 9.7**). You can ignore the X and Y positions of the button for now.

INSPECTORS

In Xcode's utility area (on the right side of the window), you'll find a row of icons along the top. These are inspector icons, and they can change depending on the type of file you have selected in Xcode. If you hover your mouse over each inspector icon, the name will appear in a help tag.

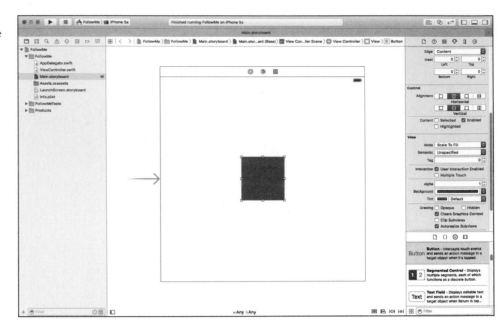

FIGURE 9.8 Changing the button color in the Attributes inspector

Once you have changed the button's size, click the Attributes inspector icon, located along the top of the utility area. In the title field, delete the "Button" text. This button will have no text in it. Scroll down in the Attributes inspector and locate the View section. Change the Background setting of the button to red by clicking the color and selecting the Color Palettes tab of the Colors window that appears (**Figure 9.8**).

Now you'll create the remaining three buttons. The simplest way to do this is to select the red button and choose Edit > Duplicate three times to create three more buttons. Change the colors of the duplicated buttons to yellow, blue, and green, and then position the buttons in a grid pattern, as in **Figure 9.9**.

Now, select all four buttons. You can do this by selecting the first button and Command-clicking the remaining three buttons. With all four buttons selected, choose Editor > Embed In > View. With this new view in place, drag the view to center it both vertically and horizontally inside of the outer view. This embeds all four buttons into a container view. The purpose of this is to make setting constraints easier, as described in the "Setting Constraints" section later in this chapter.

FIGURE 9.9 All four buttons created and positioned

FIGURE 9.11 FollowMe running in the iPhone 5s simulator

RUNNING IN THE SIMULATOR

With the buttons in place and now inside a container view, it's time to see how the app will look when it runs. Xcode conveniently lets you run your app in a simulator, which mimics the screen size and aspect ratio of a number of iOS devices. For the purposes of developing this app, use the iPhone 5s simulator for now. You can select it in the upper-left corner of the Xcode window (**Figure 9.10**).

You can now run the app in the simulator by choosing Product > Run, which builds the app and launches the chosen iOS simulator. **Figure 9.11** shows the app running.

Something looks awry, doesn't it? The buttons seem to be off-center and falling off the edge of the screen. This is due to the difference in size between the view in the editor area (600 x 600) and the iPhone 5s's screen width. To solve this, you'll dive into Auto Layout.

FIGURE 9.12 Selecting
the container view

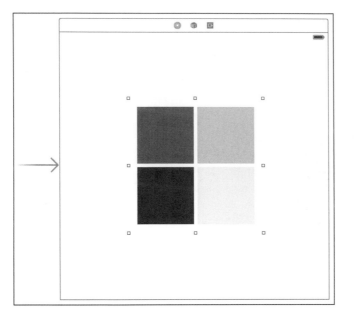

SETTING CONSTRAINTS

Apple's numerous hardware offerings for iOS include iPhones and iPads of various sizes and aspect ratios. Developing user interfaces to accommodate these different screen resolutions and sizes is made much simpler using Auto Layout, and you'll use this technology in your app.

Constraints are relationships between objects that enforce position and sizing behaviors, among other things. For instance, if you rotate your iPhone, your UI should adapt appropriately. Whether your app is running on an iPhone 6 or an iPhone 4, with a properly configured set of constraints things will look optimal.

For this app, the important constraint is that the buttons remain centered on the screen, irrespective of what device they appear on. This is achieved by setting the constraints on the container view itself, which holds the four buttons.

Quit the simulator and return to the view in Xcode. There, select the container view by clicking just outside any of the four buttons. The container view will show as selected (**Figure 9.12**).

With the container view selected, navigate to the area just to the lower-right side of the editor area, where the constraint-setting icons are located. Click the Align constraint icon (the second icon from the left), and select both the Horizontal Center in Container and Vertical Center in Container options in the pop-up window (**Figure 9.13**). Add the two constraints by clicking the Add 2 Constraints button.

Once the constraints have been set, the lines in **Figure 9.14** appear.

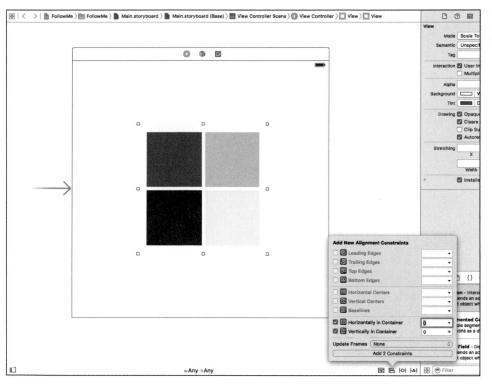

FIGURE 9.13 Setting the horizontal and vertical center constraints

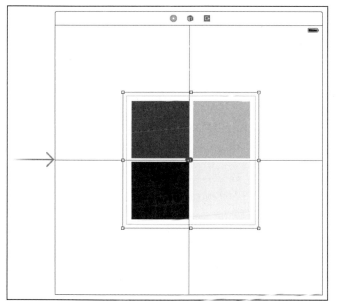

FIGURE 9.14 The view after the constraints have been set

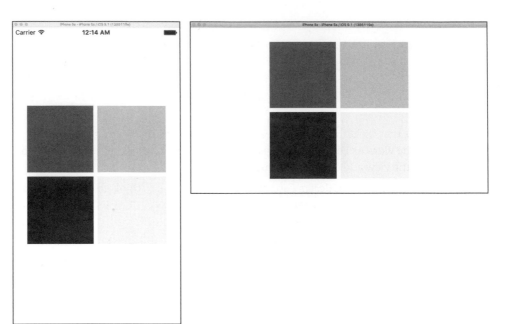

Now that the constraints have been set, run the app in the simulator again. This time the buttons remain centered. You can simulate rotation of the iPhone 5s in the simulator by holding down the Command key while pressing the Left and Right Arrow keys on the Mac. In all orientations, the buttons should align properly in the center (**Figure 9.15**).

When you're finished, quit the simulator and return to Xcode.

At this point, the user interface is nearly good enough; you'll come back to a few settings in a bit, but it's time to delve into the code that controls gameplay. But before getting to that, the next sections discuss an important design pattern that you will encounter here and should understand as you become adept at Swift.

THE MODEL-VIEW-CONTROLLER

In software development, *design patterns* are useful and common practices programmers use over and over to solve a common set of problems. Many such design patterns exist and are used in different situations, but the *model-view-controller* (MVC) in particular is pervasive in iOS and Mac app development.

As the name implies, this design pattern is composed of three distinct parts:

- **Model** represents the data and the code that manipulates and processes that data. Examples include the variables, constants, and functions that deal with the logic of games such as FollowMe.

- **View** is the visible set of objects. In FollowMe, these would be the buttons that appear on the screen.

- **Controller** is the object that orchestrates and facilitates communication between the model and the view. As FollowMe is played, the controller becomes the conduit through which both the view and the model are updated.

The advantage of the MVC design pattern is that it allows you to think about your app in terms of what data and functionality it is modeling, what it is showing the user, and how coordination happens between the two. This *separation of concerns* provides opportunity to factor your code such that components can be reused in other applications and projects.

Depending on the complexity of the app, the model, view, and controller may be composed of separate classes, or they may be combined into a single class. For FollowMe, the model and controller will be combined into a single source file; the divisions will be noted in the source code.

CODING THE GAME

Ready for some more Swift?

Locate and click the `ViewController.swift` file in Xcode's navigator area; the contents appear in the editor area. Delete the code in the editor area except for the comments and blank line (lines 1 through 8), and then type the following code:

> ### SMART EDITING
>
> As you type, the Swift compiler works in the background to find errors. Hence, you may see errors appear and disappear while typing. This is normal, so just continue typing until all the code is in place. Also, Xcode's editor may try to help you by putting ending curly braces in position when you type opening ones. It may take some getting used to such a smart editor, so be aware as you input the code.

```
import UIKit

class ViewController: UIViewController, UIAlertViewDelegate {
    enum ButtonColor: Int {
        case Red = 1
```

```swift
        case Green = 2
        case Blue = 3
        case Yellow = 4
    }

    enum WhoseTurn {
        case Human
        case Computer
    }

    // view related objects and variables
    @IBOutlet weak var redButton: UIButton!
    @IBOutlet weak var greenButton: UIButton!
    @IBOutlet weak var blueButton: UIButton!
    @IBOutlet weak var yellowButton: UIButton!

    // model related objects and variables
    let winningNumber: Int = 25
    var currentPlayer: WhoseTurn = .Computer
    var inputs = [ButtonColor]()
    var indexOfNextButtonToTouch: Int = 0
    var highlightSquareTime = 0.5


    override func viewDidLoad() {
        super.viewDidLoad()
        // Do any additional setup after loading the view, typically from a nib
    }

    override func didReceiveMemoryWarning() {
        super.didReceiveMemoryWarning()
        // Dispose of any resources that can be recreated.
    }

    override func viewDidAppear(animated: Bool) {
        startNewGame()
    }

    func buttonByColor(color: ButtonColor) -> UIButton {
        switch color {
```

```
        case .Red:
            return redButton
        case.Green:
            return greenButton
        case.Blue:
            return blueButton
        case.Yellow:
            return yellowButton
        }
    }


    func playSequence(index: Int, highlightTime: Double) {
        currentPlayer = .Computer

        if index == inputs.count {
            currentPlayer = .Human
            return
        }

        let button: UIButton = buttonByColor(inputs[index])
        let originalColor: UIColor? = button.backgroundColor
        let highlightColor: UIColor = UIColor.whiteColor()

        UIView.animateWithDuration(highlightTime,
            delay: 0.0,
options:UIViewAnimationOptions.CurveLinear.intersect(.AllowUserInteraction).
    intersect(.BeginFromCurrentState),
            animations: {
                button.backgroundColor = highlightColor
            }, completion: { finished in
                button.backgroundColor = originalColor
                let newIndex: Int = index + 1
                self.playSequence(newIndex, highlightTime: highlightTime)
            })
    }


    @IBAction func buttonTouched(sender: UIButton) {
        // determine which button was touched by looking at its tag
        let buttonTag: Int = sender.tag
```

```
        if let colorTouched = ButtonColor(rawValue: buttonTag) {
            if currentPlayer == .Computer {
                // ignore touches as long as this flag is set to true
                return
            }

            if colorTouched == inputs[indexOfNextButtonToTouch] {
                // the player touched the correct button...
                indexOfNextButtonToTouch++

                // determine if there are any more buttons left in this round
                if indexOfNextButtonToTouch == inputs.count {
                    // the player has won this round
                    if advanceGame() == false {
                        playerWins()
                    }
                    indexOfNextButtonToTouch = 0
                }
                else {
                    // there are more buttons left in this round... keep going
                }
            }
            else {
                // the player touched the wrong button
                playerLoses()
                indexOfNextButtonToTouch = 0
            }
        }
    }

func alertView(alertView: UIAlertView, clickedButtonAtIndex buttonIndex:
→ Int) {
    startNewGame()
}

func playerWins() {
    let winner: UIAlertView = UIAlertView(title: "You won!", message:
    → "Congratulations!", delegate: self, cancelButtonTitle: nil,
    → otherButtonTitles: "Awesome!")
    winner.show()
```

```
    }

    func playerLoses() {
        let loser: UIAlertView = UIAlertView(title: "You lost!", message:
        → "Sorry!", delegate: self, cancelButtonTitle: nil, otherButtonTitles:
        → "Try again!")
        loser.show()
    }

    func randomButton() -> ButtonColor {
        let v: Int = Int(arc4random_uniform(UInt32(4))) + 1
        let result = ButtonColor(rawValue: v)
        return result!
    }

    func startNewGame() -> Void {
        // randomize the input array
        inputs = [ButtonColor]()
        advanceGame()
    }

    func advanceGame() -> Bool {
        var result: Bool = true

        if inputs.count == winningNumber {
            result = false
        }
        else {
            // add a new random number to the input list
            inputs += [randomButton()]

            // play the button sequence
            playSequence(0, highlightTime: highlightSquareTime)
        }

        return result
    }
}
```

Now that you've typed in the code, let's walk through it so you understand how the program works.

THE CLASS

Since this class will deal with UI elements, importing the UIKit frameworks is important:

```
import UIKit
```

Just like the original contents of the file, the class remains named ViewController, which is a subclass of the UIViewController class. In addition, a protocol, UIAlertViewDelegate, has been added. This class must conform to this particular protocol due to alert dialogs used later in the code.

```
class ViewController: UIViewController, UIAlertViewDelegate {
```

ENUMERATIONS

The ButtonColor enumeration exists to represent all four button colors in the game: red, green, blue, and yellow.

This particular enumeration is based on the Int type, and each enumeration member is set to a unique raw value of the Int type. The reason for this will become apparent a little later.

```
enum ButtonColor: Int {
    case Red = 1
    case Green = 2
    case Blue = 3
    case Yellow = 4
}
```

Since the game is played by both the computer (who decides which buttons to highlight) and the player (a human), you need a way in the game to determine whose turn it is to play. This enumeration captures that:

```
enum WhoseTurn {
    case Human
    case Computer
}
```

Note that these two enumerations are declared inside the ViewController class; therefore, they would not be known, or accessible, outside of that class.

THE VIEW OBJECTS

Next is the declaration of the variables and constants needed for the game. All four views (UIButton objects) exist in the Main.storyboard file. The class needs a reference to those so that it can manipulate them during the game. The @IBOutlet weak keywords are a hint that you need to connect these variables to their represented objects in the storyboard. You'll do that later.

```
// view-related objects and variables
@IBOutlet weak var redButton: UIButton!
@IBOutlet weak var greenButton: UIButton!
@IBOutlet weak var blueButton: UIButton!
@IBOutlet weak var yellowButton: UIButton!
```

THE MODEL OBJECTS

Objects and variables related to the model are defined in this section. Unlike a pure model-view-controller separation, where each entity gets its own class, the controller class ViewController encompasses these model objects, which represent the data associated with the playing of the game.

The winningNumber variable is an Int that represents the victory condition: the number of consecutive button highlights the user must successfully mimic. The current value, 25, is considered somewhat difficult; you can set this number lower to make the game easier to win.

```
// model-related objects and variables
let winningNumber: Int = 25
```

To keep track of whose turn it is, currentPlayer is declared as a variable of the WhoseTurn enumeration type. Its default value is set to Computer

```
var currentPlayer. WhoseTurn = .Computer
```

The progression of the game is built on "rounds." Each round consists of the computer highlighting buttons in the previous round, along with a new random button. The player must touch the buttons in the same order. This ordering is dictated by the inputs variable, which is declared as an array of ButtonColor objects:

```
var inputs = [ButtonColor]()
```

As the player touches the buttons, the computer keeps track of the next button's index in the inputs array. This variable keeps track of that index:

```
var indexOfNextButtonToTouch: Int = 0
```

One aspect of the game that can affect the degree of difficulty is the time the computer takes to highlight the button. This variable, set to half a second, controls this time. Larger numbers slow the highlight progression and make the game easier; smaller numbers increase the game's speed, making the game harder:

```
var highlightSquareTime = 0.5
```

OVERRIDABLE METHODS

Working within the context of Cocoa Touch's UIViewController class, you will find several methods recommended to override. One such method is viewDidLoad, which is called when the view is loaded and about to appear on the iOS screen. For the purposes of this app, we'll leave this method alone.

```
override func viewDidLoad() {
    super.viewDidLoad()
    // Do any additional setup after loading the view, typically from a nib.
}
```

Another method provided to the UIViewController class is didReceiveMemoryWarning, which is called by iOS when memory is running low on the device. Apps that receive this usually try to free resources, unload images, or take other actions to relieve memory pressure. For this app, we'll simply let the method call its superclass's implementation.

```
override func didReceiveMemoryWarning() {
    super.didReceiveMemoryWarning()
    // Dispose of any resources that can be recreated.
}
```

The viewDidAppear method is called after the view is loaded but just before it appears on the screen. This is a perfect place for you to call the startNewGame method, which will begin the gameplay.

```
override func viewDidAppear(animated: Bool) {
    startNewGame()
}
```

GAME METHODS

One handy method you need during the game is buttonByColor, which takes a ButtonColor type and returns the corresponding UIButton on the screen. This is helpful to map color names with the buttons in the view they represent. The switch/case construct is used to scan through the various supported button colors, returning the appropriate UIButton reference.

```
func buttonByColor(color: ButtonColor) -> UIButton {
    switch color {
    case .Red:
        return redButton
    case .Green:
        return greenButton
    case .Blue:
        return blueButton
    case .Yellow:
```

```
      return yellowButton
   }
}
```

The following method is at the heart of the game and drives the highlighting of the button sequence by the computer. Two parameters are passed: an index into the `inputs` array, which will be used to identify the button to highlight, and a highlight time.

Because this is a fairly sophisticated method, exploring it in depth is worth the time so that you can understand exactly how it works, so let's dive in:

```
func playSequence(index: Int, highlightTime: Double) {
```

Upon entering the method, the `currentPlayer` variable is set to indicate that the computer is the current player, since it is the one in control of the game board at this juncture.

```
currentPlayer = .Computer
```

The following `if` statement performs a special check to see whether the index value passed is equal to the number of elements in the `inputs` array. If this is true and the two values are equal, it's the human's turn to play, and the method immediately returns to the caller.

```
if index == inputs.count {
   currentPlayer = .Human
   return
}
```

Three variables are declared next. The first, `button`, is set to the `UIButton` reference of the current input. The `buttonByColor` method reviewed earlier is used here to find the actual `UIButton` based on the `ButtonColor` stored in the array.

The second variable, `originalColor`, captures the background color of the button just retrieved. This saves the color so that it can be restored later. Note that the `UIColor` object here is declared as optional—because a button can have its `backgroundColor` property set to `nil`. In this game that won't happen, but the declaration still needs to be made in this way because the type of `backgroundColor` is a `UIColor?` and not a `UIColor`.

The third variable, `highlightColor`, is the color that will be used to highlight the button. It is set to white by calling the `whiteColor` method of the `UIColor` class.

```
let button: UIButton = buttonByColor(inputs[index])
let originalColor: UIColor? = button.backgroundColor
let highlightColor: UIColor = UIColor.whiteColor()
```

The following line of code is what actually causes the selected button to highlight. Here, the `animateWithDuration` method is used to perform the animation that indicates to the player that the button is to be touched. This special method, known as a *type method*, is called directly from the type name itself (`UIView` in this case) and not from a variable of that type. A type method is typically used when having an instance of a type is not necessary to perform a specific function. Type methods in Swift are analogous to *class methods* in Objective-C.

A number of parameters are used to perform the animation, but the most relevant for the game are the highlightTime, which indicates how long the animation will run, and two closures: one that indicates what will be animated, and one that indicates what happens after the animation is finished.

```
UIView.animateWithDuration(highlightTime,
    delay: 0.0,
    options: UIViewAnimationOptions.CurveLinear.intersect(.
AllowUserInteraction).intersect(BeginFromCurrentState),
```

The first closure simply sets the button's background color to the highlight color (white). This means that the button's color will change from its current color (either red, blue, green, or yellow) to white in 0.5 seconds, which you set when you created the highlightSquareTime variable.

```
    animations: {
        button.backgroundColor = highlightColor
```

After the animation has occurred and the duration has passed, the code in the second closure is executed.

In this closure, the button's backgroundColor property is restored to the original color that was obtained. In addition, a new variable, newIndex, is created and set to the value of the index passed to the method earlier, plus 1.

The final line of the closure actually calls back into the same method, playSequence, passing in newIndex and highlightTime. This action causes the next button in the inputs array to highlight.

If you find a method calling itself to be a little like a snake eating its tail, you're not alone. This concept in computer science is known as *recursion* and is useful when repetitive and related operations such as this one are executed. The terminal point of the recursion is the return statement reviewed earlier—when all buttons have been highlighted.

The finished variable is a Boolean supplied to the closure by the animation method, and it precedes the in keyword. We ignore it in the closure.

```
    }, completion: { finished in
        button.backgroundColor = originalColor
        let newIndex: Int = index + 1
        self.playSequence(newIndex, highlightTime: highlightTime)
    })
}
```

On to the next method. Here is the action method that is called when the player touches one of the four buttons (shortly, you'll hook up this action method to the buttons in the storyboard). This is another fairly involved function that we'll dive into:

```
@IBAction func buttonTouched(sender: UIButton) {
```

Every UIButton has a tag property. A tag is an integer property that can be set to a number. For convenience, all four buttons will link to this same action method. Soon, you'll set the tag of each button to correspond to the color code in the ButtonColor enumeration. This will assist the method in determining which button was touched.

```
// determine which button was touched by looking at its tag
let buttonTag: Int = sender.tag
```

This next line may look a little strange, but it is actually a common way of conditionally executing a block of code based on the value of an assignment. Known in Swift as *optional chaining*, it assigns the result of the ButtonColor creation call and checks whether the value is nil.

A new constant, colorTouched, is set to the appropriate ButtonColor enumeration member based on the value of buttonTag. Since buttonTag was declared as an Int type earlier, it must be converted to a ButtonColor using the rawValue parameter of the ButtonColor initialization method.

In the unlikely circumstance ButtonColor(rawValue: buttonTag) were to return nil, the code inside the if statement would not get executed.

```
if let colorTouched = ButtonColor(rawValue: buttonTag) {
```

At this point, the player can touch the buttons while the computer is highlighting them. If this happens, this method will be called "out of order" and can interfere with proper gameplay. Therefore, you check to see who is the current player. If it is the computer, you simply ignore this touch and return immediately.

```
if currentPlayer == .Computer {
    // ignore touches as long as this flag is set to true
    return
}
```

The colorTouched constant, which was created and assigned earlier, is checked against the current button color in the inputs array. Here the determination is made whether the user has pressed the correct button in the sequence.

```
if colorTouched == inputs[indexOfNextButtonToTouch] {
```

If so, indexOfNextButtonToTouch is incremented and checked against the size of the array (inputs.count).

```
// the player touched the correct button...
indexOfNextButtonToTouch++

// determine if there are any more buttons left in this round
if indexOfNextButtonToTouch == inputs.count {
```

If the above statement is true, the user has touched the last button in the round correctly. A call is then made to the advanceGame method (which you'll see shortly). The result of that call will determine whether there are more buttons to be touched. If not, false is returned and the user has won the game.

```
// the player has won this round
if advanceGame() == false {
    playerWins()
}
```

In either case, the round is over since the player has touched the buttons in sequence correctly, and the indexOfNextButtonToTouch variable is reset to zero.

```
    indexOfNextButtonToTouch = 0
}
```

For clarity, the else clause is placed here, but there is no specific action to take. The game keeps playing since the player has neither won nor lost, and there are more buttons to be pressed.

```
    else {
        // there are more buttons left in this round... keep going
    }
}
```

This else clause is the counterpart to the if statement earlier that checked whether colorTouched was equal to inputs[indexOfNextButtonToTouch]. If control comes to this point in the code, the player touched the wrong button in the sequence and has lost the game. The appropriate method is called, and indexOfNextButtonToTouch is reset to zero so that the game can start over.

```
    else {
        // the player touched the wrong button
        playerLoses()
        indexOfNextButtonToTouch = 0
    }
}
```

WINNING AND LOSING

An important part of gameplay is the visual cues necessary to communicate to the player whether the game is won or lost. Cocoa Touch provides a class known as UIAlertView to do this. Both the playerWins and playerLoses methods create the view with appropriate win and lose messages.

The following method is part of the `UIAlertViewDelegate` protocol, which is adopted by this class and which is called when the user taps the button to acknowledge the message. Doing so in either case starts a new game.

```
func alertView(alertView: UIAlertView, clickedButtonAtIndex: Int) {
    startNewGame()
}
```

The next two methods are called depending on whether the player wins or loses the game. In both cases, the same `UIAlertView` object is created, taking a number of parameters, including a title, a message, a delegate (for calling the above method), and optional button titles.

Finally, the `show` method is called on the `UIAlertView` object, which causes the dialog to display.

```
func playerWins() {
    let winner: UIAlertView = UIAlertView(title: "You won!", message:
    → "Congratulations!", delegate: self, cancelButtonTitle: nil,
    → otherButtonTitles: "Awesome!")
    winner.show()
}


func playerLoses() {
    let loser: UIAlertView = UIAlertView(title: "You lost!", message:
    → "Sorry!", delegate: self, cancelButtonTitle: nil, otherButtonTitles:
    → "Try again!")
    loser.show()
}
```

The element of randomness is achieved through the following method, which takes no parameters and returns a `ButtonColor`. Inside the method, a variable is declared. Its value is derived from the `arc4random_uniform` method, which is provided by iOS to generate random numbers between zero and the passed parameter minus 1 (in this case, a value of 4 cast to a `UInt32` type, as mandated by the method).

As called, the `arc4random_uniform` method returns a random whole number between 0 and 3. The number 1 is added to shift the value to between 1 and 4, corresponding to the `ButtonColor` enumeration's raw values.

That `Int` value is then passed to the `ButtonColor`'s `rawValue` creation method to return a `ButtonColor?` type. Since it's an optional, it's returned unwrapped (hence the exclamation mark at the end of the last line).

```
func randomButton() -> ButtonColor {
    let v: Int = Int(arc4random_uniform(UInt32(4))) + 1
    let result = ButtonColor(rawValue: v)
    return result!
}
```

This method starts a new game by initializing the inputs array to a set of empty ButtonColor objects, and calling the method advanceGame to start the gameplay.

```
func startNewGame() -> Void {
    // randomize the input array
    inputs = [ButtonColor]()
    advanceGame()
}
```

This final method in the code is called as the gameplay advances from round to round.

```
func advanceGame() -> Bool {
```

The assumption, based on the assignment of the result variable, is that there are more buttons for the player to touch. However, if the number of inputs in the inputs array is equal to the winningNumber constant, the game is effectively over.

```
var result: Bool = true

if inputs.count == winningNumber {
    result = false
}
else {
```

If the game is not over, a new random button is added to the inputs array using the concatenation notation. The randomButton method, which returns a random ButtonColor, is called. The returned value is wrapped and added to the end of the array, effectively increasing the button count by 1.

```
// add a new random number to the input list
inputs += [randomButton()]
```

After the addition of the random button, the playSequence method is called. This is how the computer shows the player the sequence of buttons that must be touched to continue gameplay:

```
// play the button sequence
playSequence(0, highlightTime: highlightSquareTime)
}
```

And finally, the result of the comparison at the top of the method is returned to the caller.

```
    return result
    }
}
```

BACK TO THE STORYBOARD

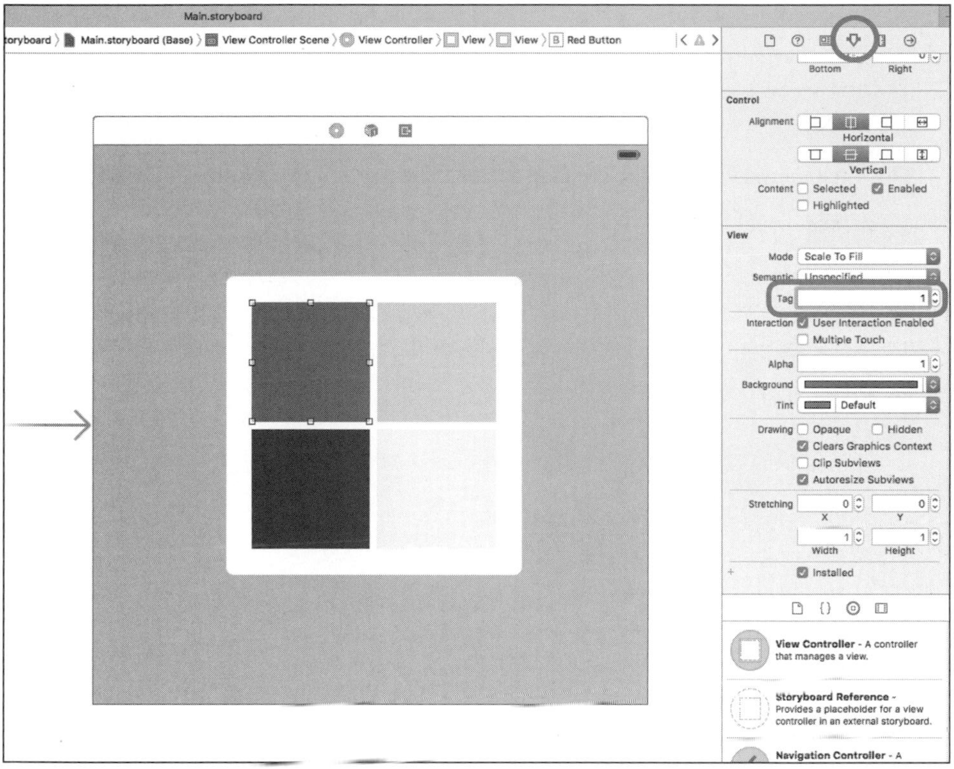

FIGURE 9.16 Setting the Tag property for the red button

With all the code added to the ViewController.swift class, we'll make a few hookups to the user interface in the storyboard.

Bring up the Main.storyboard file in the editor area, and then hook up the IBOutlets from the View Controller icon on the left of the editor area to the corresponding buttons in the view. To do this, right-click the View Controller icon, and then drag from the appropriate outlet to the button. Do this for all four outlets: blueButton, redButton, greenButton, and yellowButton.

Next, you'll set the tags for each button. In the view showing the four buttons, click the red button. From there, navigate to the utility area, click the Attributes inspector, and then scroll down and locate the Tag property. Set it to 1 (**Figure 9.16**). This value corresponds to the value Red in the ButtonColor enumeration.

Do the same thing for the green, blue, and yellow buttons, setting their tags to 2, 3, and 4, respectively. Setting up the tags this way allows the buttons to be found in the buttonTouched method in the code.

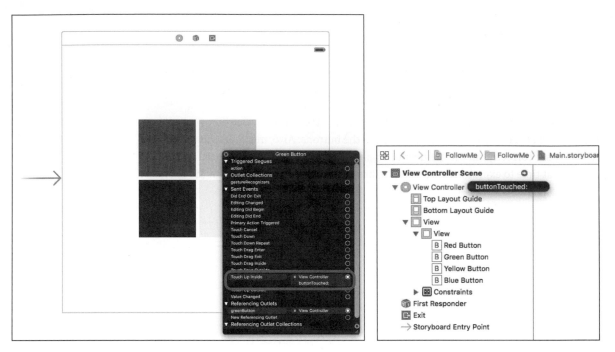

FIGURE 9.17 Making the connections between the code and user interface elements

FIGURE 9.18 Attaching to the `buttonTouched` method

Next, each button must link to the same `buttonTouched` action method. Start by clicking the red button to select it, and then right-click it so that the heads-up display appears.

Locate the Touch Up Inside event in the heads-up display that appears (**Figure 9.17**), and then click the circle on the far right of the line. Drag the line up to View Controller (to the left of the editor area), then release the mouse button to attach it to the `buttonTouched` method that appears in the second heads-up display (**Figure 9.18**). Follow this same step for the other three buttons to tie them to the same action method.

Consider making one final "touch" to the game. Select each button with the mouse, then turn on the "Shows touch on highlight" option in the Attributes inspector. Setting this option will cause the button to highlight when the user touches it, making it obvious which button was selected.

TIME TO PLAY

With the code typed in and the links made to the UI elements, it's time to play FollowMe! Run the app. If all goes well and you didn't make any typos, the iOS simulator should appear with the app running. Go through the game and play a few rounds.

If this isn't working, verify that all four buttons are attached to the action method, and that the outlet variables are connected back to the buttons. Also, make sure that the tag fields are set correctly. All the connections need to be made for the game to work. This is also a great time to experiment with setting breakpoints and tracing through the operation of the program.

Feel free to experiment with both the highlightTime and winningNumber values to adjust the difficulty of gameplay.

There are a number of other adjustments and enhancements you can consider making to improve the game as it currently stands. Consider doing the following to make playability more fun and interesting:

- Play sounds when the computer highlights each button.
- Keep a top score or a ranking based on the name of the player.
- When the user taps the wrong button, highlight the button that should have been tapped.

Congratulations on your very first iOS game written in Swift! The additional language concepts you've been exposed to in this chapter will become part of your foundation as you move forward into Swift development.

You've almost reached the end of your Swift journey... just a couple of chapters left. We'll touch on some additional language features, delve into a few advanced topics, and then finish off with a more challenging game for iOS!

Becoming an Expert

It's been an exciting journey through the Swift language, and you've made it to another chapter! You've learned how to use the REPL, tested code in playgrounds, and created both a Mac OS app and an iOS app. Between all of that, you learned about the Swift language itself.

Your learning Swift doesn't stop with this chapter, the next one, or this book for that matter. You will continue to discover plenty about the language as you use it to craft apps. Then there's the ever-expansive collection of frameworks Apple continues to improve in Cocoa and Cocoa Touch. The sky is the limit, and the fun never ends!

This chapter covers a range of Swift topics including memory management, logical operations, operator overloading, and error handling. These are areas that you should understand well if you want to eventually become a Swift expert.

MEMORY MANAGEMENT IN SWIFT

Every object, be it something as small as an Int type or as large as a blob of data, takes up memory resources. Even though your Mac, iPhone, or iPad comes with a large amount of memory, it is still a shared, finite resource that must be managed appropriately. Your app won't be the only app running on the system, so "playing nice" by using memory appropriately and wisely is part of being a good "app citizen."

If you have programming experience with other languages, you may have been waiting to see when and if this book would cover memory management. Indeed, that aspect of Swift wasn't mentioned in the previous chapters. How memory is handled is usually a detail that other programming languages force the developer to deal with, but Swift was designed to make this detail as transparent as possible.

The secret weapon in Swift's seemingly invisible memory management is Apple's use of the advanced LLVM (low level virtual machine) compiler infrastructure. More than just interpreting Swift statements into machine code, LLVM also traces code paths and determines where objects go out of scope and when their memory can be relinquished.

Even though memory management may seem transparent, you should be aware of some interesting twists as you embark on your Swift journey.

VALUE VS. REFERENCE

Early on, you were introduced to the concept of value types versus reference types. This is the notion of how types are used and passed around in the course of their lifetime.

Types such as Int and String, as well as structures and enumerations, are considered value types; when a value type is passed to a method, for instance, a copy of that value is made in memory, and the copy is passed. This makes for a relatively straightforward memory management style. By working with a copy of a String value, your method can modify it with impunity and not worry about it changing the original value that was passed.

Reference types, on the other hand, are not copied when they are passed around—instead, their *memory address* is provided to functions or methods that may use them. Closures and objects of instantiated classes are examples of reference types. If you pass a closure or an object to a method, a copy is *not* made. Instead, a reference (in the form of the memory address) is passed.

Because reference types are not copied when passed around, special care must be taken to ensure that they are properly disposed of at the right time. If the memory occupied by a reference type is given back to the system's memory pool too early, a crash or data corruption will typically result. This problem is known as the *dangling reference* and is indicative of one or more variables pointing to freed memory, then attempting to read or write into that memory area.

Conversely, if the memory occupied by a reference type is not given back to the system's memory pool after the type is no longer needed, that memory is essentially locked up and unavailable to be assigned to another type. This is known as a *memory leak*. Memory leaks are not as insidious as dangling references because they typically don't cause an app to crash, but they do waste memory resources.

What's behind the reason for value versus reference types anyway? Why not make everything a value type? In constructs such as classes and closures, where executable code exists, special memory protection constraints prohibit the copying of code. From a resource allocation and execution time point of view, passing an object as a reference instead of a value is also more efficient. Remember that values are copied, and copying data requires processor time, as well as extra memory to hold the copy. Referenced objects avoid this overhead, and in certain cases, multiple references to the same object can be used as a means of sharing data between parts of your program.

THE REFERENCE COUNT

Swift uses an innovative style of memory management for reference types. Devised by Apple and supported by the LLVM compiler, this memory management technique is known as ARC (automatic reference counting).

The basic premise of ARC is that every object has a number known as a *reference count*. This number is set to 1 when the object is created. As that object is passed around in your app, it may attain one or more "owners" who will use that object in some way or another. Each owner of the object is responsible for increasing the reference count by 1 (a *retain*) when it attains ownership and decreasing the reference count by 1 (a *release*) when it relinquishes ownership. When the reference count goes to 0 (presumably released by the last owner), the object is destroyed and the memory it occupied is returned to the free memory pool for reuse by other objects.

In Objective-C, this *retain/release* model of memory management used to be manually driven by the app developer. That is, the developer writing the code that used a referenced object would need to both retain the object (increase its reference count by 1) and release the object (decrease its reference count by 1) when he or she was finished with it.

More recently, ARC was introduced, and the burden of retaining and releasing was lifted from the developer's shoulders and given to the compiler instead. Through clever code flow analysis, the compiler can determine where to properly insert retains and releases without developer intervention. Swift is a beneficiary of this memory management model, giving you total freedom from the tedium of keeping track of when your objects should be retained or released.

Not that you can safely ignore memory management when developing in Swift, however. Sometimes the use of reference types can get you into undue trouble, so having some appreciation for what ARC does is important. In fact, you've already seen hints of ARC in code you worked with in previous chapters. It just wasn't emphasized at that point.

FIGURE 10.1
Reference cycle

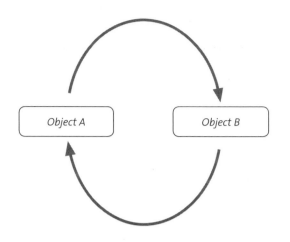

ONLY THE STRONG SURVIVE

For the most part, using classes and closures in your code involves nothing more than a simple declaration and creation. You can then pass the variable around as needed for work to be done. Although it's not obvious, when you declare a variable of a reference type and then assign an object to it, you are creating a *strong* reference to that variable, which means the variable's reference count will be incremented.

However, a unique problem—known as a *reference cycle*—can crop up when two objects reference each other, which is often the case when designing in Swift. Think of it as a deadly embrace, where object A has a reference to object B, and object B has a reference to object A (**Figure 10.1**). They both hold on to each other so strongly that when it's time to let go, they cannot.

The result of a reference cycle is that the referencing objects stay alive and the memory they occupy is never returned to the system as long as your app runs.

Let's look at a code example that exemplifies this problem. Start up Xcode, if it's not already running, and create a new OS X project by choosing File > New > Project. Select Cocoa Application from the OS X section. Be sure to select the Swift language and leave the Use Storyboards check box unselected. Name this project **ReferenceCycleExample**.

PUT IT IN A LETTER

To demonstrate a reference cycle, you will create two Swift classes: a Letter class that models a letter addressed to someone, and a MailBox class that models the mailbox the letter will be put into.

```
class Letter {
    let addressedTo: String
    var mailbox : MailBox?

    init(addressedTo: String) {
        self.addressedTo = addressedTo
    }

    deinit {
        print("The letter addressed to \(addressedTo) is being discarded")
    }
}
```

This class contains a constant named addressedTo, which is the name of the person the letter will be addressed to. There is also a variable that is a reference to an optional MailBox object.

The init method takes a String that is assigned to the addressedTo member variable that is part of the Letter class. A new method named deinit is also present. This method is called when an object is about to be deinitialized and just before the memory it occupies is returned to the system. In this method, a message is printed to indicate that the letter is being discarded.

Now on to the MailBox class:

```
class MailBox {
    let poNumber: Int
    var letter: Letter?

    init(poNumber: Int) {
        self.poNumber = poNumber
    }

    deinit {
        print("P.O. Box \(poNumber) is going away")
    }
}
```

The MailBox class looks similar to the Letter class in structure. There is a member constant named poNumber, which is an Int representing the post office box number of the mailbox. A member variable named letter is a reference to an optional Letter object.

THE TEST CODE

The code to exercise the two classes and demonstrate the reference cycle is next.

In the following code segment, two variables are declared: an optional Letter variable named firstClassLetter and an optional MailBox variable named homeMailBox.

```
var firstClassLetter: Letter?
var homeMailBox: MailBox?
```

The objects are then created with appropriate parameters and assigned to the variables:

```
// initialize the objects
firstClassLetter = Letter(addressedTo: "John Prestigiacomo")
homeMailBox = MailBox(poNumber: 355)
```

Here is where the homeMailBox object reference is assigned to the mailbox member variable of the firstClassLetter object, as well as assigning the firstClassLetter object to the letter member variable of the corresponding homeMailBox object.

```
firstClassLetter!.mailbox = homeMailBox
homeMailBox!.letter = firstClassLetter
```

Lastly, both the firstClassLetter object and homeMailBox objects are assigned to nil. This is allowable since both member variables were declared as optionals. When nil is assigned to a variable holding an optional reference, the reference to the object is destroyed and the object's reference count is decremented. If the reference count reaches zero, the object's deinit method is called, and the memory the object occupied is released back to the system.

```
// deinitialize the objects
firstClassLetter = nil
homeMailBox = nil
```

Figure 10.2 shows the placement of this code in the AppDelegate.swift file of your newly created project. The Letter and MailBox classes go at the bottom of the file on lines 41 through 65, and the test code is located on lines 19 through 31 in the applicationDidFinishLaunching method.

FIGURE 10.2
Placement of the
reference cycle
example code in
AppDelegate.swift

```
1   //
2   //  AppDelegate.swift
3   //  ReferenceCycleExample
4   //
5   //  Created by Boisy Pitre on 9/29/15.
6   //  Copyright © 2015 MyCompany. All rights reserved.
7   //
8
9   import Cocoa
10
11  @NSApplicationMain
12  class AppDelegate: NSObject, NSApplicationDelegate {
13
14      @IBOutlet weak var window: NSWindow!
15
16
17      func applicationDidFinishLaunching(aNotification: NSNotification) {
18          // Insert code here to initialize your application
19          var firstClassLetter: Letter?
20          var homeMailBox: MailBox?
21
22          // initialize the objects
23          firstClassLetter = Letter(addressedTo: "John Prestigiacomo")
24          homeMailBox = MailBox(poNumber: 355)
25
26          firstClassLetter!.mailbox = homeMailBox
27          homeMailBox!.letter = firstClassLetter
28
29          // deinitialize the objects
30          firstClassLetter = nil
31          homeMailBox = nil
32      }
33
34      func applicationWillTerminate(aNotification: NSNotification) {
35          // Insert code here to tear down your application
36      }
37
38
39  }
40
41  class Letter {
42      let addressedTo: String
43      var mailbox : MailBox?
44
45      init(addressedTo: String) {
46          self.addressedTo = addressedTo
47      }
48
49      deinit {
50          print("The letter addressed to \(addressedTo) is being discarded")
51      }
52  }
53
54  class MailBox {
55      let poNumber: Int
56      var letter: Letter?
57
58      init(poNumber: Int) {
59          self.poNumber = poNumber
60      }
61
62      deinit {
63          print("P.O. Box \(poNumber) is going away")
64      }
65  }
66
```

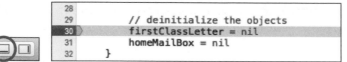

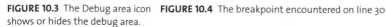

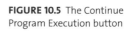

FIGURE 10.3 The Debug area icon shows or hides the debug area. **FIGURE 10.4** The breakpoint encountered on line 30 **FIGURE 10.5** The Continue Program Execution button

Because the app uses the `print` method to show when the objects are discarded in their respective `deinit` methods, the debug area must be visible. This is where the output of the `print` methods will be directed. Before running the code, ensure that the debug area is visible at the bottom of the Xcode window. If it isn't visible, just click the Debug area icon in the upper-right corner of the Xcode window (**Figure 10.3**).

With the code in place, set breakpoints on the following lines by clicking the line number to the left of the editor display (remember that the dark blue arrow indicates that the breakpoint is set):

Line 30:

```
firstClassLetter = nil
```

Line 50:

```
print("The letter addressed to \(addressedTo) is being discarded")
```

Line 63:

```
print("P.O. Box \(poNumber) is going away")
```

With the breakpoints set, run the app in Xcode by choosing Product > Run. The breakpoint at line 30 will pause execution (**Figure 10.4**).

The `firstClassLetter` object is about to be set to `nil`. This action, once it takes place, should cause the `Letter` class's `deinit` method to be called, thus triggering the second breakpoint. Will it? To find out, click the Continue Program Execution button just above the debug area (**Figure 10.5**). Instead of encountering the second breakpoint, control will continue.

A blank window appears, but since the focus of this simple app is to view the log information only, you can safely ignore it. Press Command-Q (or use the menu bar) to quit the app.

At this point, both the `firstClassLetter` and `homeMailBox` variables have been set to `nil`, but the `deinit` methods corresponding to the objects were not called. This is a clear indication that a reference cycle is in place and that the objects, though no longer referenced, are still alive and holding memory.

BREAKING THE CYCLE

Now that the reference cycle exists, how do you break it?

The problem stems from the fact that by default, variables that point to reference objects are strong references. The solution is to convince one of the variables—either `letter` in the Letter class or mailbox in the MailBox class—**not** to increment the reference count. This is known as a *weak reference,* and you actually saw the weak keyword in code in an earlier chapter.

Declaring a reference variable as weak means that the variable does not "own" the referenced object but merely "refers" to it. The assignment does not cause the retain count to increment, which breaks the deadly embrace that two objects can have on each other.

In the previous code example, it does not matter which variable is declared as weak, as long as one of them is. Modify the mailbox member variable on line 43 as follows:

```
weak var mailbox : MailBox?
```

Just adding the weak keyword in front of the var keyword is enough to let Swift know that mailbox is a weak variable. With the change in place, rerun the application.

The breakpoint on line 30 will stop execution as it did before. Now when you continue execution, you'll notice that the breakpoint on line 63 is encountered. This is the deinit method of the MailBox object being called as part of its destruction. Clicking the Continue Program Execution button then stops at the third breakpoint on line 50, corresponding to the Letter object's deinit method. Now the cycle is broken, and both objects have been properly terminated. The output from the print methods also appears in the debug area, indicating that both objects have been destroyed.

CYCLES IN CLOSURES

Closures are also reference types and, as such, can fall victim to the reference cycle, albeit in a slightly different way. Take for example the following class, which creates a MailBox object and a Letter object:

```
class MailChecker {
    let mailbox: MailBox
    let letter: Letter

    lazy var whoseMail: () -> String = {
        return "Letter is addressed to \(self.letter.addressedTo)"
    }

    init(name: String) {
        self.mailbox = MailBox(poNumber: 311)
        self.letter = Letter(addressedTo: name)
    }

    deinit {
        print("class is being deinitialized")
    }
}
```

FIGURE 10.6

Adding the code to
the applicationDid
FinishLaunching
method

```
29        // deinitialize the objects
30        firstClassLetter = nil
31        homeMailBox = nil
32
33        // create and destroy a MailCheck object
34        var checker : MailChecker? = MailChecker(name: "Mark Marlette")
35        let result : String = checker!.whoseMail()
36        print(result)
37        checker = nil
38    }
39
```

In addition to the mailbox and letter properties, this class has something new: a *lazy property* named whoseMail to check the letter's addressee. The lazy keyword is used to defer the evaluation of the property until it is actually used somewhere in the code. For this example, the reference to self.letter.addressedTo inside the closure that makes up the whoseMail property mandates the lazy keyword; otherwise, a compiler error would result.

Because the closure is referencing its enclosing MailChecker object as self, Swift insists on capturing the object as a strong reference. Likewise, the closure itself is strongly referenced by the MailChecker object that owns it, showing another example of the deadly embrace that can occur between two objects that strongly reference each other (in this case, those two objects are a class and a closure).

To illustrate this, type in the MailChecker class at the bottom of the AppDelegate.swift file, insert a blank line at line 32, then add the following lines of code at lines 33–37 inside the applicationDidFinishLaunching method (**Figure 10.6**):

```
// create and destroy a MailCheck object
var checker : MailChecker? = MailChecker(name: "Mark Marlette")
let result : String = checker!.whoseMail()
print(result)
checker = nil
```

This code instantiates an optional MailChecker object, assigns it to the checker variable, and then prints the contents of the object's whoseMail variable (which is composed of the closure I just discussed). Lastly, the checker variable is set to nil, which should cause the deinit method of the MailChecker object to be called and its memory to be returned to the system.

With all the code in place, set a breakpoint on the line of the MailChecker class's deinit method (line 87, as shown in **Figure 10.7**) and then run the application from Xcode.

When the application runs, the previously set breakpoints will be encountered. Just click the Continue Program Execution button to continue over them. However, the breakpoint on line 87 is not encountered. That's because of the reference cycle.

To break this cycle, a special notation has to be added to the closure declaration in the MailChecker class. Change line 77 to read:

```
lazy var whoseMail: () -> String = { [unowned self] in
```

The addition of [unowned self] in to the closure definition alerts Swift that the self object should not be retained, thus breaking the reference cycle.

```
68    deinit {
69        print("P.O. Box \(poNumber) is going away")
70    }
71 }
72
73 class MailChecker {
74    let mailbox: MailBox
75    let letter: Letter
76
77    lazy var whoseMail: () -> String = {
78        return "Letter is addressed to \(self.letter.addressedTo)"
79    }
80
81    init(name: String) {
82        self.mailbox = MailBox(poNumber: 311)
83        self.letter = Letter(addressedTo: name)
84    }
85
86    deinit {
87        print("class is being deinitialized")
88    }
89 }
90
```

FIGURE 10.7 Setting the breakpoint in MailChecker's deinit method

With the addition in place, run the application one more time in Xcode. Execution will stop on the breakpoint at line 87, confirming that the reference cycle no longer exists, and the MailChecker object is properly deinitialized and terminated.

THANKS FOR THE MEMORIES

Aside from the need to be cognizant of problems like reference cycles, memory management in Swift is mostly a hidden detail that is handled behind the scenes thanks to the LLVM compiler. It's one of the many things that make developing in Swift simple and straightforward. You focus on your app, and the language and compiler worry about the rest.

THINKING LOGICALLY

Although Swift has new and innovative features, in some ways it remains a beneficiary of computer languages that came before it. That's particularly true regarding basic things like mathematical expressions, which have a common, recognizable syntax across many different languages.

Another area where Swift inherits from other languages is in the use of *logical operators*. Logical operations involve determining the truth or falseness of a statement based on words like *and*, *or*, and *not*. We use these in our everyday spoken language all the time. For example:

If it is past 10 P.M. and the living room lights are on, turn them off.

or:

While it is not raining, leave the windows open.

These statements involve evaluating the truth of a clause in the statement and performing some action based on the outcome of the evaluation.

When you're programming, these types of constructs come up often, and Swift provides logical operators you can use to build expressions that evaluate to either true or false.

Let's move back to playgrounds to test out some of these ideas. In Xcode, create a playground using File > New > Playground, and select the OS X platform. Save the playground as **Chapter 10**.

TO BE OR NOT TO BE...

A common operator is the *logical NOT*, which is used to negate the outcome of an evaluation. It uses the exclamation mark (!) operator and precedes an expression.

Type the following code into your newly created playground:

```
// logical NOT
var a : String = "pumpkin"
var b : String = "watermelon"

if a == b {
    print("The strings match!")
}
```

This code snippet compares the value of a and b using the equality comparison operator (==) you learned about in Chapter 1. Obviously, "pumpkin" and "watermelon" are not equal strings, so the result is false, and the code inside the curly braces does not execute.

But by simply using the NOT operator, the logical outcome can be inverted, causing the block to execute. Type the following code into the playground and observe the Results sidebar:

```
if !(a == b) {
    print("The strings don't match!")
}
```

As you would expect, the NOT character inverts the false result, making it true, and the print method is executed. Also, the parentheses surround the comparison by necessity so that the NOT operator can invert the result of the comparison.

COMBINING WITH AND

The second logical operator that you should know about is the *logical AND*, which is used to combine two or more Boolean expressions. If any of the Boolean expressions are false, the entire expression is considered false as well.

Two consecutive ampersand characters (&&) are used to denote the logical operation. The following code snippet illustrates how to use the operator. Type the following code into your playground:

```
// logical AND
let c = true
let d = true

if c == true && d == true {
    print("both are true!")
}
```

Here, the logical AND is used when the predicate is evaluated. Both c and d are set to true, therefore the result of the logical AND is also true, and the print method is called.

If either variable were set to false instead of true, the predicate result would be false, and the code inside the curly braces would not execute.

ONE WAY OR THE OTHER

The third and final logical operator is the *logical OR*. Like the logical AND, the logical OR also combines two or more Boolean expressions, but only one of the expressions needs to be true for the entire expression to be true.

The logical OR is denoted with two vertical bar characters (||). Type the following code into your playground to see the logical OR in action:

```
// logical OR
let e = true
let f = false

if e == true || f == true {
    print("one or the other is true!")
}
```

FIGURE 10.8

Code demonstrating
the logical operators

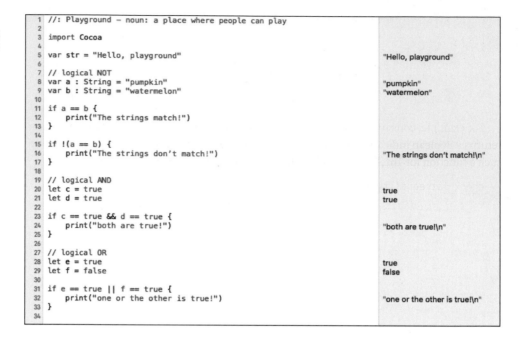

```
1   //: Playground — noun: a place where people can play
2
3   import Cocoa
4
5   var str = "Hello, playground"                              "Hello, playground"
6
7   // logical NOT
8   var a : String = "pumpkin"                                 "pumpkin"
9   var b : String = "watermelon"                              "watermelon"
10
11  if a == b {
12      print("The strings match!")
13  }
14
15  if !(a == b) {
16      print("The strings don't match!")                     "The strings don't match!\n"
17  }
18
19  // logical AND
20  let c = true                                               true
21  let d = true                                               true
22
23  if c == true && d == true {
24      print("both are true!")                               "both are true!\n"
25  }
26
27  // logical OR
28  let e = true                                               true
29  let f = false                                              false
30
31  if e == true || f == true {
32      print("one or the other is true!")                    "one or the other is true!\n"
33  }
34
```

This code illustrates that even though f is set to false, e is true; therefore, the predicate evaluates to true and the print is executed.

Figure 10.8 shows the sample code in the playground along with the results. Feel free to change the values of the variables to see how they affect the outcome of the if statements.

GENERICS

Many times in software development, you will encounter situations where you need a function or method to perform similar behavior on more than one type. In other languages, this usually means writing one method or function for every type supported.

For example, consider a simple function that takes two parameters of the same type and returns a Boolean indicating whether the first value is equal to the second value. Writing such a function for Int, Double, and String types would require three functions:

```
// check for equality between Int values
func areValuesEqual(firstValue: Int, secondValue: Int) -> Bool {
    return firstValue == secondValue
}


// check for equality between two Double values
func areValuesEqual(firstValue: Double, secondValue: Double) -> Bool {
    return firstValue == secondValue
}


// check for equality between two String values
func areValuesEqual(firstValue: String, secondValue: String) -> Bool {
    return firstValue == secondValue
}
```

Swift provides a feature known as *generics* that makes this repetitiveness a thing of the past. A generic function or method doesn't specify the type but instead specifies a placeholder.

All three functions just listed could be replaced by the following function, which makes the type a generic:

```
func areValuesEqual<T: Equatable>(firstValue: T, secondValue: T) -> Bool {
    return firstValue == secondValue
}
```

The generic method has a special syntax, with the generic placeholder T encompassed in < and >. Normally just the placeholder is required, but since the values are being used in a comparison context with ==, the placeholder is followed by a colon and the word Equatable, which is a Swift-provided protocol that requires arguments to be of types that support equality comparisons.

FIGURE 10.9

The generic method and the code that exercises it

```
34
35  func areValuesEqual<T: Equatable>(firstValue: T, secondValue: T) -> Bool {
36      return firstValue == secondValue
37  }
38
39  areValuesEqual(3, secondValue: 3)
40  areValuesEqual(3.3, secondValue: 1.4)
41  areValuesEqual("first", secondValue: "second")
42
```

(3 times)

true
false
false

Now, you simply need to exercise the generic function with Int, Double, and String values:

```
areValuesEqual(3, secondValue: 3)
areValuesEqual(3.3, secondValue: 1.4)
areValuesEqual("first", secondValue: "second")
```

Figure 10.9 shows the code and the results.

OVERLOADING OPERATORS

Early on, you learned how to enhance classes with new methods using extensions. This ability to bring new functionality into a language construct also extends to the most basic elements in Swift: operators.

With *operator overloading*, you can define how basic math operations such as addition, subtraction, multiplication, and division operate among custom classes or structures by redefining how their operators behave.

You may be wondering why you would even consider redefining the operation of the + (addition) sign or the * (multiplication) sign. Wouldn't it be confusing to change the meaning of these very basic operators and how they are used in Swift source code?

Although this is a valid observation, in some cases these basic operators can be useful outside of regular integer or floating-point mathematics. Consider linear algebra, for example, which concentrates on mathematical operations between matrices.

Addition and multiplication operations are more involved and complex in matrices than regular numbers are. Although some computer languages can inherently perform math on matrices, they are typically domain-specific languages that focus specifically on scientific computing.

With operator overloading in Swift, providing support for matrices natively is possible. Although a more general class could be constructed to perform operations on matrices of different sizes, let's keep it simple and focus on a specific case: the 2 x 2 matrix. In linear algebra, the procedure for adding two 2 x 2 matrices is as follows:

$$\begin{bmatrix} a11 & a12 \\ a21 & a22 \end{bmatrix} + \begin{bmatrix} b11 & b12 \\ b21 & b22 \end{bmatrix} = \begin{bmatrix} a11 + b11 & a12 + b12 \\ a21 + b21 & a22 + b22 \end{bmatrix}$$

Each member of the first matrix is added to the corresponding member of the second matrix, and the result is placed in the corresponding location of the result matrix.

Matrix multiplication is a little more involved. The procedure is as follows:

$$\begin{bmatrix} a11 & a12 \\ a21 & a22 \end{bmatrix} + \begin{bmatrix} b11 & b12 \\ b21 & b22 \end{bmatrix} = \begin{bmatrix} a11 * b11 + a12 * b21 & a11 * b12 + a12 * b22 \\ a21 * b11 + a22 * b21 & a21 * b12 + a22 * b22 \end{bmatrix}$$

Swift's ability to enhance basic operator behavior is useful in such a case. Consider the following structure, which is a 2 x 2 matrix:

```
struct Matrix2x2 {
    var a11 = 0.0, a12 = 0.0
    var a21 = 0.0, a22 = 0.0
}
```

The structure contains four variables of type Double. The variable name's first number is the row number, and the second number is the column number.

In Swift, defining a function with the operator's name as the function name is all you need to create new functionality for that operator. Below is the function that overrides the plus operator. Two Matrix2x2 structures are passed as parameters, and the same type is returned, representing the summation of the two matrices.

```
func + (left: Matrix2x2, right: Matrix2x2) -> Matrix2x2 {
    return Matrix2x2(a11: left.a11 + right.a11,
        a12: left.a12 + right.a12,
        a21: left.a21 + right.a21,
        a22: left.a22 + right.a22)
}
```

This function returns a new Matrix2x2 object with its a11, a12, a21, and a22 members set to the sums of the left and right matrices.

The next function defines matrix multiplication on the multiplication operator. The parameters are identical to the addition function. The code performs matrix multiplication and returns a new Matrix2x2 representing the product of the left and right matrices.

```
func * (left: Matrix2x2, right: Matrix2x2) -> Matrix2x2 {
    return Matrix2x2(a11: left.a11 * right.a11 + left.a12 * right.a21,
        a12: left.a11 * right.a12 + left.a12 * right.a22,
        a21: left.a21 * right.a11 + left.a22 * right.a21,
        a22: left.a21 * right.a12 + left.a22 * right.a22)
}
```

FIGURE 10.10

The matrix addition and multiplication code in action

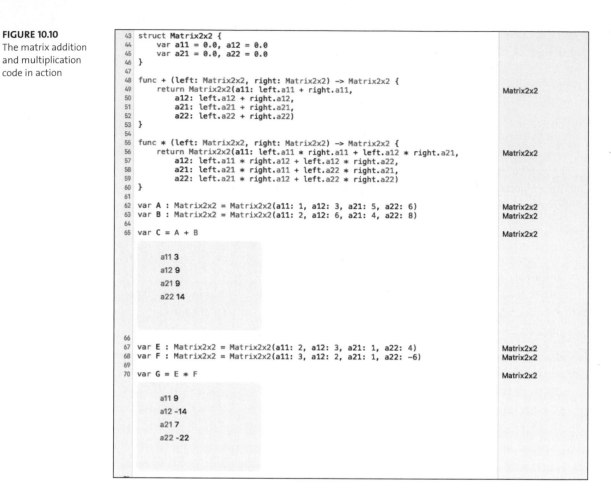

```
43  struct Matrix2x2 {
44      var a11 = 0.0, a12 = 0.0
45      var a21 = 0.0, a22 = 0.0
46  }
47
48  func + (left: Matrix2x2, right: Matrix2x2) -> Matrix2x2 {
49      return Matrix2x2(a11: left.a11 + right.a11,                          Matrix2x2
50          a12: left.a12 + right.a12,
51          a21: left.a21 + right.a21,
52          a22: left.a22 + right.a22)
53  }
54
55  func * (left: Matrix2x2, right: Matrix2x2) -> Matrix2x2 {
56      return Matrix2x2(a11: left.a11 * right.a11 + left.a12 * right.a21,   Matrix2x2
57          a12: left.a11 * right.a12 + left.a12 * right.a22,
58          a21: left.a21 * right.a11 + left.a22 * right.a21,
59          a22: left.a21 * right.a12 + left.a22 * right.a22)
60  }
61
62  var A : Matrix2x2 = Matrix2x2(a11: 1, a12: 3, a21: 5, a22: 6)            Matrix2x2
63  var B : Matrix2x2 = Matrix2x2(a11: 2, a12: 6, a21: 4, a22: 8)            Matrix2x2
64
65  var C = A + B                                                           Matrix2x2

        a11 3

        a12 9

        a21 9

        a22 14


66
67  var E : Matrix2x2 = Matrix2x2(a11: 2, a12: 3, a21: 1, a22: 4)           Matrix2x2
68  var F : Matrix2x2 = Matrix2x2(a11: 3, a12: 2, a21: 1, a22: -6)          Matrix2x2
69
70  var G = E * F                                                          Matrix2x2

        a11 9

        a12 -14

        a21 7

        a22 -22
```

Using these operators on the Matrix2x2 structure is as natural as expressing regular math in Swift. Here, two matrices, A and B, are defined, and their sum is placed in C:

```
var A : Matrix2x2 = Matrix2x2(a11: 1, a12: 3, a21: 5, a22: 6)
var B : Matrix2x2 = Matrix2x2(a11: 2, a12: 6, a21: 4, a22: 8)
```

```
var C = A + B
```

This same pattern is used to demonstrate matrix multiplication:

```
var E : Matrix2x2 = Matrix2x2(a11: 2, a12: 3, a21: 1, a22: 4)
var F : Matrix2x2 = Matrix2x2(a11: 3, a12: 2, a21: 1, a22: -6)
```

```
var G = E * F
```

To see the code in action, type it into your playground and use the Results sidebar to see the calculations, which should match those shown in **Figure 10.10**.

EQUAL VS. IDENTICAL

Early on, you learned about testing for equality among types such as Int, Double, and String. Testing whether two integers are equal is as simple as typing the following into your playground:

```
1 == 3
```

The result of such a comparison of course, would be false. What about other types? Can those objects be compared for equality? They certainly can, and such a test indicates whether two objects are *identical* as opposed to equal.

Sometimes comparing two variables to see if they are referring to the same object, rather than to two separate objects which have equal values, can be useful. Swift lets you perform this comparison by using === and !==, which are slight variants of the of the == and != operators used for comparisons between numeric and string types.

To illustrate how to determine whether objects are identical or not, type the following code into your playground:

```
// testing the identity of objects
class Test1 {
}

class Test2 {
}

var t1 : Test1 = Test1()
var t2 : Test2 = Test2()
var t3 : Test2 = Test2()
var t4 = t2


t1 === t2
t2 === t3
t4 === t2
t4 !== t2
```

The Test1 and Test2 classes are empty classes that exist merely for illustration. They could just as easily be large classes with plenty of member variables and methods.

Four variables (t1, t2, t3, and t4) are defined. Both t2 and t3 are set to new instances of the Test2 class, and t1 is set to a fresh instance of the Test1 class. The variable t4 is set equal to t2.

FIGURE 10.11
Testing for identity
among objects

```
71
72   1 == 3                                                              false
73
74   // testing the identity of objects
75   class Test1 {
76   }
77
78   class Test2 {
79   }
80
81   var t1 : Test1 = Test1()                                            Test1
82   var t2 : Test2 = Test2()                                            Test2
83   var t3 : Test2 = Test2()                                            Test2
84   var t4 = t2                                                         Test2
85
86   t1 === t2                                                           false
87   t2 === t3                                                           false
88   t4 === t2                                                           true
89   t4 !== t2                                                           false
90
```

Three comparison tests for object identity are followed by an opposite test. **Figure 10.11** shows the results of the comparisons.

The statement on line 86 evaluates to `false` because t1 and t2 are two objects of different classes. Line 87 also evaluates to `false`, because t2 and t3 are two separate instances of the same class. On line 88 is the sole test that returns `true`. The variables t4 and t2 indeed point to the same object, since t4 was assigned to t2 on line 84. Lastly, the test on line 89 is `false`. The variable t2 is equal to t4, as was just established on the previous line.

Remember that the object identity test is based on the instantiated object and not the class. Two variables can be of the same class but pointing to different instances of that class, and they would not be considered identical, as you saw in the comparison between t2 and t3 on line 87.

ERROR HANDLING

Errors are an unfortunate fact of life in programming. As a developer, you will spend a good deal of time writing code just to handle the various error cases that can crop up. Programming languages such as C++ and Objective-C have taken specific approaches to handling errors intrinsically, using constructs such as `throw`, `try`, and `catch`. Swift uses a similar method for handling errors.

THROWING AN ERROR

In Swift, errors are "thrown" by called functions and are "caught" by calling functions. When a function catches an error, it can decide what to do with it based on the *error type*.

In Swift, ErrorType is the basic protocol that can be extended to a set of errors for specific cases. For example, consider a password verification system that tests passwords for validity based on three criteria:

- Must have a minimum length of 8 characters
- Must contain at least one uppercase character
- Must contain at least one lowercase character

With those password restrictions in play, you can represent three error cases using a Swift enum that inherits from the ErrorType protocol. To get a feel for how this is done, type the following code into the playground:

```
// Error Handling Example
enum PasswordError : ErrorType {
    case TooShort
    case NoUppercaseCharacter
    case NoLowercaseCharacter
}
```

Three errors are defined and named in this enumeration, representing the three potential violations of the password rules. Now that the errors are defined, type in the password verification function below. Pay special attention to the throws keyword that follows the function definition. This keyword tells Swift that the function can throw an error.

```
func checkValidPassword(password : String) throws -> Bool {
    var containsUppercase : Bool = false
    var containsLowercase : Bool = false

    // check if password is too short
    if password.lengthOfBytesUsingEncoding(NSUTF8StringEncoding) < 8 {
        throw PasswordError.TooShort
    }

    for c in password.characters {
        if c >= "A" && c <= "Z"  {
            containsUppercase = true
            break
        }
    }

    for c in password.characters {
        if c >= "a" && c <= "z" {
            containsLowercase = true
```

```
            break
        }
    }

    if containsLowercase == false {
        throw PasswordError.NoLowercaseCharacter
    }

    if containsUppercase == false {
        throw PasswordError.NoUppercaseCharacter
    }

    return true
}
```

The function performs several checks. First, it verifies that the password is at least the minimum length (8 characters), and if it falls short, it uses the throw keyword to throw the specific error: PasswordError.TooShort. Next, it makes two passes on the characters of the string to check for upper- and lowercase. If either of those tests fail, the appropriate Boolean flag is set to true. Finally, both flags are checked, and if one or the other is true, then the corresponding error will be thrown.

CATCHING THE ERROR

With the checkValidPassword() function written, type the tryPassword function into the playground:

```
func tryPassword(password: String) {
    do {
        try checkValidPassword(password)
        print("Password is ok")
    } catch {
        print("Error: \(error)")
    }
}
```

This function uses the do/try/catch construct. Within the do clause, the method checkValidPassword() is called with the password string passed to the function. Note that the keyword try precedes the function call. This keyword is necessary because the checkValidPassword() function advertises that it will throw an error. Omitting the try keyword will cause Swift to emit an error during compile time.

```
 91  // Error Handling Example
 92  enum PasswordError : ErrorType {
 93      case TooShort
 94      case NoUppercaseCharacter
 95      case NoLowercaseCharacter
 96  }
 97
 98  func checkValidPassword(password : String) throws -> Bool {
 99      var containsUppercase : Bool = false                              false
100      var containsLowercase : Bool = false                              false
101
102      // check if password is too short
103      if password.lengthOfBytesUsingEncoding(NSUTF8StringEncoding) < 8 {
104          throw PasswordError.TooShort
105      }
106
107      for c in password.characters {
108          if c >= "A" && c <= "Z" {
109              containsUppercase = true                                  true
110              break
111          }
112      }
113
114      for c in password.characters {
115          if c >= "a" && c <= "z" {
116              containsLowercase = true                                  true
117              break
118          }
119      }
120
121      if containsLowercase == false {
122          throw PasswordError.NoLowercaseCharacter
123      }
124
125      if containsUppercase == false {
126          throw PasswordError.NoUppercaseCharacter
127      }
128
129      return true                                                       true
130  }
131
132  func tryPassword(password: String) {
133      do {
134          try checkValidPassword(password)                             true
135          print("Password is ok")                                      "Password is ok\n"
136      } catch {
137          print("Error: \(error)")
138      }
139  }
140
141  tryPassword("ValidPassword")
142
```

FIGURE 10.12

The result of passing a valid password

The catch clause contains code that is called in the event that an error is thrown in the do clause. Swift automatically assigns the ErrorType to a variable named error. In the catch clause, the error is printed.

In order to test the functions, add the following line in the playground:

```
tryPassword("ValidPassword")
```

A valid password of "ValidPassword" is passed to the tryPassword() function. Clearly it passes the tests: it's at least 8 characters long and it contains both upper- and lowercase characters. **Figure 10.12** shows the Results sidebar confirming that the checkValidPassword() function returns true on line 129 without throwing an error.

Now change the function call on line 141 to read:

```
tryPassword("2Short")
```

FIGURE 10.13
The result of passing
an invalid password

```
114      for c in password.characters {
115          if c >= "a" && c <= "z" {
116              containsLowercase = true
117              break
118          }
119      }
120
121      if containsLowercase == false {
122          throw PasswordError.NoLowercaseCharacter
123      }
124
125      if containsUppercase == false {
126          throw PasswordError.NoUppercaseCharacter
127      }
128
129      return true
130  }
131
132  func tryPassword(password: String) {
133      do {
134          try checkValidPassword(password)
135          print("Password is ok")
136      } catch {
137          print("Error: \(error)")                          "Error: TooShort\n"
138      }
139  }
140
141  tryPassword("2Short")
142
```

This time, the password doesn't pass the validity test (it's too short), and the error on line 104 is thrown, then caught and printed on line 137.

SCRIPTING AND SWIFT

If you have ever used command-line tools in the Terminal app, you have interacted with the shell. In fact, when you ran the command to launch the REPL in Chapter 1, you were using the *Bash shell*. You can run several different shells on your Mac, but Bash is the most popular.

Shell scripts are files that contain a list of executable lines of code in the language of the shell. Instead of typing a number of lines at the shell prompt, you can type those lines in a file as a shell script and then invoke that filename as though it were a command. For many developers who are command-line savvy, shell scripts are useful for repetitive tasks that are composed of many lines that need to run from time to time.

As useful as shell scripts can be, the one impediment to their adoption is that you must learn and master yet another language in order to take full advantage of them. Add to that the possibility of shell scripts also being written in other shell languages—such as the Bourne shell, C shell, or KornShell—and writing, let alone reading, an existing shell script can be a challenge.

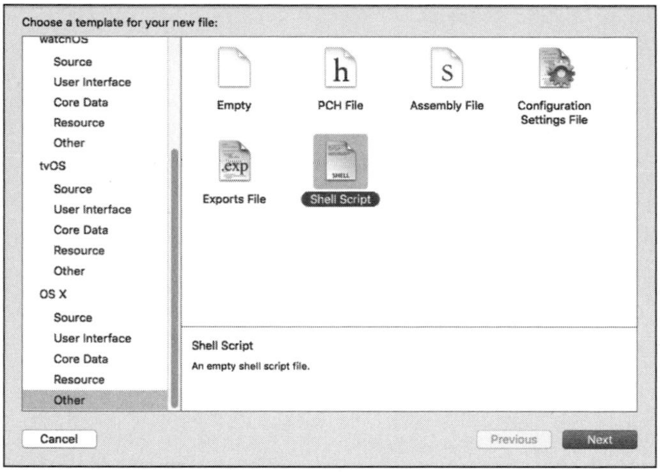

FIGURE 10.14 Creating a shell script under Xcode

This discussion about shell scripts is leading up to the fact that Swift code can run inside of a shell script! This is quite an interesting achievement given that Swift is also a compiled language, and it speaks to the power and flexibility that Apple has designed into the language. If you've used C, C++, or Objective-C, you can imagine how convenient it would be if you could use those languages in a shell script (hint: you can't).

Writing a shell script involves several steps:

1. Creating the script in an editor.
2. Setting the script's permissions so it can be executed.
3. Executing the script.

CREATING THE SCRIPT

Xcode makes a great editor, so why not use it to create a shell script?

Choose File > New > File, and then select Shell Script under the OS X Other section (**Figure 10.14**).

Click Next. In the file save dialog, name the file **SwiftScript**, and save it to your desktop (Xcode will automatically append .sh to the shell script filename). A window then appears where you can edit your script.

Xcode helps you by placing several default lines at the top of the file. The first line is the most important:

```
#!/bin/sh
```

This is known as "hash bang" syntax (named after the two characters, # and !, that start the file) and specifies the full pathlist in your file system to the shell that will run the subsequent lines of code. In this case, /bin/sh (which is the Bourne shell) is specified. For Swift scripting, you'll remove this line. In fact, delete all the lines and replace them with the following lines:

```
#!/usr/bin/env xcrun swift
import Foundation


class Execution {
    class func execute(path path: String, arguments: [String]? = nil) -> Int {
        let task = NSTask()
        task.launchPath = path
        if arguments != nil {
            task.arguments = arguments!
        }
        task.launch()
        task.waitUntilExit()
        return Int(task.terminationStatus)
    }
}

var status : Int = 0

status = Execution.execute(path: "/bin/ls")
print("Status = \(status)")

status = Execution.execute(path: "/bin/ls", arguments: ["/"])
print("Status = \(status)")
```

I'll go over the details of the script shortly. For now, type the lines into the Xcode editor, and then save the file by choosing File > Save.

SETTING PERMISSIONS

Scripts are run from the command line, so launch the Terminal application (remember that you used Spotlight in Chapter 1 to do this). When the terminal and shell prompt appear, type the following lines:

```
cd ~/Desktop
chmod +x SwiftScript.sh
```

```
1   #!/usr/bin/env xcrun swift
2   import Foundation
3
4   class Execution {
5   class func execute(path path: String, arguments: [String]? = nil) -> Int {
6           let task = NSTask()
7           task.launchPath = path
8           if arguments != nil {
9               task.arguments = arguments!
10          }
11          task.launch()
12          task.waitUntilExit()
13          return Int(task.terminationStatus)
14      }
15  }
16
17  var status : Int = 0
18
19  status = Execution.execute(path: "/bin/ls")
20  print("Status = \(status)")
21
22  status = Execution.execute(path: "/bin/ls", arguments: ["/"])
23  print("Status = \(status)")
```

FIGURE 10.15 The script file ready for execution

The first line changes the current directory to your Desktop folder (where you saved the script). The second line is needed only once to set the permissions of the script file so that it can be executed by the shell.

Now you're ready to run the script (**Figure 10.15**).

EXECUTING THE SCRIPT

Running the script is as simple as invoking the script's name at the prompt, with a little extra typing at the beginning:

`./SwiftScript.sh`

The `./` tells the shell that the script is in the current directory; you have to be explicit about this because if you leave it off, the shell won't be able to locate the script.

When the script runs, you'll see a listing of files in both your Desktop folder and the root folder of your disk. You'll also see a Status = 0 message, which indicates that the commands to list the files worked without issue.

Now that the script has executed, let's look a little closer at what this script does.

EXAMINING HOW IT WORKS

The first line is the "hash bang" mentioned earlier. In this case, the application path is /usr/bin/env, which is a special command to set up the environment for the shell script. Following that is a command that should be familiar to you: the same command you used to run the REPL:

`#!/usr/bin/env xcrun swift`

The next line should also look familiar to you. It's the import statement that you've seen in source code examples up to now. Just as in an application context, Swift scripts require a base of code to run from. Foundation is the framework that brings base functionality to Swift apps, so it is included here:

```
import Foundation
```

Next is a Swift class named Execution. Its purpose in life is to execute a command, which is something that scripts do a lot of. As you can see, setting up to execute a command in Swift takes a bit of work. Encapsulating this functionality into a class makes subsequent command execution much easier.

```
class Execution {
```

The one and only method in this class is named execute, and it takes two parameters: a String named path to an executable to run, and an array of String arguments that can be optionally passed. An Int is returned that will reveal the executed command's status.

You may recall that optional arguments allow you to either pass or not pass a parameter to a method or function. In this case, the array is also an optional, which means it can be assigned to nil.

What may look a little different to you is the keyword class in front of the method definition. This is a special method known as a *type method*. Type methods are called differently than instance methods, which is what you've been familiar with up to now.

A type method can be called directly from the class without creating an instance. Type methods are mostly for convenience, as you will see shortly.

```
class func execute(path path: String, arguments: [String]? = nil) -> Int {
```

Within the method are the steps to launch a command. A Foundation class named NSTask is used to set up the launch path and arguments:

```
let task = NSTask()
task.launchPath = path
```

In the case of the arguments parameter, there is a necessary check for the value being nil. Only if it is not nil is the parameter assigned to the arguments property of the task object, where it is unwrapped using the exclamation mark (!).

```
if arguments != nil {
    task.arguments = arguments!
}
```

Once the task object has been set up, the launch method is called to invoke the command:

```
task.launch()
```

And as per the documentation for NSTask, the waitUntilExit method must be called to allow the task to complete:

```
task.waitUntilExit()
```

Finally, the terminationStatus property of the task object is returned as an Int (within the task object, it is an Int32, so you just cast it here for the caller's convenience):

```
        return Int(task.terminationStatus)
    }
}
```

What follows the class definition is the code that actually uses the class. The variable that will hold the return status of the execute method is defined:

```
var status : Int = 0
```

Then, the execute method is used to execute the command /bin/ls (which shows files in a directory). Note the named parameter path:, which is mandated in the method's definition by repeating the parameter name. Insisting that the user specify the parameter name reinforces its purpose and makes the use of the method clear.

Also note that in this case, no arguments are being passed.

The status is returned and printed on the following line as well.

```
status = Execution.execute(path: "/bin/ls")
print("Status = \(status)")
```

The method is used again to execute the same command, but this time with an argument indicating the root path:

```
status = Execution.execute(path: "/bin/ls", arguments: ["/"])
print("Status = \(status)")
```

What you've just witnessed is the ultimate in language flexibility. You can write a class in Swift and then utilize it in the context of a shell script, which is superbly convenient. Time you invest in developing code for your apps in Swift isn't lost on scripting—the sky is the limit!

CALLING S.O.S.

FIGURE 10.16
Xcode's Help menu
gives you access to all
of Apple's documenta-
tion resources.

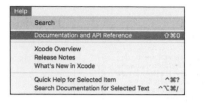

FIGURE 10.17
The Xcode documenta-
tion browser is your
central source of
information.

Having world-class documentation is one thing, but knowing how to get to it and use it is another. Apple has invested significant resources into bringing you top-notch documentation on their tools and classes, so use it. In Xcode, simply choose Help > Documentation and API Reference (**Figure 10.16**). The documentation browser appears, where you can read everything you need to know about all of Apple's technologies, including Swift, Cocoa, Cocoa Touch, and more (**Figure 10.17**).

Besides the Help menu, you have other venues for accessing documentation. You were introduced earlier to Xcode's Command-click and Option-click shortcuts for viewing details of Apple-provided Swift classes. Recall from Chapter 8 that you can hover over a Cocoa or Cocoa Touch class name in your source code and then hold down the Command key and click the underlined class name to view all the details of that class.

```
32
33          // create and destroy a MailCheck object
34          var checker : MailChecker? = MailChecker(name: "Mark Marlette")
35          let result : String = checker!.whoseMail()
36          print(result)
37          checker = nil
38      }
39
40      func applicationWillTerminate(aNotification: NSNotification) {
41          // Insert code here to tear down your applicat…
42      }
43
44
45  }
46
47  class Letter {
48      let addressedTo
49      weak var mailbo
50
51      init(addressedT
52          self.addres
53      }
54
55      deinit {
56          print("The
57      }
58  }
59
60  class MailBox {
61      let poNumber: I
62      var letter: Let
63
64      init(poNumber:
65          self.poNumb
66      }
67
68      deinit {
69          print("P.O.
70      }
71  }
72
73  class MailChecker {
74      let mailbox: Ma
75      let letter: Let
76
77      lazy var whoseM
78          return "Let
79      }
80
81      init(name: Stri
82          self.mailbo
83          self.letter = Letter(addressedTo: name)
84      }
85
```

Get into the habit of using these shortcuts—they will save you time and get you to the right place in the documentation to help you complete your work. Remember that if you hold down the Option key while hovering the mouse pointer over a type name, variable, or constant in your source, the pointer changes to a question mark. You can then click and receive a popover that shows relevant information about the item. See **Figure 10.18** for a refresher on this handy feature.

GAME TIME

This chapter covered a broad range of material, from memory management to generics to operator overloading, error handling, and more. It's a lot to take in, so feel free to review the material, then take a well-deserved break. You're almost done!

The next chapter is your final one, and it will present the largest composition of Swift code by far. Get ready for the Downhill Challenge!

CHAPTER 11

Heading Downhill

With two Xcode projects under your belt, it's time to kick things into overdrive. In Chapter 9, you wrote a game based on a fun but simple concept—testing your memory. Here, I'll show you a more elegant and detailed Swift game for iOS along with Apple technology specifically used for gaming.

GAMING THE SYSTEM

Gaming is a huge part of the app ecosystem that Apple has created with the App Store. The continuing improvements in graphics hardware performance deliver more horsepower for gaming, and these advancements have been heavily utilized by programmers. There's also the aspect of social gaming; high scores and other information can be shared with your friends and even with people you haven't met yet. Frameworks provided by Apple, such as GameKit and SpriteKit, make the task of designing and developing a full-featured game much easier than it used to be.

Besides the excitement of playing a game you've written, learning how to create one in Swift exposes you to a number of programming techniques and development tools. The work behind making a game can in itself be fun and rewarding.

Before diving into this chapter's project, I'll take a moment to discuss a few of the technologies that Apple provides for Swift developers who want to write games on both iOS and Mac OS X.

GAMEKIT

With the ubiquity of the Internet comes the opportunity for game players to be connected, and Apple has made this easy to do with GameKit. GameKit gives your app access to Game Center, Apple's central, online gaming site, where you can share scores on app leaderboards and connect with other gamers. Game Center is available for both iOS and OS X apps.

Another great feature of GameKit is the ability to connect your iOS device peer-to-peer with other iOS devices on your local network and share data in real time. Multiplayer action games benefit from such immediate interaction—it allows you to explore virtual environments and spaces with people across the room or across the world.

Finally, GameKit features voice chat for iOS devices, allowing you to hear players you're interacting with while playing a specific game. This makes for great gameplay in a virtual environment.

SPRITEKIT

Sprites are the visual elements within a game that move and animate. They can be characters such as heroes and villains, projectiles such as bullets and arrows, or even targets such as buildings and vehicles. No matter what type of game you intend to create, you'll use sprites to represent the objects.

The fundamental class that represents a sprite in SpriteKit is the SKNode. Every "actor" in a game is represented by this class. Even light sources and text labels are based on this class. You'll learn more about SKNode objects shortly.

Apple's SpriteKit emphasizes two-dimensional (2D) gameplay and is suitable for games with a "flat" appearance. For three-dimensional (3D) immersive game development, Apple offers SceneKit. Although I won't touch on SceneKit here, it's worth exploring on your own if you want to create games with field depth.

SpriteKit is perfect for games like the one you will work on in this chapter. It gives you the tools you need to create sprites and the world in which they will live. You'll need to be familiar with a number of terms as you use SpriteKit—don't worry, I'll explain them to you as you go along.

IT STARTS WITH AN IDEA

Games can run the gamut from extremely simple to vastly complex, and everything in between. Much of what makes a game compelling is the interaction that the player has with the content, as well as the degree of difficulty and types of controls.

For this chapter, you won't have to worry about game ideas—I'll introduce you to a fun and addictive game, written in Swift, named Downhill Challenge.

HEADING DOWNHILL

The premise of Downhill Challenge is simple: The player is in the form of a snowman that slides downhill in the snow. While racing down the hill, the player must move the snowman left or right to avoid trees along the path.

In addition to avoiding the obstacles, the snowman has an incentive: to catch coins along the path. As coins are caught, the score increases, and this is how the game gauges the skill of the player. The longer the player can sustain the game without hitting trees, the more opportunities there are for catching coins and increasing the score.

SOCIAL CONNECTIVITY

With the ability to keep score also comes the opportunity to advertise that score amongst other players who are playing the same game. Being able to share your score adds to the competitive and challenging aspects of gameplay.

As mentioned, Apple's Game Center is the social hub for gaming on iOS and OS X. All the support for connecting to Game Center is built into the GameKit framework, and you'll be using it in the Downhill Challenge game. You can find the Game Center app on your iPhone or iPad (and even your Mac). If you aren't already familiar with the app, now is a good time to launch it and interact with its features.

READY, SET...

FIGURE 11.1
The contents of the downloaded Downhill-Challenge folder

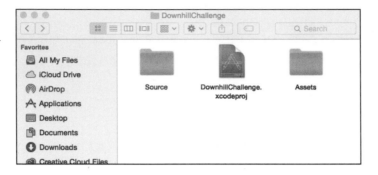

Are you ready to get started? Great! The good news is that you don't have to type in any source code. All you need to do is download the existing project. It contains all the source code and game assets, such as audio and sprites, and is ready to run on the iPhone simulator or directly on your device (in Xcode 7, Apple has lifted restrictions regarding running apps on actual devices).

Visit www.peachpit.com/swiftbeginners2 to download the project bundle.

Once you have downloaded the compressed file, it should automatically appear in your Downloads folder in a subfolder named DownhillChallenge. Double-click that folder to see its contents, which includes a number of folders as well as a file named DownhillChallenge.xcodeproj (**Figure 11.1**). Double-click that file, and the project will load into Xcode 7.

With the project loaded in Xcode, now is a great time to study how to play the game.

HOW THE GAME PLAYS

As I explained, in this game you're a snowman racing down a snow-covered hill. As you perpetually head downward, you encounter trees and coins. During gameplay, you must move left or right to avoid the many trees that are in your path while at the same time touching as many coins as you can. If you hit a tree, it's game over. If you touch a coin, your score goes up by one point.

As your snowman races along, he can attain a higher score by hitting the coins that appear randomly on the hillside. The game is over when he hits a tree, at which point the score is recorded in Game Center. You can then view the leaderboard from the Game Over scene to see how you rank against others who are playing the game on their iOS devices.

If that sounds a little monotonous, there's more. Besides just touching coins and dodging trees, the snowman must be on the lookout for two dangers that lurk: a menacing snowball and a dangerous truck. Both can appear at unexpected times, chasing the snowman down the hill and running over him.

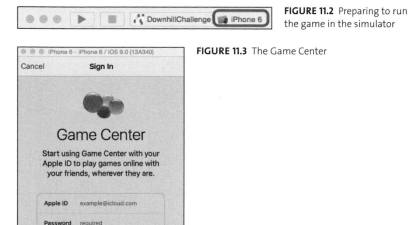

FIGURE 11.2 Preparing to run the game in the simulator

FIGURE 11.3 The Game Center

TAKE IT FOR A SPIN

The premise is quite easy and the gameplay is fun, so why not take it for a spin? In Xcode 7, select the iPhone 6 simulator at the top of the toolbar (**Figure 11.2**), then in the menu bar, select Product > Run.

When the game starts for the first time, you'll be presented with the Game Center login screen (**Figure 11.3**). Use your Apple ID to log in, and you'll see the Home scene. This is where you can start a new game or show the leaderboard from Game Center.

Tap Play and the Game scene comes into view with the message "Tap or hold sides to move" appearing in the middle of the screen. Tap anywhere to begin.

Once the game starts, tap on the left or right of the screen to dodge the trees and collect the coins (you may find using your thumbs to play the game is a natural method of control). Once you hit a tree, the game is over and you are taken to the Game Over scene, where you can tap Main Menu to go back to the Home scene or tap Restart to go to the Game scene and play another round. The most recently achieved score and best scores are also shown here (**Figure 11.4**, on the next page).

You'll want to play the game a few times to understand the flow. Notice that the snowman waves his arms as he moves, and he also leaves a trail behind him. Pay attention to the music and sound effects as you play the game. These are all important aspects of gameplay, and I'll show you how they work shortly.

FIGURE 11.4
The Home, Game,
Game Over, and
Leaderboard scenes

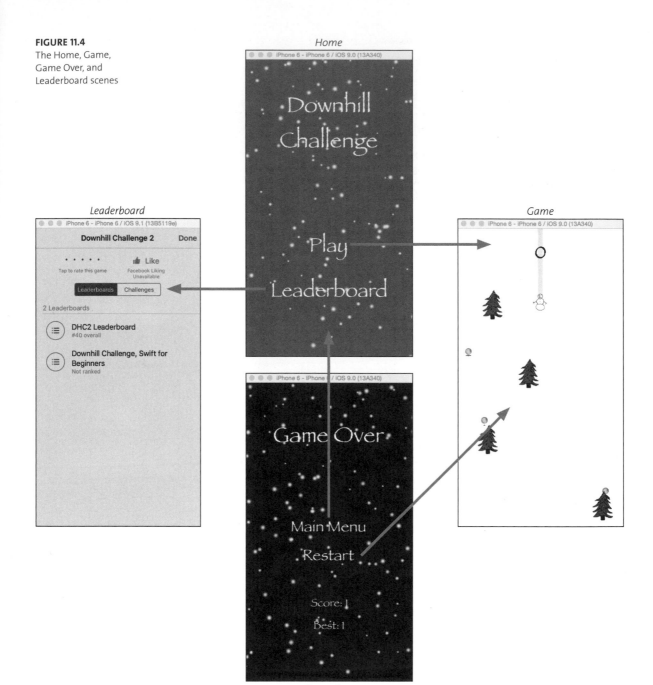

Home

Downhill Challenge

Play

Leaderboard

Game

Leaderboard

Downhill Challenge 2   Done

• • • • •   👍 Like
Tap to rate this game   Facebook Liking
                         Unavailable

Leaderboards | Challenges

2 Leaderboards

≡ DHC2 Leaderboard
   #40 overall

≡ Downhill Challenge, Swift for
   Beginners
   Not ranked

Game Over

Main Menu

Restart

Score: 1

Best: 1

Game Over

INSPECTING THE PROJECT

Now that you've played the game a bit, it's time to delve into the project and see how it's organized. Going back to Xcode 7, take a look at the navigator area to the left. There you can see a large number of groups and files that are referenced in the project (**Figure 11.5**).

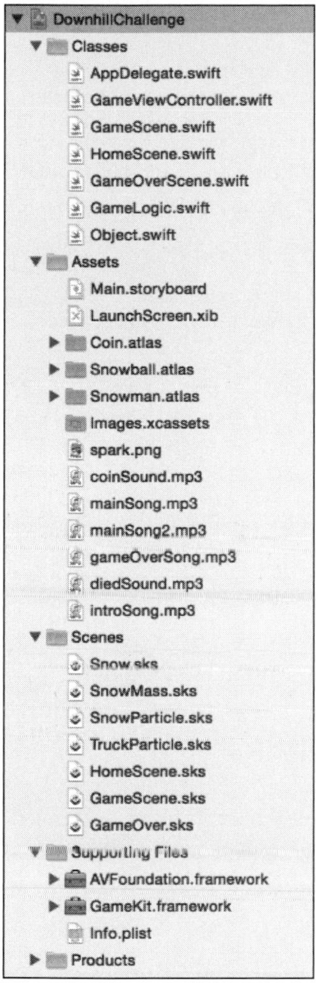

FIGURE 11.5
The navigator area shows the files in the project.

CLASSES

The Classes group contains the Swift source files that handle game logic, view controller manipulation, and more. You should become familiar with these files as you study the game:

- **AppDelegate.swift:** You have seen this file in other projects. It defines the various entry point and exit point methods for the application.
- **GameViewController.swift:** This class derives from `UIViewController` and is the code that backs up the main view of the game.
- **GameScene.swift:** This class derives from a special SpriteKit class named `SKScene`. It provides the Swift code for the environment in which sprites and other game content are rendered.
- **HomeScene.swift:** This class also derives from SpriteKit's `SKScene` class and contains code to set up the Home scene, which you see when you first start the game.
- **GameOverScene.swift:** This is another `SKScene`-derived class; it contains the logic for the Game Over scene.
- **Object.swift:** This class contains the logic that represents an object in the game: a tree or a coin, for example.
- **GameLogic.swift:** This class contains miscellaneous game logic.

ASSETS

The game assets are under the Assets group and contain sound effects, image files, and music for the game:

- **Main.storyboard:** The main storyboard for the game; it contains the `GameViewController`.
- **LaunchScreen.xib:** This file contains the screen that appears when the app is first launched.
- **Coin.atlas:** This folder contains 12 separate image files that represent the animation frames of the coin.
- **Snowball.atlas:** This folder contains four separate image files that represent the animation frames of the snowball.
- **Snowman.atlas:** This folder contains three separate image files that represent the animation frames of the snowman.

The additional files in this group contain music and sound effects for the game. The reader can click each image and sound to preview it in Xcode. This is helpful in understanding how the animations work.

SCENES

This group contains .sks files that contain graphic assets used within the game. You can view the content of each file by clicking the file from the navigator area. Try it!

- **Snow.sks:** This file contains falling snow particles that appear on the Home and Game Over scenes.
- **SnowMass.sks:** This file contains snow particles that appear behind the giant snowball as it rolls downhill.
- **SnowParticle.sks:** This file contains the snow trail that appears behind the snowman as he slides downhill.
- **TruckParticle.sks:** This file contains large snow particles that appear behind the truck as it rolls downhill.

The remaining .sks files are for the Home, Game, and Game Over scenes.

TOURING THE SOURCE

It's time to delve into some source code. Given the size and scope of the game, it's impractical to go over every line and file; instead, I'll highlight the salient parts and provide general guidance to help you discover other parts of the game on your own.

THE HOME SCENE

The Home scene is where you land to either start a game or view the Game Center leaderboard. Since this is the first scene that you see after launching the game, it's a good class to explore. It is similar to the other two scene classes in this project: GameScene.swift and GameOverScene.swift.

Click the HomeScene.swift file in the navigator area to view the source code, then turn your attention to the code starting on line 15.

The HomeScene class derives from SpriteKit's SKScene class and adopts the GKGameCenterControllerDelegate protocol. One variable and a number of constants are declared to handle the game's background music and to handle text nodes of type SKLabelNode. There's also an SKEmitterNode object, which loads the Snow.sks file that you viewed earlier.

```
class HomeScene: SKScene, GKGameCenterControllerDelegate {

    var backgroundMusic = AVAudioPlayer()

    let title1 : SKLabelNode = SKLabelNode(text: "Downhill")
    let title2 : SKLabelNode = SKLabelNode(text: "Challenge")
    let playButton : SKLabelNode = SKLabelNode(text: "Play")
```

```
    let gamecenter : SKLabelNode = SKLabelNode(text: "Leaderboard")

    let snow : SKEmitterNode = SKEmitterNode(fileNamed: "Snow.sks")!
```

Skip lines 26–33 for now, and focus on the method setupAudioPlayerWithFile() starting on line 35. This function is responsible for setting up an audio player with a specific audio file (and is called farther down, on line 56, to bring in the background music for the scene).

```
func setupAudioPlayerWithFile(file: String, type: String) -> AVAudioPlayer {
    let path = NSBundle.mainBundle().pathForResource(file, ofType: type)
    let url = NSURL.fileURLWithPath(path!)

    var audioPlayer : AVAudioPlayer?
```

The next few lines should look familiar due to the discussion of Swift's error handling in the previous chapter:

```
    do {
        audioPlayer = try AVAudioPlayer(contentsOfURL: url)
    } catch let error1 as NSError {
        print("\(error1)")
        audioPlayer = nil
    }

    return audioPlayer!
}
```

Recall that everything in the do clause is subject to evaluation for error. The try keyword precedes the function call to create an instance of AVAudioPlayer, which can presumably "throw" an error (you can confirm this by Command-clicking the class name to view the init methods that supply the throws keyword). Finally, the catch clause contains code that will be executed in the event that an error occurs.

The next method, gameCenterViewControllerDidFinish(), is a simple callback method that is invoked when the player has decided to stop viewing the Game Center leaderboard by touching the Done button. To see this called, set a breakpoint on line 51, then run the game and select Leaderboard from the Home screen. When the leaderboard screen appears, touch Done at the upper-right corner of the view.

```
func gameCenterViewControllerDidFinish(gameCenterViewController:
→ GKGameCenterViewController) {
    gameCenterViewController.dismissViewControllerAnimated(true,
      → completion: nil)
}
```

This next method is called when the Home scene comes into view. It starts by creating the backgroundMusic object, by calling the setupAudioPlayerWithFile() method that you just reviewed. The introduction song is loaded from the app bundle and will be played infinitely (numberOfLoops is set to –1).

```
// set up view
override func didMoveToView(view: SKView) {
    backgroundMusic = setupAudioPlayerWithFile("introSong", type: "mp3")
    backgroundMusic.numberOfLoops = -1
    backgroundMusic.volume = 0.25
    backgroundMusic.play()
```

The code in the next few lines sets the background color and calls the SKScene method addChild(), which adds the snow node to the Home scene. The position of the snow node is also set relative to the coordinate of the Home scene.

```
    backgroundColor = UIColor(red: 0, green: 125/255, blue: 1, alpha: 1)

    addChild(snow)
    snow.position = CGPointMake(size.width / 2, size.height)
```

The following lines of code call the method setLabel(), which is defined on lines 26–33 above (I skipped over it earlier). In essence, this is a convenience method that takes an SKLabelNode, the font name and size, the x and y position, and the color for the label. This is what builds the four labels that you see when you are viewing the Home screen in the game.

```
    setLabel(title1, labelName: "Title1", fontName: "Papyrus",
    → fontSize: 50, xPos: size.width / 2, yPos: size.height * 0.82,
    → fontColor: UIColor.whiteColor())
    setLabel(title2, labelName: "Title2", fontName: "Papyrus",
    → fontSize: 50, xPos: size.width / 2, yPos: size.height * 0.70,
    → fontColor: UIColor.whiteColor())
    setLabel(playButton, labelName: "Play", fontName: "Papyrus",
    → fontSize: 45, xPos: size.width / 2, yPos: size.height * 0.35,
    → fontColor: UIColor.whiteColor())
    setLabel(gamecenter, labelName: "Leaderboard", fontName: "Papyrus",
    → fontSize: 45, xPos: size.width / 2, yPos: size.height * 0.2,
    → fontColor: UIColor.whiteColor())
}
```

The showLeaderboard() method below is called when the user taps the Leaderboard label on the Home screen. It sets up an object of the Cocoa-supplied class GKGameCenter-ViewController and then sets the leaderboard identifier. This is the unique ID that allows app users to compare scores with each other in Game Center. Finally, it presents the view controller for the user to interact with.

```
func showLeaderboard() {
    let gcViewController: GKGameCenterViewController =
    → GKGameCenterViewController()
    gcViewController.gameCenterDelegate = self

    gcViewController.viewState = GKGameCenterViewControllerState.Leaderboards

    gcViewController.leaderboardIdentifier = "dhc-sfb.leaderboard"

    let vc : UIViewController = self.view!.window!.rootViewController!
    vc.presentViewController(gcViewController, animated: true, completion: nil)
}
```

The final method in this class overrides the touchesBegan() method. This method is called when a touch has been made on the screen, and it provides a set of UITouch objects. Each object in the set is analyzed to see whether it happened within the scene itself, and if so, which node in the scene. Since we're only interested in acting upon the Play and Leaderboard label nodes, those are checked. If a touch is made on the Play node, the background music is paused and the Game scene is presented. Otherwise, if the Leaderboard node was touched, the showLeaderboard() method is called.

```
// Called when a touch begins
override func touchesBegan(touches: Set<UITouch>, withEvent event:
→ UIEvent?) {
    for touch in (touches ) {

        let touchedScreen = touch.locationInNode(self)
        let touchedNode = self.nodeAtPoint(touchedScreen)

        if touchedNode.name == "Play" {
            backgroundMusic.pause()
            let scene = GameScene(size: self.scene!.size)
            self.scene?.view?.presentScene(scene, transition:
            → SKTransition.fadeWithColor(UIColor.whiteColor(),
            → duration: 0.5))
        }
        if touchedNode.name == "Leaderboard" {
            showLeaderboard()
        }
    }
}
```

That completes the review of the HomeScene class. Its purpose is to set up and handle the interactive elements (represented as SKNode objects) that make up the first screen the user sees when launching the game.

The other two scene class files, GameScene.swift and GameOverScene.swift, handle the Game screen and the Game Over screen. The core control of the game itself happens in GameScene.swift, so click that file in the navigation area so that it appears in the editor.

THE GAME SCENE

Much of the code that is responsible for the game's behavior is in the GameScene.swift file. It holds the logic for the GameScene class, which inherits from the SKScene class and adopts the SKPhysicsContactDelegate protocol. This protocol defines two methods that indicate when contact between two objects, or bodies, has been made. This is known as *collision detection* and is crucial to establish how sprites interact with each other.

A number of variables related to speeds and scoring are declared, as well as an SKEmitterNode object, which will carry the snow particles. An object of type GameLogic is created to handle values of various objects:

```
class GameScene: SKScene, SKPhysicsContactDelegate {

    var backgroundMusic = AVAudioPlayer()
    var coinCounter : Int = 0
    var playerSpeed : CGFloat = 240
    var pSpeed : NSTimeInterval = 200
    var upSpawn : Bool = false
    var actionCounter : Bool = false
    let trailParticle : SKEmitterNode = SKEmitterNode(fileNamed:
    → "SnowParticle.sks")!
    var gameLogic = GameLogic(tSpeed: 4.5, tRespawn: 0.5, sSpeed: 10,
    → sRespawn: 18, cSpeed: 5.2, cRespawn: 0.6, trSpeed: 4, trRespawn: 18)
    var didComeToGame : Bool = true


    let number = NSUserDefaults.standardUserDefaults()


    let player = NewObject(imageName: "Snowman", scaleX: 0.63,
    → scaleY: 0.63).addSprite()
```

The NewObject class is defined in the Object.swift file and is the basis for the snowball, tree, and coin objects that are created next. This class tracks the size and position of these objects on the screen.

```
    let snowball = NewObject(imageName: "Snowball", scaleX: 0.7, scaleY: 0.7)
    let tree = NewObject(imageName: "Tree", scaleX: 0.7, scaleY: 0.7)
    let coin = NewObject(imageName: "Coin", scaleX: 0.25, scaleY: 0.25)
```

The score and help nodes are created, and the snowman animation, which is organized as an atlas file containing a series of successive images, is loaded. You can see the atlas files in the navigator area.

```
var score : SKLabelNode = SKLabelNode(text: "0")
let help : SKLabelNode = SKLabelNode(text: "Tap or hold sides to move")

let snowmanAnimation : SKTextureAtlas = SKTextureAtlas(named:
→ "Snowman.atlas")
var snowmanArray = Array<SKTexture>()
var coinArray = Array<SKTexture>()
```

The following method, didMoveToView(), is called when the scene first appears on the screen. The coin sound is played and new background music starts. The user is instructed to tap or hold the sides to move, and once a tap is made the game begins.

```
/* Setup your scene here */
override func didMoveToView(view: SKView) {

    playCoinSound()

    snowmanArray.append(snowmanAnimation.textureNamed("Snowman1"))
    snowmanArray.append(snowmanAnimation.textureNamed("Snowman2"))
    snowmanArray.append(snowmanAnimation.textureNamed("Snowman3"))

    backgroundMusic = setupAudioPlayerWithFile("mainSong2", type: "mp3")
    backgroundMusic.numberOfLoops = -1
    backgroundMusic.play()
    backgroundMusic.volume = 0.2

    self.backgroundColor = UIColor.whiteColor()
    physicsWorld.contactDelegate = self

    trailParticle.targetNode = self.scene
    trailParticle.zPosition = 0

    // Score label
    score.position = CGPointMake(size.width / 2, size.height * 0.90)
    score.fontName = "Papyrus"
    score.fontColor = UIColor.blackColor()
    score.fontSize = 40
```

```
score.zPosition = 10

help.position = CGPointMake(size.width / 2, size.height / 2)
help.fontName = "Papyrus"
help.fontColor = UIColor.blackColor()
help.fontSize = 25
help.zPosition = 10
```

The setPlayer() method (defined on line 101) is called to set up the snowman for action, and finally the snowmanAnimate() method (defined on line 162) sets up an SKAction object to animate the snowman.

```
setPlayer()

addChild(help)
snowmanAnimate()
}
```

The next method of interest is didBeginContact() on line 216. This is the central method for determining whether the snowman collided with an object, such as a tree or a coin, and will be called automatically by SpriteKit.

Place a breakpoint on line 219, then choose Product > Run from the Xcode menu bar to run the game in the simulator. As soon as the snowman comes into contact with an object, the breakpoint will be hit:

```
if contact.bodyA.categoryBitMask < contact.bodyB.categoryBitMask {
    firstBody = contact.bodyA
    secondBody = contact.bodyB
} else {
    firstBody = contact.bodyB
    secondBody = contact.bodyA
}
let contactMask = firstBody.categoryBitMask | secondBody.categoryBitMask
```

The method is an SKPhysicsContact object that contains the two bodies that made contact. Each body carries a categoryBitMask whose values are defined in the Body enumeration on line 13 in Object.swift. The logical ORing of the categoryBitMask values of the objects yields a single contactMask that is then used in the switch statement on line 229 to determine what action to take. For example, when the snowman collides with a coin (case 10 on line 244), the coin sound is played, the score advances by 1, the text is updated, and the secondBody node (the coin) is removed from its parent node, effectively causing it to disappear.

The functions that follow are called at various points to create objects that appear on the screen. Set a breakpoint on line 286 and continue program execution.

```
func moveTree() {
addChild(tree.setMovingTree(randomTreeLocation(), destination:
→ CGPoint(x: 0, y: size.height * 2), speed: gameLogic.treeSpeed))
}
```

When this breakpoint is hit, a new tree will be added to the scene in a random location with a given speed. There are functions to spawn a snowball, a coin, and a truck too.

On line 360 is the update() method, which is part of the SKScene class and is called on every frame that is rendered in the game. This is where a certain amount of gameplay decisions are made. Here, the score, represented by the coinCounter variable, is evaluated via the switch statement. As the score increases, more objects are brought into the game and the speed of play is increased.

```
/* Called before each frame is rendered */
    override func update(currentTime: CFTimeInterval) {

        switch coinCounter {
        case 15:
            if upSpawn == false {
                gameLogic.treeRespawn = 0.3
                upSpawn = true
            }
        case 25:
            if upSpawn == false {
                gameLogic.treeRespawn = 0.22
                upSpawn = true
            }
        case 50:
            if upSpawn == false {
                playerSpeed += 5
                gameLogic.treeRespawn  = 0.18
                upSpawn = true
            }
        case 100:
            if upSpawn == false {
                gameLogic.snowballRespawn = 10
                gameLogic.treeRespawn  = 0.15
                upSpawn = true
            }
```

```
        case 200:
            if upSpawn == false {
                gameLogic.truckRespawn = 13
                upSpawn = true
            }
        default:
            upSpawn = false
        }
    }
```

This next method, didEvaluateActions(), is also a member of the SKScene class and is typically overridden by an SKScene subclass. It is called on every frame by SpriteKit and gives you the opportunity to update sprite behavior. In this function, the score is evaluated, and upon reaching specific milestones, additional actions are run. For an interesting exercise, change the case 15 on line 396 to case 2, then re-run the game and hit two coins. Soon after, you will be chased by a giant snowball!

```
override func didEvaluateActions() {
    switch coinCounter {
    case 15:
        if actionCounter == false {
            //gameLogic.treeRespawn = 0.3
            runActions(runTree: true, runSnowball: true, runCoin: false,
            → runTruck: false)
            actionCounter = true
        }
    case 25:
        if actionCounter == false {
            runActions(runTree: true, runSnowball: false, runCoin: true,
            → runTruck: false)
            actionCounter = true
        }
    case 50:
        if actionCounter == false {
            runActions(runTree: true, runSnowball: false, runCoin: false,
            → runTruck: true)
            actionCounter = true
        }
    case 100:
```

```
                if actionCounter == false {
                    runActions(runTree: true, runSnowball: true, runCoin: false,
                    → runTruck: false)
                    actionCounter = true
                }
            case 200:
                if actionCounter == false {
                    runActions(runTree: false, runSnowball: false, runCoin: false,
                    → runTruck: true)
                    actionCounter = true
                }
            default:
                actionCounter = false
            }
        }
    }
```

GAME VIEW CONTROLLER

Finally, take a look at the GameViewController.swift class. The code in this file backs up the view controller that is part of the Main.storyboard file. It is derived from the UIViewController class, which is responsible for displaying and manipulating a view on the screen.

Lines 9–11 import the necessary frameworks for the game:

```
import UIKit
import SpriteKit
import GameKit
```

You've already seen the SKNode class and its subclasses numerous times already. It is a fundamental class in the SpriteKit framework, and its job is to represent a visual element in the game. Here, an extension on the SKNode class is being declared with a single class method, unarchiveFromFile(), which takes a single parameter: a filename where the representation of a SpriteKit object exists in the file system.

```
extension SKNode {
    class func unarchiveFromFile(file : String) -> SKNode? {
        if let path = NSBundle.mainBundle().pathForResource(file, ofType:
        → "sks") {
            let sceneData = try! NSData(contentsOfFile: path, options:
            → .DataReadingMappedIfSafe)
```

```
        let archiver = NSKeyedUnarchiver(forReadingWithData: sceneData)

        archiver.setClass(self.classForKeyedUnarchiver(), forClassName:
        → "SKScene")
        let scene = archiver.decodeObjectForKey
        → (NSKeyedArchiveRootObjectKey) as! HomeScene
        archiver.finishDecoding()
        return scene
    } else {
        return nil
    }
  }
}
```

```
class GameViewController: UIViewController {
```

The first function that appears in the class is viewDidLoad(), which is called when the view has loaded and is about to be displayed. After calling the superclass's method, the localPlayer() method of the GKLocalPlayer class is invoked to create an object that will be used to connect to Game Center.

```
override func viewDidLoad() {
    super.viewDidLoad()

    let localPlayer : GKLocalPlayer = GKLocalPlayer.localPlayer()
```

The object's authentication handler is set to a closure that is called automatically when the game begins. That closure is passed a view controller and an error. Assuming the view controller is valid, it is presented to allow the user to log in to Game Center. If the user is already logged in, a notification will appear at the top of the screen, indicating that authentication has taken place.

```
    localPlayer.authenticateHandler = {(viewController, error) -> Void in
        if (viewController != nil) {
            self.presentViewController(viewController!, animated: true,
            → completion: nil)
        } else {
            if GKLocalPlayer().authenticated == false {
                print("Player will be authenticated.")
            }
        }
    }
```

The next block of code loads the HomeScene object. Assuming success, the scene variable will contain a reference to the loaded scene HomeScene (the .sks file in the navigation area). A new variable, skView, is created to point to the view of this view controller as an SKView object. The as keyword casts self.view as an SKView object (a subclass of UIView), which it happens to be. Without this keyword, self.view would be referenced as a UIView.

The SKView class has properties to show the frames per second and node counts, and those are set to false:

```
if let scene = HomeScene.unarchiveFromFile("HomeScene") as? HomeScene {
        // Configure the view.
        let skView = self.view as! SKView
        skView.showsFPS = false
        skView.showsNodeCount = false
        scene.size = skView.bounds.size

        /* Sprite Kit applies additional optimizations to improve
     →  rendering performance */
        skView.ignoresSiblingOrder = true

        /* Set the scale mode to scale to fit the window */
        scene.scaleMode = .AspectFill
```

Finally, it's time for the view to present the scene that was loaded earlier. This action causes the scene to appear in the view and on the device's screen:

```
        skView.presentScene(scene)
    }
}
```

TAKING IT ALL IN

It's time to catch your breath! This tour of the source code touched on a number of key points in the game, but it probably also leaves you with more questions. That's understandable, because a lot is going on under the hood. I encourage you to spend time going through both the source code and the Xcode documentation for SpriteKit and GameKit to learn more about these powerful frameworks.

Find a point in the source code that looks interesting, then set a breakpoint and run the game until the breakpoint is hit. Look at the stack trace and variables in the method, and snoop around to learn how the game works. Don't be afraid to change parts of the code and then re-run the game to see how your change affects gameplay. That's how you learn!

YOU DID IT!

Congratulations! You've reached the end of *Swift for Beginners*. In all honesty, though, your journey into Swift has really just begun. The investment you have made in reading the pages of this book, following the examples, and typing and running the code will begin to pay off as you practice what you've learned.

Before I send you off on your Swift adventure, I've compiled some "words of wisdom" that I hope will guide you going forward.

STUDY APPLE'S FRAMEWORKS

Cocoa and Cocoa Touch are composed of many, many frameworks and libraries. Along with all those frameworks are pages and pages of documentation available from Xcode's Help menu. It may seem overwhelming at first, but over time your knowledge of them will increase. Like a skilled carpenter who knows which tool is best for the job at hand, you too will learn to select the right framework and class to perform the task you need.

JOIN APPLE'S DEVELOPER PROGRAM

If writing an app for the App Store is in your plans, being a part of Apple's Developer Program, for $99 a year, is a must. With this resource, you'll gain access to the latest beta builds of the software, development tools, and a host of other goodies, including sample app code from Apple.

Besides the obvious benefits of being a member of the Developer Program, you also receive a number of technical support incidents that are handled by Apple Support engineers, giving you direct access to personalized support to resolve difficult problems. You also gain access to the developer forums, where developers and Apple engineers alike participate in helping each other with problems.

BECOME A PART OF THE COMMUNITY

Whether you're in a big city where there are like-minded Swift developers or in the solitude of the country, miles away from civilization, consider joining the growing number of online communities that focus on Swift and Apple development. Join publicly available forums, mailing lists, and any other online resources you can find.

If your budget allows, considering traveling to one of the many conferences that focus on iOS and Mac development. Traditionally, these technology-centric conferences, such as CocoaConf and MacTech Conference, have focused on Objective-C development, but that will undoubtedly change as Swift becomes the dominant language for Apple's family of devices. Attending conferences like these gives you the opportunity to focus on specific areas that are addressed by speakers who are well known in the community. I can attest that they are terrific folks who are very approachable and willing to help.

NEVER STOP LEARNING

The key to any investment's success is continued and sustained growth. I encourage you to continue expanding your knowledge of Swift by reading and studying the proliferation of example code on Apple's developer site and throughout the Internet. Ask questions, share knowledge and ideas, and continue to focus on the basics. Leave yourself room to poke and prod some of the esoteric nooks and crannies of the Swift language.

Websites such as stackoverflow.com are dedicated to helping you get past a compiler error or an issue with a particular class. Use the crowd-sourced wisdom of other Swift developers on this and similar websites to expand your understanding of the language—and don't forget to give back when someone else needs help.

BON VOYAGE!

It's been fun having you along for the ride; now it's time for you to go out there and use Swift to bring great products to people. You've been given a solid foundation—continue to study and explore the language. The rest is up to you.

Now go out there and change the world!

INDEX

NUMBERS

2 × 2 matrix, 264–266

600 × 600 view space, 224

SYMBOLS

./ prefix, using with shell scripts, 275

..< syntax, using, 59

-> characters, using with functions, 85

+ (addition) operation, performing, 21

&& (AND) logical operator, 261

: (colon), using with variables and
constants, 18

, (commas), using with arrays, 35

// (comments), converting lines into, 209

/ (division) operation, performing, 21–22

. (dot) notation, using with methods, 117

== (double equal) sign, 67–69

= (equal to) comparison, 24

! (exclamation mark)

   ending strings with, 10

   using with optionals, 195

   in Xcode, 186

> (greater than) comparison, 24, 69

>= (greater than or equal) comparison,
24, 69

< (less than) comparison, 24, 69

<= (less than or equal) comparison, 24, 69

* (multiplication) operation, performing,
21–22

! (NOT) logical operator, 260

!= (not equal to) comparison, 24, 69

% (modulo) operation, performing, 21

| | (OR) logical operator, 261–262

.. (periods), using with for-in loops, 58–59

+ (plus sign) operator, using with strings, 19

? (question mark), using with
dictionaries, 43

– (subtraction) operation, performing, 21

_ (underscore)

   using with numeric representations, 23

   using with parameter names, 100–101

   using with Void keyword, 97

A

action methods, using in Xcode, 187.
See also methods

actions and outlets, connecting, 188–189

addition (+) operation, performing, 21

addition and multiplication code, 266

advanceGame method, 242

aliases, using, 27

analyzing tools in IDE, 172

AND (&&) logical operator, 261

animateWithDuration method, 239–240

AppDelegate.swift file, 288

AppDelegate.swift source file, 176–177

append method, using with extensions,
163–164

Apple

   Developer Program, 301

   Game Center, 283

applicationDidFinishLaunching
method, 176

D

randomness, 221

UI design, 221–222

winning, 221

GameScene.swift class, 288

GameViewController.swift class, 288

    SKNode class, 298–299

    SKView class, 300

generic method, 263–264. *See also* methods

{ get set }, using with protocols, 152–153

gigabytes (gb), converting Int to, 161–162

Go menu, 8

greater than (>) comparison, 24, 69

greater than or equal (>=) comparison, 24, 69

gutter, clicking lines in, 206

H

hash bang syntax, 274–276

Hello, World! 10–11

:help command, typing, 10

Help menu in Xcode, 278

hexadecimal notation, 23

highlightColor variable, 239

Home scene, 286, 289–293

homeMailBox object, 254

HomeScene.swift class, 288

House constant, 150

HUD (heads-up display) window, appearance of, 188

I

@IBAction tag, appearance of, 188

@IBOutlet tag, appearance of, 188

IDE (integrated development environment), components of, 172

identical vs. equal objects, 267–268

if statements

    comparing numbers in, 69

    multiple, 70–72

    using, 66–70

    using in playground, 67

immutable String values, 36–37

implicit external parameter name, 100–101

implicitly unwrapped optional, 186–187. *See also* optionals

import statement

    in shell scripts, 276

    using in Xcode, 177, 184–185

increment, post, 63

inheritance

    and protocols, 155–156

    superclasses and subclasses, 124–125

init method, 116, 121–123, 136, 159, 253, 290. *See also* convenience initializers

inout keyword, using to modify parameters, 105

input leniency, 200

insert() method, using with arrays, 41

inspecting code, 77–80

inspector icons, locating, 225

instantiation, 115–116

    NiceDoor class, 131

    subclasses, 130–136

NSNumberFormatter class, 192, 194, 196–197, 208

  Attributes inspector, 199

  locating, 198

NSString method, 20

NULL value, 29

number formatting.
    See NSNumberFormatter class

numbers, comparing in if statements, 69

numeric representations, 23

numeric types

  mixing, 22

  upper and lower limits, 16

O

objects. *See also* first-class objects

  defining with class keyword, 115

  equal vs. identical, 267–268

  properties and behaviors, 112

  testing for identity, 268

  turning classes into, 115–116

Object.swift class, 288

octal notation, 23

OOP (object-oriented programming), 112

  base class, 125–128

  inheritance, 124

  subclasses, 128–136

operator overloading, 264–266

optional chaining, 241

optional Int, 29–30

optionals. *See also* implicitly unwrapped optional

  explained, 186

  unwrapping, 195

OR (| |) logical operator, 261–262

outlets and actions, connecting, 188–189

override keyword, 134

P

parameter names

  best practices, 102–103

  external, 102

  implicit external, 100–101

parameter values, prohibited changing of, 103–105

parameters. *See also* unnamed parameter

  defaults, 98–100

  passing to functions, 88–89

  setting values for, 100

  using temporary variables with, 104–105

  variadic, 90

passcode parameter, 97

passwords, checking and trying, 270–272

peppers example. *See* dictionaries

periods (.), using with for-in loops, 58–59

playground

  Timeline pane, 167

  using in Xcode, 64–65

playSequence method, 239–240, 244

plus sign (+) operator, using with strings, 19

Portal class, 125–128, 148

post increment and decrement, 63

prepend method, using with extensions, 163–164

print method, using, 26–27, 35

print() method, using, 10–11

profiling tools in IDE, 172

project manager in IDE, 172

project window in Xcode, 174–178

projects

MyFirstSwiftApp, 175

saving in Xcode, 174

properties, 112. *See also* Attributes inspector; computed properties; lazy property

protocols

adding variables to, 151

adopting multiple, 153–154

vs. classes, 148–151

delegation design pattern, 156–159

and inheritance, 155–156

using, 151–153

Push Button element, creating for interest calculator, 180

Q

question mark (?), using with dictionaries, 43

:quit command, typing, 10

quitting REPL, 34

R

$R3? temporary variable, 25

randomButton method, 244. *See also* buttons for FollowMe game

randomness, including in games, 243

raw values, using with enumerations, 139. *See also* values

Rectangle structure, using with protocols, 154

reference cycle

breaking, 256–257

in closures, 257–259

explained, 252

firstClassLetter object, 254–256

homeMailBox object, 254–256

Letter and Mailbox classes, 253–254

MailChecker class, 257–258

test code, 254–256

reference types vs. value types, 143–145, 250–252

repeat-while loop, 76–77

REPL (Read-Eval-Print-Loop) tool

commands, referencing, 10

quitting, 34

temporary variable, 25

Results sidebar, contents of, 77–80

returned functions, calling, 94–96

S

safety, emphasis on, 36

saving projects in Xcode, 174

scientific notation, 23

Scoville units, 42

securityDoor object, 134

self keyword, 122, 162

setLabel() method, calling for Home scene, 291

shell scripts

./ prefix, 275

arguments parameter, 276

/bin/sh, 274

creating, 272–274

executing, 275

hash bang syntax, 274–276

import statement, 276

launch method, 276–277